An Introduction to Theories of Popular Culture

Second Edition

Dominic Strinati

Routledge
Taylor & Francis Group
LONDON AND NEW YORK

First published 1995
by Routledge

Reprinted 1995, 1996, 1997, 1998, 1999, 2000, 2001, 2002, 2003

Second edition published 2004 by Routledge
11 New Fetter Lane, London EC4P 4EE

Simultaneously published in the USA and Canada
by Routledge
29 West 35th Street, New York NY 10001

Routledge is an imprint of the Taylor & Francis Group

Typeset in Bell Gothic and Perpetua by
Florence Production Ltd, Stoodleigh, Devon
Printed and bound in Great Britain by
MPG Books Ltd, Bodmin, Cornwall

British Library Cataloguing in Publication Data
A catalogue record for this book is available from the British Library

Library of Congress Cataloging in Publication Data
Strinati, Dominic.
An introduction to theories of popular culture / Dominic Strinati –
2nd ed.
p. cm
Includes bibliographical references and index
1. Popular culture. I. Title
HM621.S834 2004
306–dc22 2003026815

ISBN 0-415-23499-9 (hbk)
ISBN 0-415-23500-6 (pbk)

An
con
fro
pro
trie

cult
tur
fem
how
hav
to

new
disc
gen

and

Do
Lei
and
contemporary forums of popular culture. He is the author of *An Introduction to Studying Popular Culture* (2000) and co-editor, with Stephen Wagg, of *Come on Down? Popular Media Culture in Post-war Britain* (1992).

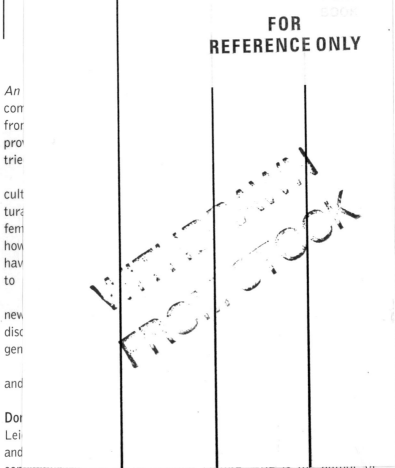

To the memory of my mother,
Francesca Aloyisia Maria Strinati (1916–1984),
my father, Giovanni (John) Strinati (1913–1990), and my brother, John Edward Strinati (1950–1957).

Contents

Acknowledgements

THANKS ARE DUE TO former and present students and colleagues (at Leicester and elsewhere) for the help they have given, whether consciously or not, in the writing of this book in both its editions. Among those I wish to thank are Richard Courtney, Ros Gill, Abigail Gilmore, James Fulcher, Roman Horak, Derek Layder, John Scott, Sallie Westwood and John Williams. I would especially like to thank Graham Murdock, for the help and guidance he provided when this book was no more than a draft proposal, and Rebecca Barden, for wanting to publish the book in the first place, for asking for a second edition, and for her advice and tolerance during the time it took me to write and revise it. I am grateful to Bill Mackeith for the highly efficient way he has copy edited this book, and to Felicity Watts for her careful proofreading of the final manuscript. I am also very grateful to Helen Faulkner, Lesley Riddle and Ruth Whittington for all their work in making sure this second edition has finally seen the light of day. Needless to say, the ultimate responsibility for what follows is mine, though I should add that Adam does like rap ('mmm') and Jonny definitely likes vinyl.

Introduction

THIS BOOK OUTLINES AND critically assesses some leading theories of popular culture. It does this in what is hoped is a clear and accessible style. There is no reason why readability should be confined to textbooks and not become a more common practice in writing social science generally; nor are all textbooks that accessible. But it is probably its coverage and readability which have led to a second edition of this book being published. The book itself has been substantially rewritten in order to make it even clearer and more accessible. Every sentence has been scrutinised and relatively few have remained unscathed. The coverage has, on the whole, been left alone, though criticisms have been added in a number of chapters, and some of the theoretical emphases have been changed from the original book. These changes will most likely be evident from the new Conclusion which has been written for this second edition. This Introduction has been rewritten although there seemed little need to change the content that much, since most of it is still relevant to the book's arguments. Again, any significant changes have been left to the Conclusion.

The study of popular culture is becoming a part of the educational curriculum, at the same time that it has begun to attract more attention from theorists and researchers in the humanities and social sciences. And this is even truer now than when this book was first published in 1995. The emergence and consolidation of popular culture as a subject to be analysed and taught has meant that it has been assessed and evaluated by a number of different theories. This book examines some of these theories to see how far they have advanced the study of popular culture.

However, it is not only this development which makes popular culture and its analysis a relevant topic of inquiry. More important is the increasing extent to which people's lives in western capitalist societies appear to be affected by the popular culture presented by the modern mass media. It is clearly important in other societies, both past and present, but in these societies the sheer volume of popular media culture which is made available gives it a specific significance which needs to be considered. Again, this sheer volume must not be exaggerated.[1] Just as there are international inequalities in the distribution of the media, so in western capitalist societies there are domestic, economic and cultural inequalities which prevent people from sharing in the increased availability of popular media culture.[2] Notwithstanding this, the scale of popular culture in the modern world suggests that looking at theories which have tried to explain and evaluate it may have some relevance to the overall debate on popular culture and the mass media.

The focus of the book is theories and perspectives on popular culture. It does not discuss particular traditions of research, such as audience research and the methodological issues it raises.[3] This is not because these traditions are not important, for, in fact, they are crucial to the development of the study of popular culture. However, this area of study has been dominated by different theoretical perspectives and the arguments and debates they have produced. This means that any assessment of the development of the study of popular culture has to come to terms with these theoretical perspectives. Of course, not all theories and perspectives are under-represented by research. Feminism, for example, has built up a strong body of research while still being involved in extensive and relevant theoretical debates. But what this book does assume is that the importance of theory should be balanced more evenly by the importance of research. A good example of this lack of balance is to be found in postmodernism which is considered below.

While this book presents an outline and critique of theories of popular culture, it does not pretend to be comprehensive in its range and detail. The theories discussed in this book have been chosen for a number of reasons. First, they are directly concerned with the analysis and evaluation of popular culture. Some theories, such as Marxism and feminism, are about a lot more than this, but are restricted here to what they have to say about popular culture. Other theories, which may seem relevant, are not considered if they have not looked directly at popular culture: for example, some variants of postmodernism and post-structuralism have not directed their attention to this area. So, whatever potential their proponents may think they have, they are not directly addressed in this book. This is one reason why the version of postmodern theory outlined below is a composite picture drawn from differing sources. Second, the theories covered in this book have all played an important part, at different times, in moulding arguments about how popular culture can and should be interpreted. They may not all have been equally supported by empirical research, but their ideas have all formed an important point of reference for any attempt to analyse and evaluate popular culture. The focus on popular culture, not more general developments in social and cultural theory, is the reason why the theories considered in this book have been selected.

Third, the theories chosen deal directly with popular culture rather than the mass media. It is almost impossible to look at one without looking at the other, especially since popular culture today is so closely bound up with the mass media; and the links between the two are recognised in this book. Yet insofar as a difference has arisen between theories and studies which concentrate upon the mass media, and those which concentrate upon popular culture, this book will confine itself to the latter. Some of the theories considered, such as the political economy variant of Marxist theory, are as concerned with explaining the role of the mass media as they are with understanding popular culture. None the less, in view of the focus of this book, approaches such as these will be outlined and assessed primarily by the theory of popular culture they put forward, without their theories of the mass media being thereby undervalued.

In addition, the theories and perspectives which are discussed in the following chapters are assessed by their adequacy as sociological theories of popular culture. The development of the study of popular culture has been based upon the contributions of a number of different disciplines. These include literature, literary criticism, history and psychoanalysis, as well as sociology. The inter-disciplinary character of this process, and the intellectual cross-fertilisation it has entailed, have proved useful in establishing this area of study, and in fostering conceptual innovations, empirical research and theoretical disputes.

However, the value of inter-disciplinary work and the contribution it can make is easily exaggerated. This is not a subject which can be pursued in detail here. What can be noted is that different disciplines do use different concepts, present different explanations, study different things, or study similar things with different methods, contain different ways of forming their arguments, and of providing empirical proof for their arguments; some do not even seem to be that concerned with explanations or empirical proof. These differences cannot be ignored or wished away for the sake of an imprecise, nebulous and ineffectual inter-disciplinarity.

It is not even a question of striking a balance between different approaches and disciplines, because they are often incompatible: this is the case, for example, with the difference between the methodologies of history and psychoanalysis and the explanations offered by sociology and literary criticism. It is also clear that the inter-disciplinary accord rarely extends to biology and genetics; and if it were, the problems we have noted would become more intractable. The claim that the 'cultural studies' approach to the study of popular culture is truly inter-disciplinary fails to recognise this argument: that different disciplines have different traditions, theoretical assumptions, empirical and historical concerns, methodologies, and so on, which prevent them from being simply and effortlessly integrated into an over-arching 'interdisciplinary' perspective. In the light of these problems, this book stresses most of all the importance of sociological contributions to the study of popular culture.

While this book attempts to outline and criticise some leading theories of popular culture, it is not written as a history of the study of popular culture. The theories selected are discussed in terms of their assumptions and arguments about how to explain and evaluate popular culture. They are not discussed as stages in an introspective history of how popular culture has been studied; nor is it the intention of this book to review them like this. Books which do this, or which deal with specific aspects of this history, are already available. There is, for example, Turner's outline (1990) of the tradition of British cultural studies closely associated with the Centre for Contemporary Cultural Studies at Birmingham University. There is also McGuigan's critique (1992) of the populism associated with this tradition which is based upon its neglect of the wider dimensions of political and economic power.[4] Similarly, there is Ross's account (1989) of the changing relationship between intellectuals and popular culture in America. One problem with books such as these is that they are often more concerned with the internal mechanics of intellectual debates, or the uneven development of the field of study, than with the analysis and evaluation of popular culture. In any event, a sociology of knowledge is required to do a proper job with their material but is usually lacking in such work.

This book does not, thus, pretend to provide an internal history of popular cultural study, but assesses the theories discussed in their own terms: as ways of accounting for popular culture. Nor does it pretend to present an alternative theory of popular culture, though there are implied preferences which the more discerning reader might notice. These preferences are made clearer in the Conclusion. Elements of an alternative approach are evident in some of the criticisms made of the theories outlined. But to have indulged in the presentation of an alternative theory would have got in the way of the more modest aims of the book.

Although this is a book about popular culture, not much time will be wasted defining it in this Introduction. A working definition of the sort of things that can be called popular culture will have to do here. The meaning of popular culture used in this book covers 'a set of generally available artefacts: films, records, clothes, TV programmes, modes of transport, etc.' (Hebdige 1988: 47). Popular culture can be found in different societies, within different groups in societies, and among societies and groups in different historical periods. It is therefore preferable not to have a strict and exclusive definition, so the straightforward definition just mentioned will do for the purposes of this book. The range of artefacts and social processes covered by the term popular culture will emerge as the discussion of the book unfolds, particularly since examples are used to illustrate the claims of the different theories considered.

Discussion of the various conceptual attempts to define popular culture has also been avoided for the simple reason that this is one of the things theories of popular culture predictably do. However implicitly or explicitly they address the problem, these theories provide definitions of popular culture which are more or less consistent with their general conceptual frameworks. Any attempt to define popular culture inevitably involves its analysis and evaluation. It therefore seems difficult to define popular culture independently of the theory which is designed to explain it.

A few examples may help clarify this point. Popular culture for the mass culture critics is either folk culture in pre-industrial societies or mass culture in industrial societies. For the Frankfurt School, popular culture is the culture produced by the culture industry to secure the stability and continuity of capitalism. The Frankfurt School thus shares a theory which sees popular culture as a form of dominant ideology with other versions of Marxism, such as those put forward by Althusser and Gramsci.[5] The Marxist political economy perspective comes close to this understanding of popular culture, while variants of feminist theory define it as a form of patriarchal ideology which works in the interests of men and against the interests of women. While semiology stresses the role of popular culture in obscuring the interests of the powerful – in Barthes's view the bourgeoisie – some structuralist theories see popular culture as an expression of universal and unchanging social and mental structures. Those writers who advocate cultural populism define popular culture as a form of consumer subversion which is precisely how they wish to evaluate and explain it (Fiske 1989b: 43–47). Lastly, according to post-modernist theory, popular culture embodies radical changes in the role of the mass media which wear away the distinction between image and reality.

The conclusion which can be drawn from these examples is that popular culture is defined by how it is explained and evaluated theoretically. Popular culture can be defined descriptively as covering a specific set of artefacts. But the possibility of a theoretically informed definition receiving widespread agreement is a long way off. It is especially difficult to envisage at the moment because the attempt to achieve this involves competing conceptions of the nature of the social relationships (or the lack of them) within which these artefacts are located. Popular culture cannot be properly defined except in relation to particular theories, so the problem of definition is best left to the chapters which follow. Some of the more general problems raised by the critical assessment of theories of popular culture will be taken up in the conclusion.

Chapter 1

Mass culture and popular culture

THE SOCIAL SIGNIFICANCE OF popular culture in the modern era can be charted by the way it has been identified with mass culture. The coming of the mass media and the increasing commercialisation of culture and leisure gave rise to issues, interests and debates which are still with us today. The growth of the idea of mass culture, very evident from the 1920s and 1930s onwards, is one of the historical sources of the themes and perspectives on popular culture which this book discusses.

This is not to say that the debate over mass culture represents something totally new. Lowenthal (1957), for example, has traced some of its central arguments back to the writings of Pascal and Montaigne in the sixteenth and seventeenth centuries, and linked their emergence to the rise of a market economy. Others argue they have always been with us, pointing to the 'bread and circuses' function of popular culture in the Roman empire. More convincingly, Burke suggests that the modern idea of popular culture is associated with the development of national consciousness in the late eighteenth century, and results from the attempt by intellectuals to turn popular culture into national culture. The distinction, for example, between popular culture and 'high' or 'learned' culture is to be found in this period in the writings of the German poet Herder (Burke 1978: 8).

The contrasting implications associated with the history of the idea of popular culture are clearly noted by Williams (1976). Referring to a 'shift in perspective' between the eighteenth and nineteenth centuries, he notes that 'popular' meant 'being seen from the point of view of the people rather than from those seeking favour or power over them'. However, 'the earlier sense had not died.' This meant that 'popular culture was not identified by the people but by others.' It also 'carries two older senses: inferior kinds of work (cf. popular literature, popular press as distinguished from quality press); and work deliberately setting out to win favour (popular journalism as distinguished from democratic journalism, or popular entertainment); as well as the more modern sense of well liked by many people'. Last, 'the recent sense of popular culture as the culture actually made by people for themselves is different from all these; it is often displaced to the past as folk culture but it is also an important modern emphasis' (Williams 1976: 199).

The development of the idea of popular culture is linked to arguments about meaning and interpretation which predate but become strikingly evident in the debates over mass culture. In particular, three related themes can be found in the work referred to above which, while not being exhaustive, have been central to theories of popular culture ever since.[1] The first concerns what or who determines popular culture. Where does popular culture come from? Does it emerge from the people themselves as an autonomous expression of their interests and modes of experience, or is it imposed from above by those in positions of power as a type of social control? Does popular culture rise up from the people 'below', or does it sink down from elites 'on high', or is it rather a question of an interaction between the two? The second theme concerns the influence of commercialisation and industrialisation upon popular culture. Does the emergence of culture in commodity forms mean that criteria of profitability and marketability take precedence over quality, artistry, integrity and intellectual challenge? Or does the increasingly universal market for popular culture ensure that it is truly popular because it makes available commodities people actually want? What wins out when popular culture is manufactured industrially and sold according to the criteria of marketability and profitability – commerce or quality? The third theme concerns the ideological role of popular culture. Is popular culture there to indoctrinate the people, to get them to accept and adhere to ideas and values which ensure the continued dominance of those in more privileged positions who thus exercise power over them? Or is it about rebellion and opposition to the prevailing social order? Does it express, in however an imperceptible, subtle and rudimentary manner, resistance to those in power, and the subversion of dominant ways of thinking and acting?

These are issues which are still very much alive in the study of popular culture today, but they (as well as others) received systematic and substantial attention in the debates about mass culture which started to gather pace from the 1920s onwards.[2] The 1920s and 1930s are significant turning points in the study and evaluation of popular culture. The coming of cinema and radio, the mass production and consumption of culture, the rise of fascism and the maturing of liberal democracies in certain western societies, all played their part in setting the agendas of these debates.[3]

The very fact that culture came to be almost infinitely reproducible due to the development of techniques of industrial production posed considerable problems for traditional ideas about the role of culture and art in society (Benjamin: 1973). Cultural products such as films were not, of course, mass produced in the same way as motor cars. However, the introduction of mass production techniques into the making of films, and the mass consumption afforded by cinemas, meant they could be regarded as commercial products.[4] For a number of the writers we shall look at in this chapter, this meant that cultural products, such as cinema, could not be authentic and genuine works of art. Equally, they could not be 'folk' culture because they no longer came from the 'people', and therefore could not reflect or satisfy their experiences and interests.

Apart from the popular press, cinema and radio were arguably the first archetypically modern mass media to emerge. They fuelled fears about the commercialisation of culture, and raised concerns about the potential they conferred upon political regimes (particularly but not exclusively fascist ones) for mass propaganda. The existence of highly efficient means of reaching large numbers of people within societies with centralised, totalitarian political systems was seen by many as another way, along with coercion, of further entrenching such systems and suppressing democratic alternatives. Mass media such as radio and film transmitted and inculcated the official ideology of the fascist state because they could be controlled centrally and broadcast to the population at large. The absence of countervailing political organisations in totalitarian societies just added to the efficiency of this equation: mass media equalled mass propaganda equalled mass repression. This potential was also marked by the deliberate and conscious attempt by the Nazi party in Germany in the 1930s to establish official Nazi ideology in all areas of culture and art, and eradicate alternative political and aesthetic ideologies. The aim was to enlist the help of intellectuals, writers, novelists, poets, painters, sculptors, musicians, academicians, architects, etc., in ensuring that Nazi ideology prevailed as Nazi aesthetics. Totalitarian societies, along with liberal democracies, have been viewed as types of mass society. The concept of mass society has formed one important perspective on the role of mass media and mass culture in modern capitalist societies. It has been the fears and anxieties of intellectuals, in societies such as Britain and America, about the rise of what they have seen as a mass society and a mass culture which have served to organise and inform the debates about these developments.[5]

Mass culture and mass society

Although what follows may look something like an identikit picture which nobody can be or wants to be identified with, I shall single out the main points advanced by mass society theory. This should illustrate its relevance to debates about the nature of popular culture as mass culture.[6]

The major claim of mass society theory refers to the disruptive consequences of industrialisation and urbanisation. The rise of large-scale and mechanised industrial production, and the growth of massive and densely populated cities, are argued to have destabilised and then eroded the societies and values which previously held people together. These radical changes included the eradication of agrarian work tied to the land, the destruction of the tightly knit village community, the decline of religion and the secularisation of societies; and they have been associated with the growth of scientific knowledge, the spread of mechanised, monotonous and alienating factory work, the development of large anomic cities populated by anonymous crowds, and the relative absence of moral integration. These processes are thought to lie behind the emergence of a mass society and mass culture.

The theory argues that industrialisation and urbanisation serve to create what is called 'atomisation'. This defines precisely what is meant by a mass society. A mass society consists of people who can only relate to each other like atoms in a physical or chemical compound. Mass society consists of atomised people, people who lack any meaningful or morally coherent relationships with each other. These people are clearly not conceived of purely and simply as isolated atoms, but the links between them are said to be purely contractual, distant and sporadic rather than close, communal and well integrated. In a mass society, the individual is left more and more to his or her own devices, has fewer and fewer communities or institutions in which to find identity or values by which to live, and has less and less idea of the morally appropriate ways to live.

People find themselves in this situation as 'atomised individuals' because industrialisation and urbanisation lead to the decline of mediating social organisations. These are organisations, such as the village, the family and the church, which once provided a sense of psychological identity, social conduct and moral certainty for the individual. In contrast, their modern counterparts, such as the city or science, do not work in the same way; they cannot foster identity, define conduct and fashion morality. According to the theory, people in a mass society are atomised both socially and morally. Not only are the contacts between people purely formal and contractual, but they lack any deeper sense of moral integrity since moral order declines in a mass society. The point here is that if no appropriate framework of moral order is forthcoming, if people do not have a secure sense of moral value, then a spurious and ineffectual order will emerge instead, and people will turn to surrogate and fake moralities. This will thereby aggravate rather than resolve the moral crisis of mass society. Mass culture plays a part here in that it is seen as one of the major sources of a surrogate and ineffective morality. Without appropriate mediatory organisations, individuals are vulnerable to manipulation and exploitation by core institutions such as the mass media and popular culture. There is no moral order to prevent this happening. Religious certainties and communal verities give way to the amoral immediacy of rational individualism and secular anomie associated with the rise of mass consumption and mass culture, the moral placebos of a mass society.

Though this claim is not integral to every version of the theory, mass culture theorists have suggested that democracy and education can be harmful developments in that they may contribute to the pathological condition of mass society. This point is particularly relevant to the debate about Americanisation which will be discussed more fully later in this chapter. Fears about Americanisation in the nineteenth century concerned the effects of democracy and education in a number of areas: breaking down traditional hierarchies of class and taste; allowing the 'mass' or the 'mob' to be the majority in the polity and culture, and to thus determine political decisions and lower cultural standards; supposedly realising the tyranny of the ignorant majority over the cultivation of minority taste; and ensuring the reduction of all questions of moment to the lowest common denominator.

From this point of view, democracy means that everyone is entitled to full political citizenship, and that, potentially, everyone's general cultural preferences are as valuable and as worthy of being respected and fulfilled as those of traditional elites. Furthermore, as part of this process of democratisation, education means that the capacity to engage more fully in cultural activities – the abilities to read, write, discriminate, demand, know, understand – becomes more accessible, formally at least, to more and more people. Just as the mass or the population at large began to be regarded as the main influence upon government and political decisions because of the extension of political citizenship rights, so the expansion of this trend in culture, combined with the effects of universal elementary education, is seen to result in the popular determination of the culture of mass societies.

This has not, however, always been seen in a favourable light. On the contrary, it is argued that because the masses lack taste and discrimination, culture is thereby debased and trivialised. If the tastes of the masses are to be satisfied, then everything has to be reduced to the lowest common denominator of the average or the mass. The people have to have a culture of their own, one which reflects their status and judgement as a mass. Democracy and education entail the breakdown of cultural distinctions between art and folk culture on the one hand, and mass culture on the other, in the same way that industrialisation and urbanisation entail the breakdown of traditions of community and morality. These fears continued well into the twentieth century, and could be argued to be present, in differing guises, at subsequent points of major cultural change.

However, mass society theory does not necessarily have a democratic theory of power, and if it does it does not think that it is a good thing. It tends to argue that the processes it describes invest power in the central institutions of the society, the commercial industries, the state and the mass media. Mass society theory is one attempt to understand the rise of mass propaganda, the potential for elites to use the mass media to more systematically and pervasively cajole, persuade, manipulate and exploit the people than had previously been possible. Those who control the institutions of power pander to the tastes of the mass in order to control them. If traditional communal and moral frameworks, and respected hierarchies of class and status, are breaking down, and there are no institutions left to mediate the relationships between the atomised individual and the centralised powers of mass society, the individual is open to the persuasive, manipulative and coercive force exercised by the combined or separate power of capitalism, the state and the mass media. Alternatively, if a specific variant of the theory complains about the rise of political and cultural democracy because they appear to work, and uses elitist criteria of taste and discrimination to criticise mass culture, then it is the power of the mass, and not its lack, which is emphasised. But again it is not welcomed or celebrated.

Before going on to look directly at the theory of mass culture an important definition needs to be clarified. This concerns the differences between elite culture or art, popular or folk culture, and mass culture, and arises because theories of mass society and mass culture usually rely upon a clear division between the past and the present. The division is normally taken to refer to a process of social change from a 'better' or preferable past to a degenerating and uninviting present and future. The pre-mass society is viewed as a communal and organic whole in which people accept and abide by a shared and agreed-upon set of values which effectively regulate their integration into the community, and which recognise hierarchy and difference. There is a place for art, the culture of elites, and a place for a genuinely popular folk culture which arises from the grass roots, is self-created and autonomous, and directly reflects the lives and experiences of the people. This authentically popular folk culture can never aspire to be art, but its distinctiveness is accepted and respected. With industrialisation and urbanisation this situation changes. Community and morality break down, and individuals become isolated, alienated and anomic, caught up in increasingly financial and contractual social relationships. They are absorbed into an increasingly anonymous mass, manipulated by their only source of a surrogate community and morality, the mass media. In this society, mass culture suppresses folk culture and undermines the integrity of art.

To indicate the relevance of this to the themes of this chapter we can quote a leading theorist of mass culture:

> Folk art grew from below. It was a spontaneous, autochthonous expression of the people, shaped by themselves, pretty much without the benefit of High Culture, to suit their own needs. Mass Culture is imposed from above. It is fabricated by technicians hired by businessmen; its audiences are passive consumers, their participation limited to the choice between buying and not buying. . . . Folk Art was the people's own institution, their private little garden walled off from the great formal park of their master's High Culture. But Mass Culture breaks down the wall, integrating the masses into a debased form of High Culture and thus becoming an instrument of political domination.
>
> (MacDonald 1957: 60)[7]

This statement summarises concisely how this perspective defines the differences between elite, folk and mass culture. We now have to consider more fully the implications of these differences, and the meaning of the idea of mass culture.

The mass culture debate

Put simply, we can say that mass culture refers to popular culture which is produced by the industrial techniques of mass production, and marketed for profit to a mass public of consumers.[8] It is commercial culture, mass produced for a mass market. Its growth means there is less room for any culture which cannot make money, and which cannot be mass produced for a mass market, such as art and folk culture. This also indicates how mass culture theory can be understood as a response to the industrialisation and commercialisation of popular culture on a grand scale which began to gather momentum in the 1920s and 1930s. The terms of the theory and its implications need to be made clear before we show how, in this country, it has been bound up with the debate about Americanisation. This will be followed by a critical examination of its claims.

First, we can note that industrialisation and urbanisation gave rise to an atomised and anonymous mass ripe for manipulation, a mass market for the mass media best catered for by mass culture. Both mass production industries and mass markets encouraged the spread of mass culture. For this approach, the main determinant of mass culture is the profit its production and marketing can make from its potential mass market. If culture can't make money then it is unlikely to be produced. The theory also stresses the effects of the mass production of mass culture. The use of mass production techniques, along with the commercial need to make a profit, are seen to have a harmful and corrupting influence on the culture produced in mass, industrial societies. It is argued that aspects of mass production such as the assembly line, a highly specialised division of labour, the strict separation of different stages of production, and output quotas (some of which could be said to have characterised the Hollywood studio system between the 1920s and the 1950s) stamp mass culture with the features associated with the products of mass production industries.

From this point of view, there is no real difference between material and cultural products, between, say, the production of cars and the production of films. The standardised, formulaic and repetitive products of mass culture are the result of the manufacture of cultural commodities by means of routine, specialised, assembly-line types of production. Art, for example, cannot be produced in this way. The alleged aesthetic complexity, creativity, experiments and intellectual challenges of art cannot be achieved by the techniques or conditions which produce mass culture. Instead, art depends upon the inspired genius of the individual artist working outside the constraints of the commercial market, and without the tried and tested formulas and standard techniques of mass culture. Equally, folk culture has to be produced by an integrated community which knows what it is doing, and which can thereby guarantee the authenticity of its products.

This argument is associated with a specific idea of the audience for mass culture, the mass public which consumes mass-produced cultural products. This audience is understood to be a mass of passive consumers, susceptible to the manipulative persuasions of the mass media, acquiescent with the appeals to buy mass-produced commodities such as mass culture, supine before the false pleasures of mass consumption, and open to the commercial exploitation which motivates mass culture. The picture is of a mass of people which, almost without thinking or reflecting, accepts mass culture and mass consumption. The emergence of mass society and mass culture means it lacks the intellectual and moral resources to do otherwise. It cannot think of alternatives since its cultural universe is reduced to one common mass. Art lies beyond its aspirations, and it has already lost its folk culture. The nature of this audience therefore means that culture can be profitably mass produced.

The bland and standardised formulas of mass culture are developed to sell things to this mass consuming public because they can be made to appeal to everyone since everyone, every atomised person, is open to manipulation. Also, mass cultural products can be made in large numbers by mass production industries. There is thus no point in making demands upon or challenging this audience in the way that art might do, or drawing it into genuine and authentic forms of communal participation as folk culture might do, since their conditions can no longer be sustained. Instead, the mass audience is there to have its emotions and sensibilities manipulated, to have its needs and desires distorted and thwarted, to have its hopes and aspirations exploited for the sake of consumption, by the meretricious sentiments, the surrogate fantasies, the false dreams of mass culture. In effect, mass society delivers up people to mass exploitation by mass culture.

This idea of the audience is quite common to theories of popular culture. According to one of its leading proponents, mass culture theory argues that if 'people are organized . . . as masses, they lose their human identity and quality . . . they are related to one another neither as individuals nor as members of communities'. Instead, every individual exists as 'a solitary atom, uniform with and undifferentiated from thousands and millions of other atoms who go to make up "the lonely crowd" as David Reisman well calls American society.' By contrast, 'a folk or a people . . . is a community, i.e., a group of individuals linked to each other by common interests, work, traditions, values, and sentiments' (MacDonald 1957: 69; cf. Frith 1983: 252).

From this point of view, mass culture is a standardised, formulaic, repetitive and superficial culture, one which celebrates trivial, sentimental, immediate and false pleasures at the expense of serious, intellectual, time-honoured and authentic values. MacDonald laments what he calls the 'spreading ooze of Mass Culture', and argues 'it is a debased, trivial culture that voids both the deep realities (sex, death, failure, tragedy) and also the simple, spontaneous pleasures'. This occurs because 'the realities would be too real and the pleasures too lively' to encourage 'a narcotized acceptance of Mass Culture and of the commodities it sells as a substitute for the unsettling and unpredictable (hence unstable) joy, tragedy, wit, change, originality and beauty of real life.' The result is that 'the masses, debauched by several generations of this sort of thing, in turn come to demand trivial and comfortable cultural products' (MacDonald 1957: 72–73).

Mass culture is therefore a culture which lacks intellectual challenge and stimulation, providing instead the undemanding ease of fantasy and escapism. It is a culture which discourages the effort of thinking and creates its own emotional and sentimental responses. It does not demand that its audience thinks for itself, works out its own responses, and entertains responses which are intellectual and critical. In this sense, it begins to define social reality for the mass public. It therefore tends to simplify the real world and gloss over its problems. If these problems are recognised, it usually treats them superficially by presenting glib and false solutions. It equally encourages commercialism and celebrates consumerism, together with the virtues of profit and the market. Also, just as it denies intellectual challenge, it tends to silence other opposing voices because it is a stultifying and pacifying culture.

The rise of mass culture would, on its own, be considered enough of a danger by some of the writers we consider in this chapter. But there is more to the argument than what has been described so far. The eclipse of folk culture could not be resisted by the 'people', but high culture and the role of the traditional intellectual elite are equally at risk. This is the core of many of the anxieties, fears and hostilities expressed by this elite about mass culture. Another culture, an elite culture – what might be termed 'art' – has remained in place above the already doomed folk culture being deserted by the masses in favour of mass culture. Nevertheless, the position and security of the high cultural elite, its privileged judgement and arbitration of taste, the voice it has to speak on behalf of those excluded from high culture, have been challenged both by the spread of mass culture and its general trivialisation of all culture, and by the presumed loss among the mass of the skills and abilities required to appreciate and understand high culture.

For some, like MacDonald, this would not be that much of a problem if the people could keep to their own folk cultural pastimes, and leave art to the elite. For others, however, it served as a warning of just how pernicious the hold of mass culture could be. Writing in the early 1930s in an interesting study of the book market, the English literary and social critic, Q.D. Leavis (1906–1981), expressed her concerns as follows:

> It is not perhaps surprising that, in a society of forty three millions so decisively stratified in taste that each stratum is catered for independently by its own novelists and journalists, the lowbrow public should be ignorant of the work and even of the names of the highbrow writers, while to the highbrow public 'Ethel M. Dell' or 'Tarzan' should be convenient symbols, drawn from hearsay rather than first-hand knowledge. But what close at hand is apparently trivial becomes a serious development when we realise that this means nothing less than that the general public – Dr Johnson's common reader – has now not even a glimpse of the living interests of modern literature, is ignorant of its growth and so prevented from developing with it, and that the critical minority to whose sole charge modern literature has now fallen is isolated, disowned by the general public and threatened with extinction. Poetry and criticism are not read by the common reader; the drama, in so far as it ever overlapped literature, is dead, and the novel is the only branch of letters which is now generally supported.
>
> (Leavis 1932: 35)[9]

Her study is designed to show how the serious, high-brow novel is next.

According to MacDonald, mass culture is a threat because it is a homogeneous culture which levels down or debases all culture. He argues it 'is a dynamic, revolutionary force, breaking down the old barriers of class, tradition, taste, and dissolving all cultural distinctions . . . producing what might be called homogenized culture.' As such, it 'destroys all values, since value judgements imply discrimination.' He therefore concludes that 'mass culture is very, very democratic: it absolutely refuses to discriminate against, or between, anything or anybody' (MacDonald 1957: 62).

This argument is clearly similar to those we hear today regarding the postmodern traits of contemporary culture. It also shows, as does Q.D. Leavis's argument, just how the intellectual elite's arbitration of cultural taste is open to the democratising threat posed by mass culture. The real problem sometimes seems to be that mass culture, unlike folk culture, refuses to stay in its place and stick with the masses, but has pretensions beyond its station and merits; it refuses to recognise traditional hierarchies of taste, and the cultural distinctions generated by those at the top. For these theorists, mass culture is a danger because it can undermine the distinctions established between elite and popular culture. It can co-opt, while at the same time debasing and trivialising, what high culture has to offer.

Q.D. Leavis makes this clear in her analysis of the fate of the then modern novel. She notes the effects of the growing taste for mass culture as follows:

> The training of the reader who spends his leisure in cinemas, looking through magazines and newspapers, listening to jazz music, does not merely fail to help him, it prevents him from normal development, partly by providing him with a set of habits inimical to mental effort . . . whereas the eighteenth century and nineteenth century helped the reader, the twentieth century hinders. . . . This meant . . . an inability to be bored and a capacity to concentrate, due in part, no doubt, to the fact that there was no competition of amusements provided. Life was not then a series of frivolous stimuli as it now is for the suburban dweller, and there was time for the less immediate pleasures. The temptation to accept the cheap and easy pleasures offered by the cinema, the circulating library, the magazine, the newspaper, the dance-hall, and the loud-speaker is too much for almost every one. To refrain would be to exercise a severer self-discipline than even the strongest-minded are likely to practise, for only the unusually self-disciplined can fight against their environment and only the unusually self-aware could perceive the necessity of doing so.
>
> (Leavis 1932: 224–225)

This conclusion is confirmed for Leavis by the 'disappearance of poetry from the average man's reading', and by the fact that book clubs don't improve taste but rather standardise it (ibid.: 229). Thus, 'the general reading public of the twentieth century is no longer in touch with the best literature of its own day or of the past.' This occurs because 'the idiom that the general public of the twentieth century possesses is not merely crude and puerile; it is made up of phrases and clichés that imply fixed, or rather stereotyped, habits of thinking and feeling at second-hand taken over from the journalist' (ibid.: 235, 255); and, we might add, from other producers of mass culture as well.

The threat posed to high culture by mass culture is given a slightly different slant by MacDonald. He suggests that in the 1920s the mass culture of Hollywood cinema (which was mitigated to a limited extent by avant-garde and folk art) and the high culture of Broadway theatre were clearly and sharply distinguished from each other in terms of production – commercial versus artistic criteria; texts – popular pleasure versus intellectual stimulation; and audience – the masses versus the metropolitan upper class. However, with the arrival of the sound film these distinctions began to break down. He notes that

> plays are now produced mainly to sell the movie rights, with many being directly financed by the film companies. The merger has standardised the theatre expunging both the classical and the experimental . . . and . . . the movies . . . too have become standardised . . . they are better entertainment and worse art
>
> (MacDonald 1957: 64–65)

If it is the case that mass culture has threatened to unseat high culture and take over, where does this leave art and the avant-garde? What role if any can they play in the era of mass culture? As with so many who hold to this understanding of popular culture, MacDonald adopts a position of cultural pessimism. For him, 'bad stuff drives out the good, since it is more easily understood and enjoyed' (ibid.: p. 61). But he does see the artistic avant-garde having a defensive role to play because it is, by definition, outside the market place, and can maintain artistic standards. It can therefore oppose mass culture. The modernist avant-garde between the late nineteenth century and the 1930s (MacDonald cites Rimbaud, Joyce, Stravinsky and Picasso) tried to preserve an area outside the market and mass culture where 'the serious artist could still function'. In this it was 'remarkably successful', producing the only worthwhile art in this period (ibid.: 63).

But for MacDonald it is doubtful whether this intellectual community can sustain itself. His is a cultural pessimism in which the future is truly dark, and in which alternatives are being closed off. It is only the modernist avant-garde which seems to hold out a faint glimmer of hope. There is no sense here of the idea that mass or popular culture may not be the monolithic or homogeneous phenomenon mass culture theory makes it out to be, and that therefore diversity, innovation and opposition may well exist within as well as outside this culture. Also, whether popular culture is in itself a bad thing is something which is not questioned. There are notable similarities in these respects between mass culture theory and the Frankfurt School's analysis of modern culture. However, the Frankfurt School does have a more systematic idea of the role an avant-garde can play as the guardian of truth and values in an age of mass culture.

Indeed, Q.D. Leavis puts forward a somewhat comparable argument in pointing to ways of preventing mass culture from undermining literary standards and destroying the reading public. What she argues is that the cultural rot can only be stopped by the efforts of a committed intellectual elite: 'all that can be done, it must be realised, must take the form of resistance by an armed and conscious minority' (1932: 270). The role of this elite, this conscious minority, is two-fold. First, it must carry out research to show just how bad things have become, how far the literary standards and reading capacities of the general public have declined and how restricted a role the serious novel and writer have to play in cultural life. This will equip the elite with the information it needs to carry out its mission to reverse the decline produced by mass culture, rather than enlightening the people directly. The result of this research would not only be books to increase 'general awareness': 'it would also mean the training of a picked few who would go out into the world equipped for the work of forming and organising a conscious minority' (ibid.: 271).

This leads us to the second role of this minority, that of 'educational work in schools and universities' (ibid.). Here the function of the 'conscious minority' is, first, to constitute an elite avant-garde which will substantiate and disseminate its interpretation of the rise of mass culture, and warn the population about, and try to reverse, the decline of serious culture; and, second, to regain its position of authority in education, and hence its position of authority as the ultimate arbiter of cultural and artistic taste and values. For Leavis, 'the possibilities of education specifically directed against such appeals as those made by the journalist, the middleman, the best-seller, the cinema, and advertising, and the other more general influences discussed in this study, are inexhaustible; some education of this kind is an essential part of the training of taste' (ibid.). This minority may be the only hope Leavis holds out for the future, but she does not share MacDonald's ambiguity about the influence that an intellectual avant-garde can exercise. Her analysis is therefore instructive not only for what it says about what she sees as the debasing effect of mass culture upon literary standards, but also for its political response to this situation which involves a coherent theory of the role of an intellectual and elite avant-garde.

So far this chapter has presented an outline of the theory of mass culture. It has done this by relating it to the theory of mass society with which it shares much in common. It has been shown how the concept of mass culture involves the mass production and consumption of culture, the threatened subversion of folk culture and high culture, and the relationship between cultural pessimism and the role played by an intellectual avant-garde. It has been argued that the concept of mass culture provides a picture of a debased, trivialised, superficial, artificial and standardised culture which saps the strength of folk and high culture, and challenges the intellectual arbitration of cultural taste. This account may be somewhat simplified and exaggerated. It is always open to the charge that it does not do justice to the work of X, the ideas of Y, or the concept Z. While recognising this argument, we can still insist that what has been outlined can be found, in whole or in part, in most accounts of mass culture as popular culture. It could also be argued that nobody thinks in terms of mass culture any more, that we now know how to appreciate popular as well as high culture. However, as we shall see, ideas similar to mass culture can still be found in subsequent theories of popular culture, even though it may not be described and understood in quite the same way.

Mass culture and Americanisation

The theory of mass culture outlined above has also been concerned about the process of Americanisation. The fears and anxieties expressed by critics of mass culture have been equally directed at the threat of Americanisation.[10] The reason for this is that American popular culture is seen to embody all that is wrong with mass culture. Mass culture is thought to arise from the mass production and consumption of culture. Since it is the capitalist society most closely associated with these processes, it is relatively easy to identify America as the home of mass culture. So much mass culture comes from America that if it is a threat then Americanisation is a threat as well. For domestic critics of mass culture, Americanisation threatens not just aesthetic standards and cultural values, but national culture as well.

It is therefore interesting that intellectual concern in Britain about the harmful effects of American influence can be found in the nineteenth century, before the mass production and consumption of culture began to be fully realised. This is where American populism and the consequences of mass democracy and education become important. Q.D. Leavis, for example, cites Edmund Gosse, writing in 1889, as follows:

> One danger which I have long foreseen from the spread of the democratic sentiment, is that of the tradition of literary taste, the canons of literature, being reversed with success by

> a popular vote. Up to the present time, in all parts of the world, the masses of uneducated or semi-educated persons, who form the vast majority of readers, though they cannot and do not appreciate the classics of their race, have been content to acknowledge their supremacy. Of late there have seemed to me to be certain signs, especially in America, of a revolt of the mob against our literary masters. . . . If literature is to be judged by a plebiscite, and if the plebs recognise its power, it will certainly by degrees cease to support reputations which give it no pleasure and which it cannot comprehend. The revolution against taste, once begun, will land us in irreparable chaos
>
> (Leavis 1932: 190)

The similarity between this kind of argument and the theory of mass culture should be obvious. America is the home of the mass revolt against literary taste, and what is happening there can happen here if the 'democratic sentiment' is allowed to spread.

It is not that difficult to find early examples of anti-American sentiment. In his book Culture and Anarchy, originally published in 1869, the English poet and literary critic Matthew Arnold (1822–1888) wrote: 'in things of the mind, and in culture and totality, America, instead of surpassing us all, falls short.' America here is 'that chosen home of newspapers and politics' (cited in Webster 1988: 180). Arnold's fears about Americanisation were part of his concern that democracy should not 'just give power to the masses, but should entail a polity guided and directed by the state and a properly constituted culture.' As such, the latter should involve the 'pursuit of our total perfection by means of getting to know, on all the matters which most concern us, the best which has been thought and said in the world' (Arnold 1932: 6).

It would probably be correct to say that the equation Arnold draws is between Americanisation and mass democracy rather than Americanisation and mass culture. However, as a number of writers have suggested, democratisation and mass culture are not that easily distinguished from each other. Johnson notes, for example, that Arnold feared 'vulgarity, loss of distinction and, above all, that eccentricity of thought which arises when each man, no matter what his training or gifts, may feel that the democratic doctrine of equality allows him to consider his ideas of equal worth with those of his neighbour'. He thus 'used America as a case study to analyse the possible dangers and trends of democracy', and 'thereafter, in English thought America or "Americanization" was often seen as the epitome of what was most dangerous in the development of modern industrial society.' For Arnold Americanisation 'meant two things': 'a tendency towards fragmentariness' [the absence of a powerful central authority be it an aristocracy or the state to guide, educate, establish standards]; 'and an addiction to the banal' [the absence of standards of excellence and the cultural and moral degeneration of society which could only be halted by a proper cultural and moral education] (Johnson 1979: 21; cf. Webster 1988: 180–181).

This seems to be a consistent line of argument, although it has obviously undergone subsequent changes in context and content. It is thus worth considering the work of the English literary and social critic F.R. Leavis (1895–1978), who was responding directly to a clearly emergent mass culture. He assumed that Americanisation was an accomplished fact: 'it is a commonplace that we are being Americanised' (cited in Webster 1988: 180–181; originally published 1933).

Leavis was a critic of mass society and mass culture, and saw America as an embodiment of both of these dangers. As Hebdige has noted with respect to the anxieties expressed about Americanisation in post-1945 British society, one of the main processes which caused concern was the 'levelling-down' that Americanisation represented (Hebdige 1988: chapter 3). This levelling-down, the apparent potential for greater economic, political and cultural equality, appears also to have worried Leavis. He saw mass society as involving mass production and standardisation, generating an almost irrepressible shift to a mass culture dominated by the mass media. This involved the soporific pleasures of a superficial culture, and the exploitation of a rootless and uneducated public, which consequently became indifferent to the standards of great art. Americanisation was thus the nub of the problem for Leavis because American society had the most developed mass culture, and thus represented the future towards which other comparable societies, such as Britain, were heading: 'American conditions are the conditions of modern civilization, even if the "drift" has gone further on the other side of the Atlantic than on this' (cited in Johnson 1979: 96).

These fears about Americanisation have not been confined to a backward-looking and elitist conservatism, but can be found on the left as well. In this context an interesting socialist writer on Americanisation is the English novelist Orwell (1903–1950), who voices many of the concerns of the more traditionally conservative critics. Perhaps something of the flavour of Orwell's stance is captured in the following quote on the 'decline of the English murder':

> it is significant that the most talked of English murder of recent years should have been committed by an American and an English girl who had become partly Americanized. But it is difficult to believe that this case will be so long remembered as the old domestic poisoning dramas, product of a stable society where the all-prevailing hypocrisy did at least ensure that crimes as serious as murder should have strong emotions behind them.
>
> (Orwell 1965: 13; originally published 1946)

This was Orwell's conclusion to a short and presumably partly comic essay on changes in the nature of murder in which he set the traditional English murder, one which 'can have dramatic and even tragic qualities which make it memorable and excite pity for both victim and murderer', against the newer 'Americanised' murder cited in which there is 'no depth of feeling'. He continues: 'it was almost by chance that the two people concerned committed that particular murder, and it was only by good luck that they did not commit several others.' According to Orwell, the two murderers were an English woman who had said 'she wanted to do something dangerous, "like being a gun-moll"', and an American army deserter who had, untruthfully, 'described himself as a big-time Chicago gangster'. Significantly, 'the background' to the murder 'was not domesticity, but the anonymous life of the dance halls and the false values of the American film' (ibid.: 11–12).

Orwell was equally critical of the moral cynicism of the 'Americanised' crime novel. The example he had in mind was *No Orchids For Miss Blandish*, which featured a gangster as its 'hero'. This he compared with the less morally ambivalent 'Raffles' books which were also about the activities of a criminal hero figure. In contrasting these crime novels, the latter dating from the turn of the century, the former being published in 1939, Orwell was concerned with 'the immense difference in moral atmosphere between the two books, and the change in popular attitude that this probably implies' (ibid.: 63; the author of the 'Raffles' books was E.W. Hornung). In view of the Americanised and popular character of the *No Orchids* novel, Orwell argued that there were 'great numbers of English people who are partly Americanised in language and, one ought to add, in moral outlook'. He cites as evidence the fact that 'there was no popular protest against *No Orchids*', though 'the ordinary reader ought to have objected to – almost certainly would have objected to, a few decades earlier – . . . the equivocal attitude towards crime.' The novel implies 'that being a criminal is only reprehensible in the sense that it does not pay' and that therefore 'the distinction between crime and crime prevention practically disappears.' By contrast, 'even a book like Raffles . . . is governed by powerful taboos, and it is clearly understood that Raffles's crimes must be expiated sooner or later.' But, 'in America, both in life and fiction, the tendency to tolerate crime, even to admire the criminal so long as he is successful, is very much more marked' (ibid.: 73).

If such Americanisation is indeed a trend then, for Orwell, 'there would be good grounds for dismay'. Raffles may have been a criminal but he was also a 'gentleman' and subscribed to a code of moral honour, even if this in the end turned out to be no more than 'the reflexes of a gentleman'. On the other hand, in books like *No Orchids*,

> there are no gentlemen and no taboos. Emancipation is complete. Freud and Machiavelli have reached the outer

> suburbs. Comparing the schoolboy atmosphere of the one book with the cruelty and corruption of the other, one is driven to feel that snobbishness, like hypocrisy, is a check upon behaviour whose value from a social point of view has been underrated.
>
> (ibid.: 79)

After all, according to Orwell, intellectuals, unlike the 'common people', had by then got used to reading 'serious novels' which no longer dealt in the 'world of absolute good and evil', and which no longer provided a clear division 'between right and wrong' (ibid.: 77–78).

For writers such as Orwell, Americanisation did not pose the threat to folk culture that it did for those critics of mass culture we discussed earlier. Rather, it threatened his notion of Englishness. However, it also posed a threat to his idea of the established working-class community which shared many of the qualities ascribed by mass culture critics to the rural folk community, even if it was a product, not of an agrarian society, but of an industrial and urban capitalism. These included organic harmony, shared authentic values, a moral sense of communal and individual worth, autonomous leisure pursuits, and genuine patterns of social integration.

The better known and more extensive presentation of this position is that put forward by the English cultural critic Richard Hoggart (b. 1918). Hebdige links Orwell and Hoggart together in what he calls a 'negative consensus' since they knew what they wanted to preserve – the traditional working-class community – rather than what they wanted to change. He argues that 'Orwell and Hoggart were interested in preserving the "texture" of working-class life against the bland allure of post-war affluence – television, high wages, and consumerism' (Hebdige 1988: 51; cf. pp. 50–52).

In his justly famous book *The Uses of Literacy*, first published in 1957 (a book which has been central to the development of the study of popular culture in Britain) Hoggart tried to document how the traditional and closely knit working-class community was being taken over by what he called 'a shiny barbarism'. Writing about the background in which he grew up, he said his was not simply a critical attack upon mass culture and Americanisation, nor a statement of a particular set of preferences. He viewed what he was doing, in part, as providing a sociology of the uses of popular culture, and of the role of media in people's lives. As Passeron has noted, Hoggart's book draws 'attention to the fact that the reception of a cultural message should not be dissociated from the social conditions in which it occurs and thus from the ethos which essentially characterises a social group' (cited in Dyer 1973: 40).

The 'shiny barbarism' Hoggart feared was defined by mass culture and Americanisation. In particular, he was concerned about the manipulative and exploitative influence exercised over the working-class community, most especially over its more vulnerable younger members, by the America of the Hollywood film, the cheap and brutal crime novel, 'milk bars' and juke-box music. As Webster has pointed out (1988: 187), Hoggart's view of the value and influence of American culture is not totally dismissive or negative. He recognises, for example, the vibrancy and relevance of the more realistic and straightforward qualities of the 'tough-guy' American crime novel in its appeal to working-class readers. However, there is little doubt that, in the end, Hoggart lumps together Americanisation and working-class youth in an elegantly argued moral warning about the debasement of working-class life and the gradual wearing down of the traditional working-class community. Hoggart saw the 'newer mass arts' such as 'sex-and-violence novels', 'the "spicy" magazines', 'commercial popular songs' and the 'juke-box' enticing working-class people to lose themselves and their culture in a mindless and trivial 'candy-floss world', the 'hollow brightness' of a 'shiny barbarism', a world brought to them from across the Atlantic.

Some of Hoggart's most extended condemnations of the impact of Americanisation are reserved for working-class youth. The 'juke-box boys', who frequented what were known in the 1950s and early 1960s as 'milk bars', get special attention:

> the milk-bars indicate at once, in the nastiness of their modernistic knick-knacks, their glaring showiness, an aesthetic breakdown so complete that, in comparison with them, the layout of the living-rooms in some of the poor homes from which the customers come seems to speak of a tradition so balanced and civilized as an eighteenth-century town house . . . most of the customers are boys aged between fifteen and twenty, with drape-suits, picture ties, and an American slouch. Most of them cannot afford a succession of milk-shakes, and make cups of tea serve for an hour or two whilst – and this is their main reason for coming – they put copper after copper into the mechanical record-player . . . The young men waggle one shoulder or stare, as desperately as Humphrey Bogart, across the tubular chairs.
>
> (Hoggart 1958: 203–204)

Hoggart's view is clear: American mass culture leads the 'juke-box boys' away from the lived authenticity of their working-class backgrounds and into the empty fantasy world of Americanised pleasures.

During the period after the end of the Second World War in Britain, Americanisation had become an aspect of some more general fears and anxieties about the increasing capacity of the young and the working class to participate in the slowly emerging consumer society. Booker defined Americanisation, in his idiosyncratic social and cultural history of post-war Britain, as 'a brash, standardised mass-culture, centred on the enormously increased influence of television and advertising, a popular music more marked than ever by the hypnotic beat of jazz, and the new prominence, as a distinct social force, given to teenagers and the young' (Booker 1969: 35). As Americanisation came to be associated with increased consumerism on the part of the young and the working class, America itself came to be an object of consumption. As Frith notes, 'the American dream became an inextricable part of mass cultural fantasies. In German film director Wim Wenders's words, "The Americans colonised our sub-conscious" . . . America, as experienced in film and music, has itself become the object of consumption, a symbol of pleasure' (1983: 46).[11] Consequently, Hebdige can argue that invoking 'the spectre of Americanisation could be used to stand in for any combination of the following ideological themes: the rebellion of youth, the "feminisation" of British culture, the collapse of authority, the loss of Empire, the breakdown of the family, the growth in crime, the decline in attendance at places of worship, etc.' (1988: 58).

These themes inform Hoggart's arguments, but he was just as interested in what was being lost in the process. For example, he associated Americanisation and the milk bar with the loss of the communal sociability of the working-class pub for they represented 'a sort of spiritual dry rot amid the odour of boiled milk'. He came to this conclusion because 'many of the customers – their clothes, their hair-styles, their facial expressions all indicate – are living to a large extent in a myth-world compounded of a few simple elements which they take to be those of American life' (Hoggart: 1958: 204). There is thus in Hoggart's work the idea that the 'genuine' working-class community is in the process of being dissolved into cultural oblivion by mass culture and Americanisation (ibid.: 164–165 and 282–285).

Americanisation and the critique of mass culture theory

The criticisms that can be made of this particular understanding of Americanisation can be used to introduce a more general critique of mass culture theory. There are other ways of understanding the process of Americanisation in Britain, and we shall now look at some of these before proceeding to the general critical conclusions of this chapter.

Many nineteenth-century cultural critics were concerned about Americanisation because they identified it with mass democratic populism, and thus feared it would allow the masses to run the government and lower cultural standards. Others, however, associated America with democracy, modernity, rationality and science. The scientist T.H. Huxley, for example, saw America as representing the promise of a scientific and rational future. Huxley was an optimist who saw little benefit in trying to preserve social and cultural forms which were in decline. Instead, he saw immense possibilities being opened up for everybody by the forward march of a progressive and scientific modernity. According to Johnson, 'Huxley was optimistic about the way in which society was developing, an attitude which he exhibited quite explicitly in his reaction to America'. When Huxley described 'his first sight of America, he remarked on the excitement he felt on seeing the towers and buildings of the post office and other communication centres, instead of the spires of churches'. This symbolised, for him, 'the Americans' interest in knowledge rather than superstition' (1979: 50).

The example of a scientist like Huxley is instructive since his views illustrate an alternative understanding of America and Americanisation which can be used to offer a critical commentary on mass culture theory. In looking at this alternative we can begin with the reading public and the decline of literary standards stressed by Q.D. Leavis and Orwell. Other arguments indicate that the issues involved are more complex than a simple decline of standards. In his discussions with working-class people about their past lives, part of an attempt to construct an oral history, Worpole (1983) found that a surprising number of the people he talked to said that one type of reading matter they had preferred had been American crime and detective fiction. This led Worpole to the tentative speculation that, in the 1930s and 1940s, this fiction gave male, urban, working-class readers access to a language, a style and a subject matter that was more realistic, more relevant to their own lives, conditions and circumstances, more like the way they spoke and thought and dealt with other people, and which were not available in the literature written by and for the English upper and middle classes. As he writes:

> it was in American fiction that many British working class readers . . . found a realism about city life, an acknowledgement of big business corruption, and an unpatronising portrayal of working class experience and speech which wasn't to be found in British popular fiction of the period,

> least of all in the crime novel obsessed as it was with the corpse in the library, the colonel's shares on the stock market, and thwarted passion on the Nile.
>
> (Worpole 1983: 35)

Among other things, this provides an interesting contrast to Orwell's complaints about the 'decline of the English murder' and the popularity of the American crime novel. It also perhaps opens up the difference between the critical arbitration of taste and a sociology of culture (cf. Bourdieu 1984: 11–57).

Worpole's speculations are given support by White's historical study of a working-class street in north London, near Finsbury Park. This area, Campbell Bunk, had a reputation as one of the roughest and toughest in London, and White (1986) presents a historical overview of its development and eventual demise. With respect to the theme of Americanisation he remarks that 'the cinema forged . . . links between the male youth of Campbell Road and outside.' This applied particularly to 'American films' which 'offered heroes and heroines who were less hidebound by class than their technically inferior British counterparts.' For example, 'the glamourised male (especially young male) violence of films like *Little Caesar* (with Edward G. Robinson, 1930), *Public Enemy* (with James Cagney, 1931), *Scarface* (with George Raft, 1932), helped working-class youngsters see themselves as heroes rather than bystanders, the subject of life rather than its object.' As such, 'the adopted American accents, dress-styles and mannerisms, which many observers bemoaned as slavish emulation of a new trash culture, can be interpreted' as 'a self-conscious identification with a more democratic discourse than anything British society (including its labour movement) had to offer them' (White 1986: 166).[12]

The debate over the nature and effects of Americanisation in Britain can be traced back to the nineteenth century. But it seems to have become more significant and more contentious after 1945. In this context it is possible to contrast Hebdige's arguments with those put forward by Hoggart. For Hebdige, fears about Americanisation in the post-war period were linked to fears about the threat posed to traditional intellectual elites and their judgements about taste by the 'levelling-down process'. Ideas about America being more populist and democratic fed into concerns about increasing working-class affluence and consumption which threatened the intellectual arbitration of taste and middle-class consumption as forms of symbolic and positional power. Both Hebdige and Webster have argued that these fears reflected, to some degree, worries on the part of the 'British establishment' over the decline in Britain's world role and its increasing dependence upon the American state (Hebdige 1988: 58; Webster 1988: 183–184 and the conclusion). But what Hebdige is at pains to question is whether the working class, and particularly young, white, working-class men living in the centres of large cities and involved in putting together their own sense of subcultural styles, could be described and understood in Hoggart's terms.

Hebdige's point is that Americanisation did not result in the greater cultural uniformity and homogeneity which the mass culture critics had predicted. On the contrary, he notes 'the sheer plethora of youth cultural options currently available . . . most of which are refracted through a "mythical America"' (1988: 74). This is so because, for him, 'American popular culture – Hollywood films, advertising images, packaging, clothes and music – offers a rich iconography, a set of symbols, objects and artefacts which can be assembled and re-assembled by different groups in a literally limitless number of combinations.' In this process, 'the meaning of each selection is transformed as individual objects – jeans, rock records, Tony Curtis hair styles, bobby socks, etc. – are taken out of their original historical and cultural contexts and juxtaposed against signs from other sources' (ibid.; cf. Hebdige 1979).

According to Hebdige, young working-class males – his version of the 'juke-box boys' – do not consume their imaginary America in a passive and unreflective manner. They construct it with the popular cultural materials available, rather than being constructed by them. It does not matter that their America is 'imaginary' because that is the point – it possesses its 'magic' because it is 'imaginary'. They consume styles in images, clothes and music in an active, meaningful and imaginative fashion, one which transforms the meanings of Americanisation and converts them into distinct subcultural tastes. Hebdige suggests that these young, urban, working-class men have used the images, styles and vocabularies of American popular culture in their own distinctive and positive ways as a form of resistance, albeit not a radical one, to middle-class and upper-class culture, and as a spirited defence against their own subordination.

Moreover, this assimilation and transformation of a 'mythical America' has gone along with the adoption of European styles and fashions. For example, the 'mods', a young working-class subculture based in the central areas of large cities which emerged first in the early 1960s, borrowed as much from Italy (suits and scooters), as they did from black American popular culture (modern jazz and soul music). In fact, Hebdige quotes the anonymous working-class spy hero of Len Deighton's first novel, *The Ipcress File*, in this context. He notes that 'until the 1960s the romantic affirmation of American culture tended to be left to such unashamedly "popular" weeklies as *Titbits* and to the undergrowth of literature – the novelettes, comics and Hollywood ephemera – which were aimed at a predominantly working-class market'. However, 'by 1960, this market – at least significant sections of it, particularly amongst the young – had swung again – away from the exuberant vocabularies of streamlining and rock' (1988: 74).

This change was marked for Hebdige by the appearance of Deighton's novel in 1962. The words of the novel's narrator and anti-hero early on in the book identify the character of the transition: 'I walked down Charlotte Street towards Soho . . . I bought two packets of Gauloises, sank a quick grappa with Mario and Franco at the Terrazza, bought a *Statesman*, some Normandy butter and garlic sausage' (Deighton 1978: 22). 'What is so remarkable here', according to Hebdige, 'is the defection of a man like Harry Palmer not to Russia – still less to America – but to Italy . . . to the Continent.' He continues: 'it is perhaps the final irony that when it did occur the most startling and spectacular revolution in British "popular" taste in the early 1960s involved the domestication not of the brash and "vulgar" hinterland of American design but of the subtle "cool" Continental style which had for so many decades impressed the British champions of the modern movement' (1988: 75). Harry Palmer 'is a fictional extension of mod' (ibid.).[13] Moreover, 'the "spy masters", Burgess and Maclean (followed later by Philby) – motivated, or so the story goes, by a profound contempt and loathing for America, for American cultural, economic and military imperialism, for the "Americanization" of the globe, had flown the roost leaving men like Palmer to take care of things' (ibid.: 76).

The contrast between elitist and populist evaluations of Americanisation is made evident for Hebdige by the example of the spy novel, which he also uses to show how 'foreign' cultural influences, other than those deriving from America, were crucial to subcultures and to popular culture more generally. Indeed, if he had continued to trace out these differences in the spy novel, he would have noted that the motives which led the mole in John Le Carré's novel *Tinker, Tailor, Soldier, Spy*, to betray his country, arose from a deeply felt anti-Americanism. In his confession at the end of the novel, the mole, very much a Leavisite rather than a mod, cites Britain's global decline and irrelevance, and America's capitalist exploitation and materialism, as his reasons for his secret defection to the Soviet Union (Le Carré 1975: 306).

However, it is not at all clear how much can be argued about wider social and cultural developments on the basis of a small number of conveniently selected novels. Also, novels may be used to write social history, but whether they are works of social history is another matter. It has equally to be noted that the spy novel may not be as representative as Hebdige suggests, in that it is a genre of popular fiction which has tended to be dominated by British writers. Furthermore, as Hebdige notes himself, the influence of the Continent was experienced by a subculture which took its music from black American culture. Thus, the argument Hebdige makes may not be as easy to substantiate as he appears to suggest.

None the less, Hebdige's argument provides an effective contrast to that offered by Hoggart, and the comparison highlights some of the interesting problems associated with the analysis of the Americanisation of popular culture. Hebdige also begins to outline some of the difficulties confronted by mass culture theory. The debate about Americanisation has continued on into the 1970s and 1980s and has focused, for example, upon the threats posed to national cultural identities by popular American television programmes. For example, in her study of the Americanising influence of US soaps such as *Dallas*, Ang (1989) has shown how audiences can interpret them with ideologies of mass culture or populism. The discussion of Americanisation has tried to provide a relevant and useful illustration of some of the issues and problems raised by mass culture theory and its approach to the analysis of popular culture. It now remains to extend some of the critical points made above into a more general critique of this perspective.

A critique of mass culture theory

Nowadays, it seems, few would openly and willingly subscribe to mass culture theory. Yet it is still popular with those, for example, who are committed to the defence of what they see as great literature and great art. And though it may not always be swallowed whole, some of its specific arguments, such as those on the value of distinguishing between art and popular culture, or the claim that popular culture isn't as good as it used to be, are still widely shared. Some theorists of postmodernism, for example, lament the lowering of aesthetic standards which contemporary popular culture has achieved, echoing the fears expressed by mass culture critics about the threat posed by mass culture to folk and elite culture (Jameson 1984; Collins 1989: chapter 1). The idea of an audience manipulated and pacified by the ideological appeals of advertising and consumerism can be found in variants of Marxist, feminist and structuralist theory. Even those perspectives which pride themselves on 'taking popular culture seriously' sometimes seem too apologetic and self-conscious when they make this case.

The first line of criticism I want to look at claims that mass culture theory is elitist. This was a charge F.R. Leavis rejected because he thought 'the word "elitism" is a product of ignorance, prejudice and unintelligence . . . appealing as it does to jealousy and kindred impulses and motives.' He insists 'there must always be elites, and, mobilizing and directing the ignorance, prejudice and unintelligence' through the charge of elitism merely 'aims at destroying the only adequate control for "elites" there could be' (cited in Johnson 1979: 98).

However, it can be argued that the term elitism is highly relevant to any critical assessment of mass culture theory. Elitism can refer to a set of unexamined values which give rise to opinionated judgements about popular culture. The first problem which this suggests concerns the privilege conferred upon those positions from which popular or mass culture can be understood and interpreted. An elitist position assumes that popular or mass culture can only be understood and interpreted properly from the vantage point of the aesthetics and 'taste' of cultural and intellectual elites, that is high culture or 'high' theory. This is a problem because the principles or values which underlie this position are either taken for granted or remain unexamined. Elite values and aesthetics are assumed to be valid and authoritative and therefore capable of assessing other types of culture, without any questions being raised about these assumptions and their ability to pass cultural judgements. Mass culture theory can be criticised for being elitist because elitism rests upon a set of unexamined values which shape the perceptions of popular culture held by its exponents.

Elitism also fails to recognise that mass culture can be understood, interpreted and appreciated by other groups in distinct, 'non-elitist' social and aesthetic positions within societies. On what basis can it be argued that some groups' perception of popular culture is better or more valid than that of other groups? In the discussion of Americanisation, we saw how working-class evaluations of mass culture have, at times, been strikingly different from those made by mass culture critics. Elitist judgements fail to recognise interpretations of popular culture developed from alternative vantage points, and the value these alternatives possess. In part, this occurs because elitism usually lacks any kind of sociology. Its usual response to the problem is to minimise the importance of the mass consumers of popular culture because they do not share the aesthetic assumptions of the elite. Hence mass culture theory's view of the consumers of mass culture as passive, manipulable, and exploitable 'cultural dopes'.

Equally, elitism, like mass culture theory, tends to ignore the range and diversity of popular culture, and the tensions and contradictions within it. It usually sees mass culture as necessarily and inevitably homogeneous and standardised. We have seen how the critique of the Americanisation thesis argued that popular culture is not homogeneous or standardised but offers diversity and difference, especially when it is reinterpreted and re-evaluated outside its original context. This argument makes two points which need to be noted here. First, popular culture is diverse because it is open to different uses and interpretations by different groups in society. Second, popular culture itself has to be seen as a diverse and varied set of genres, texts, images and representations which can be found across a range of different media. For example, representations of women in advertising differ from those in soap operas because the latter portray women in a greater variety of roles (cf. Collins 1989: 10–11 on television). While mass culture does at times make use of standardised formats, this is not unique to it but can equally be found in elite culture.[14] Moreover, it is perfectly possible to appreciate some forms of popular or mass culture without accepting it all. If popular culture is not homogeneous, it need not be consumed as a whole. It can be consumed selectively due to the influence of more specific social and cultural factors than mass culture theory seems capable of recognising.

To some extent, the consumption of popular culture by the general public has been a problem for intellectuals, political leaders, and moral and social reformers. These groups have often taken the view that ideally people should be occupied with something more enlightening and worthwhile than popular culture. Q.D. Leavis's work suggests, for example, that readers would be better off with a novel from the great tradition of English literature than a pulp fiction magazine, while MacDonald implies that audiences should confine themselves to the theatre or silent and avant-garde films rather than mainstream Hollywood cinema. There are at least three points to this argument. The first is that mass culture takes up time and energy which should be devoted to other more preferable, constructive and useful pursuits such as art, politics or resuscitating folk cultures. The second is that mass culture has positively harmful effects on its audiences, making them passive, enervated, vulnerable and thus open to manipulation and exploitation. The third point is that bad mass culture drives out good culture, both folk culture and art.

But how is it possible to determine what people should consume, what popular culture they should like and dislike?; and what enables some people to pass judgement on the tastes of others? Taste and style are socially and culturally determined. It is the power to decide upon the definitions of taste and style which circulate within societies which is important, rather than the remote possibility of finding universal and objective reasons for validating aesthetic judgements. The power to determine popular culture and the standards of cultural taste is not restricted to the economic and political power exercised by the mass culture industries, though they are obviously crucial for any adequate explanation of the overall process. It also includes, even if only as a secondary phenomenon, those intellectuals, or producers of ideas and ideologies, with the power to attempt to set down guidelines for cultural discrimination, and the position from which to try to decide what people should like and dislike. As Ang has pointed out, the ideology of mass culture influences the evaluations audiences make of popular culture even if it gives them obvious pleasure (1989: chapter 3). The production of aesthetic value judgements, and hierarchies of cultural taste, together with the conflicts they give rise to, are therefore relevant to this argument.

One way to claim objectivity for the critique of mass culture is to speak on behalf of the people, and praise the authenticity of their culture while condemning the artificiality of mass culture. Mass culture, unlike a genuine and authentic popular or folk culture, cannot arise from, nor be relevant to, the lives and experiences of people. However the definitions used in this argument are questionable. What does 'authentic' mean, and how can we know that a culture is authentic? Is there such a thing as a 'pure' culture, rooted in authentic communal values, and untainted by outside influences and commercial considerations?

Popular music is an area in which the roots and authenticity of particular styles are important issues, and are used to champion the superiority of certain genres such as folk, blues or country over the artificial and superficial character of commercial and mainstream popular music. Yet the criteria of originality, roots, community and authenticity can be deployed as marketing strategies to appeal to particular segments of the music audience while presumably most musicians have to make a living. Also, how do authenticity or inauthenticity affect the pleasures music can afford its audience? Is it not possible for popular music with a wide appeal to be 'good', 'quality' music? Is it really the case that only authentic music is 'good' music? Questioning the idea of authenticity shows just how difficult it is to define, and how it may derive from a particular set of cultural tastes and values, rather than from a considered analysis of popular music.

The idea of authenticity is linked to mass culture theory's view of the past which is often said to be idealised and romanticised, picturing a society and culture fated to be ruined by the rise of mass culture. This version of the past is vividly captured by F.R. Leavis, who argues that 'what we have lost is the organic community with the living culture it embodied'. In this society 'folk-songs, folk-dances, Cotswold cottages and handicraft products are signs and expressions of something more: an art of life, a way of living, ordered and patterned, involving social arts, codes of intercourse and a responsive adjustment, growing out of immemorial experience, to the natural environment and the rhythm of the year' (cited in Johnson 1979: 96).

It may be the case that this view of the past is not fanciful but merely an attempt to show what has been lost, and the subsequent consequences of that loss. Yet it is difficult to resist the conclusion that an idealised 'golden age', in which an authentic folk culture and a truly great high culture knew their places in an ordered world, is an intrinsic part of mass culture theory. If this is so, we can argue that the theory overestimates the past and underestimates the present. What about the standards of education and literacy in the kinds of community evoked by Leavis? What about the qualities and pleasures of contemporary popular culture? Are not the continuing economic, political and cultural inequalities to be found in the past and the present to some extent bound up with the differences between folk, elite and mass culture? Equally, this idea of the past again brings out the elitism of the theory, for the idealised past is based upon a cultural hierarchy dominated by the standards of the elite, to which the people are expected to defer.

This sense of a decline from a past when things were better is by no means unique to mass culture theory. Nonetheless, its version of the past remains unclear. At what precise period of time and in what specific places could the communities and cultures referred to be found apart from the Cotswolds? Were they in their heyday in an age of mass illiteracy? As with most 'golden ages', this past is difficult to pin down historically and geographically. Moreover, when did the decline begin? With the emergence of a commercial market for popular culture? With the rise of the modern mass media? With the spreading ownership of the radio, the dominance of Hollywood cinema, or the location of a television set in most people's homes? Or is it all the fault of America? Representations of the past may themselves be cultural constructs and tell us more about the present than the past. Notwithstanding this, the questions raised suggest that mass culture theory is unclear about its terms, lacks a sense of history, and harbours an unfounded nostalgia for a romanticised and imaginary past.

Two further points emerge out of this problem. The first is that mass culture theory lacks an adequate understanding of social and cultural change. It registers and criticises the appearance of mass culture but fails to explain it. In this sense, it limits itself in not fully understanding something it attacks. Inevitably, this limits both its explanatory and its critical power. It is not enough to say mass culture is a consequence of industrialisation because a more precise argument about the links between the two is needed for an adequate explanation to be sustained. Second, the theory seems to imply a resentment on the part of certain groups of intellectuals to the threats posed by mass culture and mass democracy (popular culture, education, literacy, etc.) to their roles as cultural educators and arbiters of taste. Within a well defined and traditional social hierarchy, the production and protection of cultural standards and the arbitration of taste are carried out by elite intellectuals. The judgements they make apply both to those classes which share a position of power and privilege, and to those in subordinate positions who participate in their own popular culture, while respectfully deferring to elite culture. Mass culture threatens this hierarchy. Dominant classes engage in the commercial production of mass culture, disregarding the standards set by intellectuals, and the people have access to a popular culture beyond the bounds of the traditional hierarchy and the criteria of cultural taste and distinction it embodies. The symbolic power of intellectuals over the standards of taste which are applied to the consumption of cultural goods becomes more difficult to protect and sustain when people can consume a mass culture which does not depend on intellectuals for its appreciation and its definitions of pleasure.

The distinctions drawn by mass culture critics between mass and high culture are not as clear cut or as static as they claim. The boundaries drawn between popular culture and art, or between mass, high and folk culture, are being constantly blurred and changed. They are not necessarily given, or consistently objective and historically constant, but are often indistinct and historically variable. Mass culture theory tends to condemn mass culture as a whole. F.R. Leavis, for example, is said to have dismissed cinema as a serious cultural form, though MacDonald was prepared to count some examples of cinema, such as Eisenstein's films, as art. Some jazz is now appreciated as art, though in the first half of the last century it was condemned as mass culture by mass culture theory and the Frankfurt School. Alfred Hitchcock made commercial films within the Hollywood system but has since been defined as an auteur, an original and creative genius. Early rock-'n'-roll records, once dismissed as mindless pap by music critics, are now accorded 'classic' status by changing critical standards. It would be possible to go on, but what comes out of the examples cited is the difficulty of maintaining a clear divide between art and popular culture. This, in turn, suggests that analysing distinctions between types of culture should take account of the historically shifting power relations between the groups involved, and the categories of taste at stake in the making of these distinctions (Levine 1988; DiMaggio 1986).

The evaluations developed of popular culture can embody different types of politics. In this sense, mass culture theory has the potential to draw anti-democratic conclusions. It would be unfair to suggest that all writers in this tradition are unrepentant elitist reactionaries. None the less, there is a tendency for the critical stance of mass culture theory to lament the emergence of mass democracies, and mass cultural markets, and to see an elite avant-garde as the only potential saviour of cultural standards. This tendency can be found in theories which claim to be democratic, but mass culture theory can seem to be anxious about the equalitarian effects of democracy which allow the masses rather than elites to determine what counts as culture.

A problem which needs to be dealt with in this critique concerns mass culture theory's inadequate understanding of the role of the audience in popular culture. In putting forward a feminist critique, Modleski (1986a; cf. Chapter 5 below) has pointed out how mass culture theory tends to 'feminise' mass culture. It attributes to mass culture qualities which are culturally equated with the feminine, such as consumption, passivity and sentiment or emotion, and contrasts these with qualities such as production, activity and intellect, which are culturally equated with the masculine, and defined as art or high culture. The hierarchical relationship between art and mass culture is equivalent to, and reinforced by, the hierarchical relationship between masculinity and femininity. The power of men over women is reflected in the cultural distinction between art and mass culture. This means that one major reason for the critical dismissal of mass culture arises from its allegedly 'feminine' qualities. For example, mass culture, such as cinema or the soap opera, is denigrated because it is sentimental and plays on people's emotions. It can be dismissed because it evokes reactions associated with the feminine. Hence, one of the threats posed by mass culture, according to its critics, is that it will feminise its audience. For example, the language used in some accounts of mass culture refers to its seductive power to conquer a passive and vulnerable audience through fantasies of romance and escape.

Another way of looking at this problem is to be found in Ang's analysis (1989) of the ideologies used by viewers to account for their reasons for watching and evaluating the American television soap *Dallas*. She found those who disliked or hated the series, and those who watched but laughed at it from a carefully cultivated and 'ironic distance', were confident and secure in the judgements they made and the grounds upon which they could make them. However, those who liked the series tended to be far less confident about expressing and rationalising their preference. Some dealt with this anxiety by bringing out what they saw as the serious qualities of the series, indicating, for example, how its message is that money cannot buy happiness. However, others seemed apologetic and diffident about deriving pleasure from such an obviously inferior, Americanised, mass cultural product.

Ang accounts for this contrast by suggesting that two distinct, discursive and publicly available ideologies are at work. Without necessarily succumbing to the evaluations these ideologies imply, she distinguishes between an ideology of mass culture and an ideology of populism.[15] The first, which has things in common with the theory outlined in this chapter, is the one the first set of viewers resort to in accounting for their hostile and ironic response. This ideology of mass culture appears to be more prominent as a public discourse about cultural evaluations of what is good and bad. It underpins the confident critique of the series as yet another example of Americanised mass culture. From this point of view, *Dallas* serves as a resonant symbol of the Americanisation of Europe. By contrast, the ideology of populism, which tolerates, in an equalitarian way, different kinds of cultural taste and accepts that people know what they like, is used to account for the pleasures the viewers who liked the series derived from watching it. It lay behind their response, though it was expressed with much less confidence and vigour than the ideology of mass culture. One implication of this analysis, apart from its study of how viewers can evaluate what they watch on television, is that it sees the relationships between audiences and popular culture not as mass culture theory does, but as an aspect of the shifting association between power and knowledge.

Mass culture theory generally tends to see the audience as a passive, vulnerable, manipulable, exploitable and sentimental mass. It is resistant to intellectual challenge and stimulation but easy prey to consumerism and advertising and the dreams and fantasies they have to sell. It has little awareness of good taste, and is devoted to the repetitive formulas of mass culture. A number of criticisms can be made of this idea of the audience. First, is there any such thing as a mass audience? Producers of popular culture may not need to reach a mass audience, but sections of a market divided and stratified by tastes, values and preferences as well as money and power. The need for producers to maximise their audiences is a specific instance of cultural production and consumption, and not a guaranteed outcome in societies where mass consumption prevails. The mass audience may not even exist at the point of consumption because the evaluations and effects of popular culture will vary in line with the social character of consumers. The conclusions reached by mass culture theory are difficult to substantiate without knowledge of the social positions occupied by consumers of popular culture in the wider society.

Second, can people's consumption of popular culture be characterised in the way mass culture theory suggests? Can the view that the audience for popular culture is an undifferentiated mass of passive consumers be sustained? To answer these questions adequately we need to see audiences as socially and culturally differentiated, and to recognise that cultural taste is socially constructed. We also need to acknowledge that audiences may be more knowing, active and discriminating in their consumption of popular culture than has usually been conceded by popular culture theory. This theory has tended to speak on behalf of the audience rather than finding out what it has to say for itself. However, this point need not imply that audiences are somehow as powerful, if not more powerful, than the producers of popular culture.[16] We shall return to this below when we consider cultural populism.

Further reading

Ang, I. (1989) *Watching Dallas*, London, Routledge.

Bennett, T. (1982) 'Theories of the media, theories of society', in M. Gurevitch *et al.* (eds), *Culture, Society and the Media*, London, Methuen.

Brookeman, C. (1984) *American Culture and Society since the 1930s*, London and Basingstoke, Macmillan.

Frith, S. (1983) *Sound Effects*, London, Constable.

Hebdige, D. (1988) *Hiding in the Light*, London, Routledge (chapter 3).

Hoggart, R. (1958) *The Uses of Literacy*, Harmondsworth, Penguin.

MacDonald, D. (1957) 'A theory of mass culture', in B. Rosenberg and D. White (eds), *Mass Culture*, Glencoe, Ill., Free Press.

Modleski, T. (1986a) 'Femininity as mas(s)querade: a feminist approach to mass culture', in C. MacCabe (ed.), *High Theory/Low Culture*, Manchester, Manchester University Press.

Strinati, D. (1992a) 'The taste of America: Americanisation and popular culture in Britain', in D. Strinati and S. Wagg (eds), *Come On Down?: Popular Media Culture in Post-war Britain*, London, Routledge.

Webster, D. (1988) *Looka Yonder: The Imaginary America of Populist Culture*, London, Routledge.

Williams, R. (1963) *Culture and Society 1780–1950*, Harmondsworth, Penguin.

Chapter 2

The Frankfurt School and the culture industry

THOSE FAMILIAR WITH THE study of popular culture might well ask if it is worth bothering any longer with the Frankfurt School. Even if it still has something relevant to say, there are now better ways of saying it. The School's perspective, it is often argued, has become both narrow and outmoded. This view is not quite so prevalent as it would have been a few years ago.[1] But it is not unusual for critiques of elitist views of popular culture to use the work of Theodor Adorno, one of the School's key figures, as a prime example of the target at which their criticisms are directed. This stance is even less surprising when it is realised how much common ground the School shares with mass culture theory.

The debate between the Frankfurt School and the other theories discussed in this book, as well as the influence it has had, indicate its continuing significance. Along with mass culture theory, the work of the Frankfurt School has set the terms of debate and analysis for the subsequent study of popular culture. The contemporary analysis of popular music still occasionally traces its heritage back to Adorno's theory, however critical it now is of his arguments. And his name is sometimes used to invoke a whole way of thinking about theory and culture. It would be very difficult to understand the study of popular culture without understanding the work of the Frankfurt School.

In this chapter we shall first place the School in context, as this may help us understand some of its ideas. This context will only be discussed insofar as it is relevant to the School's analysis of popular culture. Next, we shall look briefly at the School's general theory, before outlining in more detail its cultural theory and analysis. The discussion will generally be restricted to Adorno's work, although other representatives of the School, such as Herbert Marcuse, will also be considered. The specific examples of Hollywood cinema and popular music (especially Adorno's theory of the latter) will be used to clarify and illustrate the

School's ideas. Adorno's theory of popular music will also be used to develop a critique of these ideas. The conclusion will evaluate the School's contribution to the study of popular culture by looking at some of the arguments presented by Walter Benjamin, another member of the School but one whose work is not that representative of its approach.

The origins of the Frankfurt School

The Frankfurt Institute for Social Research (the Frankfurt School) was set up in 1923. Its founders tended to be left-wing German, Jewish intellectuals drawn from the upper and middle classes of German society. Among its activities was the development of critical theory and research. This work aimed to reveal the social contradictions underlying the emergent capitalist societies of the time, and their typical ideologies, so as to construct a theoretical critique of modern capitalism. Among the many prominent intellectuals at one time or another associated with the School, the most important are Adorno (1903–1969), Max Horkheimer (1895–1973) and Herbert Marcuse (1898–1979). An equally important figure, but one more marginal to the major tenets of the School's theory, is Walter Benjamin (1892–1940) who will be considered more fully at the end of this chapter.

The Nazi party's rise to power in Germany in the 1930s, its racist oppression of Jews, and its totalitarian repression of the left all meant that members of the School were forced to flee to other parts of western Europe and North America.[2] In the early 1940s the School was temporarily situated in New York although some members spent time in Los Angeles, including Hollywood. It eventually returned to Germany in the late 1940s, along with leading figures such as Adorno and Horkheimer. Some members stayed on in America after the war and, turning to liberalism and empirical social science, renounced the School's theory and politics. By contrast, others, in particular Marcuse, extended the School's analysis of modern society to post-war American capitalism. The fascist state of Nazi Germany, Soviet, Marxist totalitarianism, and American monopoly, consumer capitalism were crucial features of the context in which the Frankfurt School's analysis of popular culture and the mass media emerged and developed. In the eyes of the Frankfurt School, 'it seemed as though the possibility of radical social change had been smashed between the twin cudgels of concentration camps and television for the masses' (Craib 1984: 184).

There are now a number of books which present a detailed history of the School and its work.[3] Here it is merely useful to make a few general points about the School's relevance to the study of popular culture. For a start, it is useful to note what the School was reacting against in developing its own perspective. It was engaged in a critique of the Enlightenment. It thought that the promise of the Enlightenment to extend human freedom through scientific and rational progress had turned into a nightmare because science and rationality were instead stamping out human freedom. For Adorno, 'the total effect of the culture industry is one of anti-enlightenment, in which . . . enlightenment, progressive technical domination, becomes mass deception and is turned into a means of fettering consciousness.' As such, 'it impedes the development of autonomous, independent individuals who judge and decide consciously for themselves . . . while obstructing the emancipation for which human beings are as ripe as the productive forces of the epoch permit' (Adorno 1991: 92).

This critique of the Enlightenment is linked to the theory of modern capitalism and the culture industry which Adorno and others began to develop in the 1930s and 1940s. This theory rejects the prospect of rational emancipation offered by the Enlightenment but also involves a critique of Marxism. The argument here is more complicated because the School draws upon while at the same time criticising Marxist theory. The Frankfurt School's perspective is an obvious variant of Marxism. But its distance from orthodox Marxism can be gauged by its attempt to get away from the emphasis placed upon the economy as the major explanation of how and why societies work as they do; and by its development of a theory of culture relevant to the contemporary phase of capitalism. The concept of 'the culture industry' captures the continuing commitment to Marxism (industry as the basic power of capitalism) and the original character of the School's contribution (culture as a causal factor in its own right). In emphasising the position and importance of culture and ideology, the School can be seen as trying to fill in a part of the picture of capitalism Marx did not deal with. However, in doing this it broke with some of his major arguments. In particular, as the twentieth century progressed, the School became increasingly pessimistic about the prospects for a working-class, socialist revolution in the West. An important objective of their analysis was to explain why such a revolution had not occurred and was unlikely to occur in the future.

This critique of Marxism coincided with the critique of the Enlightenment. The potential for extensive and effective social control produced by scientific rationality, as outlined by the School's idea of anti-enlightenment, undermined Marxism's political optimism. Historically, the School was confronted with a situation in which the erosion of the revolutionary, working-class movement was accompanied by the rise of fascism. The latter's political logic represented one type of rational domination identified by the critique of the Enlightenment. The historical and political context of the School's work fostered a concern with the decline of socialism and working-class radicalism. This was seen to result from the increasingly centralised control exercised over ever larger numbers of people by the expanding 'totalitarian' power of modern capitalism. The School's understanding of popular culture relies upon its theory of modern capitalism and the control it sees the culture industry exerting over the minds and actions of people. Before turning to this we need to note the School's indebtedness to a particular aspect of Marx's work.

The theory of commodity fetishism

Adorno once wrote that 'the real secret of success . . . is the mere reflection of what one pays in the market for the product. The consumer is really worshipping the money that he himself has paid for the ticket to the Toscanini concert' (1991: 34). Few statements could more graphically summarise the relevance of Marx's theory of commodity fetishism for Adorno's attempt to use the idea of the culture industry to understand modern popular culture. For Adorno and the Frankfurt School, commodity fetishism is the basis of a theory of how cultural forms such as popular music can secure the continuing economic, political and ideological domination of capitalism.[4]

Adorno's argument is that money – the price of commodities or goods, including a ticket to a concert – defines and dominates social relations in capitalist societies. The inspiration for this view is Marx's theory of commodity fetishism, which suggests that 'the mystery of the commodity form . . . consists in the fact that in it the social character of men's labour appears to them as . . . a social natural quality of the labour product itself, and that consequently the relation of the producers to the sum total of their own labour is presented to them as a social relation, existing not between themselves, but between the products of their labour.' Thus, 'a definite social relation between men . . . assumes, in their eyes, the fantastic form of a relation between things.' This is what Marx calls 'fetishism which attaches itself to the products of labour as soon as they are produced as commodities, and which is therefore inseparable from the production of commodities' (Marx 1963: 183).

According to Adorno, 'this is the real secret of success', since it can show how 'exchange value exerts its power in a special way in the realm of cultural goods' (1991: 34). Marx distinguished between the exchange value and use value of the commodities circulating in capitalist societies. Exchange value refers to the money that a commodity can command on the market, the price it can be bought and sold for, while use value refers to the usefulness of the good for the consumer, its practical value or utility as a commodity. For Marx, exchange value will always dominate use value in capitalism because the production, marketing and consumption of commodities will always take precedence over people's real needs. This idea is central to Adorno's theory of capitalist culture. It links commodity fetishism with the predominance of exchange value. Money exemplifies how social relations between people can assume the fantastic form of a relation defined by a 'thing', that is money, and is the basic definition of the value of commodities for people in capitalist societies. This is why we are supposed to venerate the price we pay for the ticket to the concert rather than the concert itself.

What Adorno has in fact done has been to extend Marx's analyses of commodity fetishism and exchange to the sphere of cultural goods or commodities. The example cited concerns the market for music for which he elaborates a 'concept of musical fetishism'. Adorno argues that 'all contemporary musical life is dominated by the commodity form; the last pre-capitalist residues have been eliminated' (ibid.: 33). This means that what Marx said about commodities in general also applies to cultural commodities which 'are produced for the market, and are aimed at the market' (ibid.: 34). They embody commodity fetishism, and are dominated by their exchange value, as both are defined and realised by the medium of money. What is, however, unique to cultural commodities is that 'exchange value deceptively takes over the functions of use value. The specific fetish character of music lies in this quid pro quo' (ibid.). With other commodities, exchange value both obscures and dominates use value. Exchange value not use value determines the production and circulation of these commodities. However, cultural commodities such as music bring us into an 'immediate' relation with what we buy – the musical experience. Therefore their use value becomes their exchange value such that the latter can 'disguise itself as the object of enjoyment' (ibid.).

So we come back to the statement we started with, hopefully now more aware of its rationale. We are said to worship the price we pay for the ticket to the concert, rather than the performance itself, because we are victims of commodity fetishism whereby social relations and cultural appreciation are objectified and dominated by money. This, in turn, means that exchange value or the price of the ticket becomes the use value as opposed to the musical performance itself, the real underlying use value. This is only part of a more general analysis of popular music to which I shall return below. We have seen here how the School's theory has been based on some of Marx's ideas despite its challenge to some of the fundamental principles of classical Marxism. These ideas have played their part in the School's interpretation of the development of modern capitalism, and in Adorno's formulation of the concept of the culture industry.

The Frankfurt School's theory of modern capitalism

The School's theory argues that modern capitalism has managed to overcome many of the contradictions and crises it once faced, and has thereby acquired new and unprecedented powers of stability and continuity. A good example of this theory is to be found in the work of the philosopher Marcuse, a member of the School who stayed in America after the Second World War, and witnessed its economic growth, affluence and consumerism, as well as its continuing problems of inequality, poverty and racism.[5] This theory also brings out the intellectual and political distance between the School and Marx's analyses of capitalism, which usually defined it as a crisis-ridden and unstable system. The School does not deny that capitalism contains internal contradictions; for Adorno, the art of dialectical thinking necessarily involves identifying these contradictions. But insofar as capitalist societies can provide higher levels of economic well-being for large sections of their populations, including their working classes, their eventual overthrow and the rise of socialism appear less likely to occur. The School sees a durability in capitalism many others have doubted, and argues this rests upon affluence and consumerism, and the more rational and pervasive forms of social control afforded by the modern state, mass media and popular culture.

The School's theory argues that capitalist productive forces can generate vast amounts of wealth through waste production such as military expenditure which means that 'false needs' can be created and met. In this way, people can be unconsciously reconciled to capitalism, guaranteeing its stability and continuity. The rise of monopoly capitalist corporations, and the rational and efficient state management of economy and society, equally contribute to the perpetuation of the system. For example, monopoly has allowed corporations greater control over their markets and prices and thus their waste production, while state intervention can prevent the periodic eruption of economic crises and extend the power of rational organisation over capitalist societies more generally. Moreover, possible contradictions – and hence possible reasons for conflict – between abundance (the productive potential of the economic forces of capitalism) and waste (consumer and military expenditure which could otherwise be used to alleviate poverty and inequality) are no longer integral to the capitalist system and the struggle between capital and labour. Instead they become focused upon marginal groups (such as ethnic minorities) or societies (such as so-called 'third world' countries) lying outside the system. The affluence and consumerism produced by the economies of capitalist societies, and the levels of ideological control possessed by their culture industries, have ensured that the working class has been thoroughly incorporated into the system. Its members are more financially secure, can buy many of the things they desire, or think they desire, and no longer have any conscious reasons for wanting to overthrow capitalism and replace it with a classless and stateless society.

The idea that the working class has been pacified into accepting capitalism is central to the theory of the Frankfurt School and its analyses of popular culture. It links up with the critique of the Enlightenment in that rational domination is the domination of the masses in modern capitalist societies. Its debt to the theory of commodity fetishism is also evident in that commodities of all kinds become more available and therefore more capable of dominating people's consciousness. This fetishism is accentuated by the domination of money, which regulates the relationships between commodities. In keeping with these ideas is the School's concept of false needs, which connects what has been said so far with the concept of the culture industry.

The concept of false needs is identified particularly with the work of Marcuse, but is derived from the general theoretical framework of the School, and is implicit in the writings of some of its other members (Marcuse 1972: 5). It is based upon the assumption that people have true or real needs to be creative, independent and autonomous agents, in control of their own destinies, fully participating members of meaningful and democratic collectivities, able to live free and relatively unconstrained lives, and to think for themselves. It claims, however, that these true needs cannot be realised in modern capitalism because the false needs, which this system has to foster in order to survive, come to be superimposed upon them. False needs work to deny and suppress true or real needs. The false needs which are created and sustained, such as the desires encouraged by consumerism, can be fulfilled at least temporarily, but only at the expense of the true needs, which remain unsatisfied.

This occurs because people do not realise their real needs remain unsatisfied; as a result of the stimulation and fulfilment of false needs, they have what they think they want. Take the example of freedom. People who live in capitalist societies think they are free but they are deluding themselves. They are not free in the sense that the Frankfurt School uses the term. They are not free, autonomous, independent human beings, consciously thinking for themselves. Rather their freedom is restricted to the freedom to choose between different consumer goods or different brands of the same good, or between political parties who in fact look and sound the same. The false needs of consumer and voter choice offered by advertising and parliamentary democracy suppress the real needs for useful products and genuine political freedom. The cultivation of false needs is bound up with the role of the culture industry. The Frankfurt School sees the culture industry ensuring the creation and satisfaction of false needs, and the suppression of true needs. It is so effective in doing this that the working class is no longer likely to pose a threat to the stability and continuity of capitalism.

The culture industry

According to the Frankfurt School, the culture industry reflects the consolidation of commodity fetishism, the domination of exchange value and the ascendancy of state monopoly capitalism. It shapes the tastes and preferences of the masses, thereby moulding their consciousness by instilling the desire for false needs. It therefore works to exclude real or true needs, alternative and radical concepts or theories, and genuinely threatening political opposition. It is so effective in doing this that people do not realise what is going on.

In a reconsideration of the concept of the culture industry (1991) first published in 1975, Adorno reiterated his endorsement of these ideas. He clearly distinguished the culture industry from mass culture since the latter idea assumes the masses bear some responsibility for the culture they consume, that it is determined by the preferences of the masses themselves. Instead, Adorno saw this culture as something which is imposed upon the masses, and which makes them prepared to welcome it insofar as they do not realise it is an imposition.

Looking back to the book he and Horkheimer wrote entitled *Dialectic of Enlightenment* (1973; originally published in 1947), Adorno defined what he meant by the concept of the culture industry:

> In all its branches, products which are tailored for consumption by masses, and which to a great extent determine the nature of that consumption, are manufactured more or less according to plan . . . This is made possible by contemporary technical capabilities as well as by economic and administrative concentration. The culture industry intentionally integrates its consumers from above. To the detriment of both it forces together the spheres of high and low art, separated for thousands of years. The seriousness of high art is destroyed in the speculation about its efficacy; the seriousness of the lower perishes with the civilizational constraints imposed on the rebellious resistance inherent within it as long as social control was not yet total. Thus, although the culture industry undeniably speculates on the conscious and unconscious state of the millions towards which it is directed, the masses are not primary but

> secondary, they are an object of calculation, an appendage of the machinery. The customer is not king, as the culture industry would have us believe, not its subject but its object.
>
> (Adorno 1991: 85)

The commodities produced by the culture industry are governed by the need to realise their value on the market. The profit motive determines the nature of cultural forms. Industrially, cultural production is a process of standardisation whereby the products acquire the form common to all commodities, such as 'the Western, familiar to every movie-goer'. But it also confers a sense of individuality in that each product 'affects an individual air'. This attribution of individuality to each product, and therefore to each consumer, obscures the standardisation and manipulation of consciousness practised by the culture industry (ibid.: 86–87). This means that the more cultural products are actually standardised the more they appear to be individualised. Individualisation is an ideological process which hides the process of standardisation. The Hollywood star system is cited as an example: 'The more dehumanised its methods of operation and content, the more diligently and successfully the culture industry propagates supposedly great personalities and operates with heart throbs' (ibid.: 87).

In response to the claims that modern mass culture is a relatively harmless form of entertainment, a democratic response to consumer demand, and that critics like himself adopt elitist intellectual positions, Adorno stresses the vacuity, banality and conformity fostered by the culture industry. He sees it as a highly destructive force. As he puts it, 'the colour film demolishes the genial old tavern to a greater extent than bombs ever could. . . . No homeland can survive being processed by the films which celebrate it, and which thereby turn the unique character on which it thrives into an interchangeable sameness' (ibid.: 89). To ignore the nature of the culture industry, as Adorno defines it, is to succumb to its ideology.

This ideology is corrupting and manipulative, and underpins the dominance of the market and commodity fetishism. It is equally conformist and mind numbing, enforcing the general acceptance of the capitalist order. For Adorno, 'the concepts of order which it [the culture industry] hammers into human beings are always those of the status quo' (ibid.: 90). Its effects are profound and far-reaching: 'the power of the culture industry's ideology is such that conformity has replaced consciousness' (ibid.). This drive to conformity tolerates no deviation from, or opposition to, nor an alternative vision of, the existing social order. Deviant, oppositional and alternative ways of thinking and acting become increasingly impossible to envisage as the power of the culture industry is extended over people's minds. The culture industry deals in falsehoods not truths, in false needs and false solutions, rather than real needs and real solutions. It solves problems 'only in appearance', not as they should be resolved in the real world. It offers the semblance not the substance of resolving problems, the false satisfaction of false needs as a substitute for the real solution of real problems. In doing this, it takes over the consciousness of the masses.

The masses, in Adorno's eyes, become completely powerless. Power lies with the culture industry. Its products encourage conformity and consensus, which ensure obedience to authority and the stability of the capitalist system. The ability of the culture industry to 'replace' the consciousnesses of the masses with automatic conformity is more or less complete. Its effectiveness, according to Adorno, 'lies in the promotion and exploitation of the ego-weakness to which the powerless members of contemporary society, with its concentration of power, are condemned.' For example, 'it is no coincidence that cynical American film producers are heard to say that their pictures must take into consideration the level of eleven-year-olds. In doing so they would very much like to make adults into eleven-year-olds' (ibid.: 91). The power of the culture industry to secure the dominance and continuity of capitalism resides, for Adorno, in its capacity to shape and perpetuate a 'regressive' audience, a dependent and passive consuming public. We can illustrate some of these ideas by looking at the example of popular music.

The culture industry and popular music

Adorno's theory of popular music is perhaps the most well known aspect of his analysis of the culture industry. It is bound up with the theories of commodity fetishism and the culture industry. A trained musician, practising composer, music theory expert and champion of avant-garde and non-commercial music himself, Adorno had little time for the music produced by monopoly corporations and consumed by the mass public, except as a way of illustrating the power of the culture industry and the alienation to be found among the masses in capitalist societies.

According to Adorno, the popular music produced by the culture industry is dominated by two processes: standardisation and pseudo-individualisation. The idea here is that popular songs come to sound more and more like each other. They are increasingly characterised by a core structure, the parts of which are interchangeable with each other. However, this core is hidden by the peripheral frills, novelties or stylistic variations which are attached to the songs as signs of their supposed uniqueness. Standardisation refers to the substantial similarities between popular songs, pseudo-individualisation to their incidental differences. Standardisation defines the way the culture industry squeezes out any kind of challenge, originality, authenticity or intellectual stimulation from the music it produces, while pseudo-individualisation provides the 'hook', the apparent novelty or uniqueness of the song for the consumer. Standardisation means that popular songs are becoming more alike and their parts, verses and choruses more interchangeable. Pseudo-individualisation disguises this process by making the songs appear more varied and distinct from each other.

The contrasts which Adorno draws between classical and avant-garde music on the one hand, and popular music on the other, allow him to extend this argument. According to Adorno, with classical or avant-garde music, every detail acquires its musical sense from the totality of the piece, and its place within that totality. This is not true of popular or light music where 'the beginning of the chorus is replaceable by the beginning of innumerable other choruses . . . every detail is substitutible; it serves its function only as a cog in a machine' (1991: 303). The difference is not primarily one drawn between complexity and simplicity. Rather, the key distinction is that between standardisation and non-standardisation which establishes the superiority of serious over popular music. An important reason for this is that 'structural standardisation aims at standardised reactions'. These features are not characteristic of serious music:

> To sum up the difference: in Beethoven and in good serious music in general . . . the detail virtually contains the whole and leads to the exposition of the whole, while at the same time it is produced out of the conception of the whole. In popular music the relationship is fortuitous. The detail has no bearing on a whole, which appears as an extraneous framework.
>
> (ibid: 304)

In Adorno's view, one of the few possible challenges to the culture industry and commodity fetishism comes from serious music which renounces the commodity form because it cannot be contained by standardised production or consumption.

One reason for this is that those who listen to popular music are taken in by 'the veneer of individual "effects"' (ibid.: 302), which masks the standardisation of the music, and makes the listeners think they are hearing something new and different. Adorno distinguishes between the framework and the details of a piece of music. The framework entails standardisation which elicits 'a system of response-mechanisms wholly antagonistic to the ideal of individuality in a free, liberal society' (ibid.: 305). This means that the details must confer on the listener a sense of this suppressed individuality. People would not necessarily put up with musical standardisation for very long, so the sense of individualism within the process of musical consumption must be maintained. Hence, 'the necessary correlate of musical standardization is pseudo-individualization' (ibid.: 308). This involves

> endowing cultural mass production with the halo of free choice or open market on the basis of standardization

> itself. Standardization of song hits keeps the customers in line by doing their listening for them, as it were. Pseudo-individualization, for its part, keeps them in line by making them forget that what they listen to is already listened to for them or 'pre-digested'.
>
> (ibid.)

Examples of pseudo-individualisation include improvisation, such as that associated with certain forms of jazz, and the 'hook' line of a song, the slight variation from the norm which makes the song catchy and attractive, and gives it the semblance of novelty.

With respect to the audience, Adorno then goes on to argue that 'the counterpart to the fetishism of music is a regression of listening' (1991: 40). The listeners drawn to popular music are often thought to have infantile or childlike characteristics: they are 'arrested at the infantile stage . . . they are childish; their primitivism is not that of the undeveloped, but that of the forcibly retarded . . . the regression is really from . . . the possibility of a different and oppositional music' (ibid.: 41). Listeners' real need is for this latter type of music, but due to their infantile mentality they continue to listen to popular music: 'regressive listeners behave like children. Again and again and with stubborn malice, they demand the one dish they have once been served' (ibid.: 45). Accordingly, they suffer from the delusion that they are exercising some degree of control and choice in their leisure pursuits (ibid.: 46).

According to Adorno, regressive listening, 'the frame of mind to which popular music originally appealed, on which it feeds, and which it perpetually reinforces, is simultaneously one of distraction and inattention. Listeners are distracted from the demands of reality by entertainment which does not demand attention either' (1991: 309–310). The capitalist mode of production conditions regressive listening. Higher pursuits such as classical music can only be appreciated by those whose work or social position means that they do not need to escape from boredom and effort in their leisure time. Popular music offers relaxation and respite from the rigours of 'mechanised labour' precisely because it is not demanding or difficult, because it can be listened to in a distracted and inattentive manner. People desire popular music, partly because capitalists 'hammer' it into their minds and make it appear desirable. But their desire is also fuelled by the symmetry between production and consumption which characterises their lives in a capitalist society.

People desire popular music because their consumption of standardised products mirrors the standardised, repetitive and boring nature of their work in production. For Adorno, people

> want standardized goods and pseudo-individualization, because their leisure is an escape from work and at the same time is moulded after those psychological attitudes to which their workaday world exclusively habituates them . . . there is . . . a pre-established harmony today between production and consumption of popular music. The people clamour for what they are going to get anyway.
>
> (ibid.: 310)

Standardised production goes hand in hand with standardised consumption. Pseudo-individualisation saves people the effort of attending to the genuinely novel or original in their precious leisure-time. Both of these processes comprise the distraction and inattention which define regressive listening.

The last aspect of Adorno's theory that we need to look at concerns his claim that cultural phenomena such as popular music act as a type of 'social cement', adjusting people to the reality of the lives they lead. Adorno's idea is that most people in capitalist societies live limited, impoverished and unhappy lives. They become aware of this, or are made to become aware of it, from time to time. Popular music and film do not deny this awareness, but can reconcile people to their fate. The fantasies and happiness, the resolutions and reconciliations, offered by popular music and film make people realise how much their real lives lack these qualities, and thus how much they remain unfulfilled and unsatisfied. However, people continue to be adjusted to their conditions of life since 'the actual function of sentimental music', for example,

> lies rather in the temporary release given to the awareness that one has missed fulfilment. . . . Emotional music has become the image of the mother who says, 'Come and weep, my child.' It is catharsis for the masses, but catharsis which keeps them all the more firmly in line. . . . Music that permits its listeners the confession of their unhappiness reconciles them, by means of this 'release,' to their social dependence.
> (ibid.: 313–314)

Here we can see how Adorno conceives of popular culture (including popular music) as a type of 'social cement'. Popular culture does not necessarily hide reality from people; nor are they directly duped or tricked by it. Rather, they are led to recognise how difficult it is to change the world, and to value the respite popular culture offers. They therefore accept the world as it is. The comforts and cathartic effects of popular culture enable people to resign themselves to the harsh and unfulfilling reality of living in a capitalist society. The popular song and Hollywood film dissuade people from resisting the capitalist system, and from trying to construct an alternative society in which individuals could be free, happy and fulfilled.

Adorno's theory of popular music, Cadillacs and doo-wop

In an extremely useful article entitled 'Theodor Adorno meets the Cadillacs' (1986), Gendron has tried to assess Adorno's theory of popular music by applying it to the example of doo-wop music. In doing this, he introduces a critical assessment of Adorno's theory. The Cadillacs mentioned in the title of the article is a reference to both the car and a doo-wop group.

Gendron uses the example of car production in order to clarify what Adorno means when he argues that capitalism functions to standardise commodities. Standardisation involves the interchangeability of parts together with pseudo-individualisation. The parts of one kind of car can be interchanged with those from another as a result of standardisation, while the use of style or pseudo-individualisation – like the addition of a tail-fin to a Cadillac – distinguishes cars from each other, and hides the fact that standardisation is occurring. According to Gendron, Adorno argues that what is true of cars is also true of popular music. Both are distinguished by a core and a periphery, the core being subject to standardisation, the periphery to pseudo-individualisation. The process of standardisation marks the lives that people have to live in capitalist societies and ensures that popular music is inferior to classical and avant-garde music. Gendron says that for Adorno standardisation also occurs diachronically (that is to say, over time as popular musical standards are set) as well as synchronically (the standards which apply at any particular point in time).

Gendron uses the example of doo-wop,[6] as well as other styles of pop music, to critically assess Adorno's theory. He is not totally dismissive of Adorno's work. For example, he suggests that 'industrial standardization is an important feature of popular music, and must be taken seriously in any political assessment of the form' (1986: 25). He also argues that Adorno's theory has the potential both to combine political economy and semiological perspectives, or culture and economy, and to provide a critique of the argument that consumers can draw from popular culture any meanings and interpretations they wish (ibid.: 34–35). We might also note that Adorno's theory of popular culture is more complicated than is often recognised in that he does not see ideology as simply obscuring the reality of capitalism.

However, Gendron argues that Adorno takes his claims about standardisation too far, and he uses the example of doo-wop to develop his critique. Doo-wop is defined by Gendron as:

> a vocal group style, rooted in the black gospel quartet tradition, that emerged on inner city street corners in the mid-fifties and established a major presence on the popular music charts between 1955 and 1959. Its most distinctive feature is the use of background vocals to take on the role of instrumental accompaniment for, and response to, the high tenor or falsetto calls of the lead singer. Typically, the backup vocalists create a harmonic, rhythmic, and contrapuntal substructure by voicing phonetic or nonsense syllables such as 'shoo-doo-be-doo-be-doo,' 'ooh-wah, ooh-wah,' 'sha-na-na,' and so on. (ibid.: 24)

Gendron suggests this music was standardised diachronically and synchronically: the former because it relied on the long-established song patterns of either Tin Pan Alley or rhythm and blues; and the latter because of the close resemblance between doo-wop songs and the interchangeability of their parts, for example the swapping of the shoo-be-dos of one song with the dum-dum-de-dums of another.

According to Gendron, one of the major difficulties with Adorno's work is its failure to distinguish between functional artefacts such as cars and Cadillacs, and textual artefacts such as pop music and doo-wop groups, for example, the Cadillacs. The use of technological innovations in the production of functional artefacts usually encourages standardisation since it can increase the extent to which the parts of, say, one type of car can be interchanged with those of another. However, with textual artefacts, technological innovations, such as the use of experimental tape techniques by the Beatles, can differentiate between, say, pop groups or music styles rather than making them more alike (ibid.: 26). The production of textual artefacts is also different in that what is initially produced is a single 'universal' statement, the song or a series of songs, and not a commodity which can be industrially manufactured in large quantities. What is produced is a particular or unique song in a recording studio by a group of singers, musicians, engineers, etc. It only becomes a functional artefact when it is produced in large numbers as a record. Functional and textual artefacts are the result of distinct processes of production. This means that music, like most popular culture, cannot be treated as if it were just another commercial product.

Functional and textual artefacts, as Gendron goes on to note, are equally the object of different kinds of consumption. If functional artefacts are purchased and found to be useful, then they will be purchased again when required. This would even be true of commodities such as cars, which are only bought relatively infrequently. But if a textual artefact such as a record is bought and liked, this doesn't mean that the very same one will be bought again. No matter how impressed you are with this book, you are unlikely to go out and buy a second copy. What you might do, however, is buy a similar kind of book (if you could find one). If you like doo-wop you might buy different examples of the style, but not the same record twice. This is one of the reasons for the emergence of 'genres' in popular culture, and for their importance in the organisation of consumption and pleasure. Despite Adorno's argument, popular songs advertise both their individuality (it is this song, this example of doo-wop, and not any other) and their interchangeability (if you like this song, this example of doo-wop, then you might well like others in the same style or genre). In this sense, 'we might consider standardization not only as an expression of rigidity but also as a source of pleasure' (ibid.: 29). The pleasure people derive from popular music arises as much from their awareness of standardisation as it does from any perceived difference or individuality they attach to any particular song.

Gendron is equally critical of Adorno's notion of diachronic standardisation because it implies that popular musical styles never change. Going back to the distinction between core and periphery, he makes the following point: 'Adorno approached popular music from the point of view of western "classical" music; if we view popular music in terms of its own conventions, the line between core and periphery will be drawn quite differently' (ibid.: 30). For western classical music, songs share the same musical core if they share the same melodies, harmonies and chord progressions, while the sound, 'feel' and connotations of the song form its periphery. However, there is no reason to suppose that this hierarchy has universal relevance. Nor need it be closed to changes. 'Western classical music focused on melody and harmony, whereas contemporary pop music focuses on timbre and connotation', the connotation of doo-wop being 'fifties teen pop culture' and 'urban street corners' (ibid.: 31). It is by no means obvious what constitutes the core and periphery of textual artefacts; they may differ radically between different types of music.

This may be taken a step further since Gendron questions the extent to which the ideas of core and periphery can be applied to pop music. He does this on the basis of the rapidity with which popular musical styles change:

> the constant shifts in musical genres constitute at least prima facie evidence that important transformations occur in the history of popular music. Before rock 'n' roll, people listened to ragtime, dixieland, swing, crooning, be-bop, rhythm and blues, among others. Whatever their harmonic and melodic similarities, these styles differed quite substantially in timbre, evocation, connotation, and expressiveness. With the coming of rock 'n' roll, the pace of change has accelerated. The thirty years of the rock era have seen the coming and going of Doo-Wop, rockabilly, the girl group sound, surf music, the British invasion, psychedelic rock, folk rock, heavy metal, and punk, to name just a few. While it might be argued that these have only been fashion changes, and hence merely surface changes, this sort of response simply fails to attend to the important differences noted earlier between textual and functional artefacts. In the latter the fashion can change while the mechanism remains the same; fashion is at the periphery, the mechanism at the centre. In the text, there is no mechanism to distinguish from the fashion, since a text is all style or all fashion.
>
> (ibid.: 32)

According to Gendron, Adorno's notion of diachronic standardisation has difficulties handling evidence of this kind. He argues that Adorno would probably regard it as evidence of continuity rather than change, of how the inevitable standardisation of popular music has been neatly masked by the transient novelty of style. But for Gendron, this response fails to appreciate how difficult it is to define the standardised core of popular music independently of its shifting fashions and genres. To introduce the latter into the analysis raises considerations of such issues as sound, context and pleasure. However, Adorno might equally take comfort from the way Gendron establishes the extent to which popular music has been standardised and how the music industry can shape its meanings (ibid.: 24–25 and 34–35).

The Frankfurt School: a critical assessment

The Frankfurt School is rooted in a theoretical tradition different from that of mass culture theory, yet there are similarities in their of view of popular culture. This may mean that certain points already made will be repeated in the following comments. The Frankfurt School has often been singled out for two particular failings: its failure to provide empirical proof for its theories; and the obscure and inaccessible language in which its ideas have been expressed.[7]

It should be evident from the outline above that Adorno makes few attempts to substantiate empirically the claims he makes. For example, his discussion of regressive listening makes no reference to audience studies but instead relies on inferences from his theory. His ideas are confirmed by his analysis because they cannot be contradicted by empirical evidence. It would probably be Adorno's case that real listeners have regressed so far, have become so 'infantile', that nothing could be gained by studying them. However, his analysis of the culture industry is also drawn from the features of its products his theory identifies and not from an empirical and historical analysis (cf. Murdock and Golding 1977: 18–19). Even the Hollywood film can reveal something of the reality of capitalism, but if the society we live in is as Adorno envisages it, then for him non-fetishised, non-ideological forms of empirical knowledge and proof are not possible.

The same defence can be made to the criticism that the ideas of the School are conveyed in an obscure and inaccessible language. A society dominated by commodity fetishism, exchange value and the culture industry, and whose language is similarly tainted, can only be understood by a language which resists fetishism, ideology and the market. For this task, only an obscure and inaccessible language will do. Popular culture cannot be analysed in its own terms but only by the language of a theory which protects itself against contamination by its obscurity. This is also why Adorno supports the cause of avant-garde music because, in rejecting popularity, standardisation and accessibility, it is rejecting commodity fetishism, exchange value and the culture industry.

This rejection of stylistic clarity is linked to the School's idea of the role of theory. Sometimes termed critical theory, the ideas of the Frankfurt School stress that theory is a form of resistance to the commercial impulses of capitalist production and the ideological hold of commodity fetishism. But it can only function in the way that avant-garde music does if it rejects the empiricism which demands that theories be based upon some kind of evidence, and protects itself behind an obscure and inaccessible language. The School's theory and language allow it to stand outside and criticise the 'one-dimensional' world of capitalist thought and culture. However, this stance is only possible if its theory is correct. But is it?

The School's views of theory and language, as well as the wisdom of trying to communicate if most people are thought to be incapable of understanding what is being communicated, are all open to question. For example, empirical evidence can pinpoint weaknesses in the School's analysis of popular culture, as Gendron's article has shown. To develop a critique of the School's theories, we can return first to the problem of elitism, which was raised in the last chapter. Bearing in mind what was said there, it can be argued that elitism describes the role Adorno assigns to critical theory and avant-garde music. The select and enlightened few, by undertaking their intellectual and cultural practices, cut themselves off from the mundane activites of the masses, and thereby resist the power of the culture industry. Elitism describes the way Adorno assumes that other kinds of music can be judged and found wanting by the standards of western classical music. The standards which Adorno uses to discriminate between cultures are exemplified by his conception of the universal values of classical and avant-garde music. They derive from the position of the elite intellectual. Consider, in this respect, his following comment: 'a fully concentrated and conscious experience of art is possible only to those whose lives do not put such a strain on them that in their spare time they want relief from both boredom and effort simultaneously' (1991: 310). However, elitism usually encounters problems when it engages in social and cultural analysis because the standards upon which it bases itself often turn out to be arbitrary not objective, normally a reflection of the social position of particular groups not universal values (cf. Bourdieu 1984: 11–57).

The School's analysis of capitalism appears to be of a society which has discovered the secret of eternal stability. The culture industry provides capitalism with the means by which it can effectively contain any threats posed to it by radical and alternative social forces. Indeed, it is increasingly capable of suppressing such social forces altogether. This degree of stability and consensus is hardly consistent with the sociology and history of capitalist societies. Admittedly, these societies have not had to face a proletarian revolution, but there is little evidence that this was ever on the cards in the first place. Capitalism is arguably less stable than the Frankfurt School theory recognises, but neither has it been continually confronted by the implicit or explicit threat of a revolutionary working-class movement. If this is the case, popular culture cannot be seen as playing a functional role in ensuring the continued stability of capitalism. In short, just how extensive and effective is the ideological domination exercised by the culture industry (cf. Abercrombie *et al.* 1980)?

As we have seen, Adorno argues that the production and consumption of culture in capitalist societies are inevitably standardised. As Gendron suggests, this ignores the differences between functional and textual artefacts. However, it also fails to recognise how much elite or folk culture may be standardised and how some element of standardisation is required for communication to take place at all. Equally, the evident standardisation of popular culture need not necessarily be a direct outcome of the functions of the culture industry, since these could be just as easily achieved by a varied and disordered popular culture. Also, popular cultural genres involve catering for audience expectations and tastes as well as the industrial standardisation of production and consumption.[8] If the culture industry is so powerful, why does it find it difficult to determine precisely where the next hit record or block-buster film is coming from (cf. Gendron 1986: 33)?

One of the major points of contention raised by Adorno's theory is his view of the audience which consumes the products of the culture industry. Studies have shown how audiences for popular culture are more active and discriminating about what they consume than the theories of mass culture or the culture industry allow.[9] (Indeed, this is to some extent true of other theories discussed in this book.) Adorno's discussion of the regressive listener does not appear to be an empirically plausible account of what audiences do when they consume popular culture. Obviously, audiences are nowhere near as powerful as the industries which produce popular culture, but it does not therefore follow that they can be defined as 'cultural dopes'.

This problem is not helped by the way Adorno often characterises the audience. Sometimes it is 'feminised', as in his references to the consumer as 'the girl behind the counter', or 'the girl whose satisfaction consists solely in the fact that she and her boyfriend "look good"' (1991: 35; cf. Modleski 1986a). At other times he argues that adults are turned into children by the culture industry, using the metaphor of infantilism to characterise the regressive listener and regressive listening. His case is that this results from consuming the products of the culture industry. However, according to much evidence, this does not convey adequately what adults or children do when they consume popular culture.[10]

The Frankfurt School's attempt to maintain a distinction between false and true needs, between the false needs for popular cultural goods which are imposed and met by the culture industry, and the true or real needs for freedom, happiness and utopia which are suppressed by the culture industry, has equally been heavily criticised. The argument itself is most closely associated with the writings of Marcuse. However, Adorno also argues that 'the substitute gratification which it [the culture industry] prepares for human beings cheats them out of the same happiness which it deceitfully projects . . . it impedes the development of autonomous, independent individuals who judge and decide consciously for themselves' (1991: 92).

There are two related problems with this: how is it possible to distinguish between false and true needs?; and how can true needs be recognised? Why should the need for a consumer good such as a washing machine be defined as a false need? In principle, a washing machine makes a household chore that much easier to perform. It may therefore be meeting a very real need. People may need intellectual fulfilment, but they also need clean clothes. Likewise, consumer goods are being invested with more importance than they may actually possess. What may appear to be a sign of cultural control may merely be a more efficient way of doing something necessary. As Goldthorpe *et al.* have insisted, 'perhaps Marcuse and like thinkers . . . need to be reminded that "a washing machine is a washing machine is a washing machine"' (1969: 184). They continue in the same vein:

> it is not to us self-evident why one should regard our respondents' concern for decent, comfortable houses, for labour-saving devices, and even for such leisure goods as television sets and cars, as manifesting the force of false needs; of needs, that is, which are 'superimposed upon the individual by particular social interests in his repression' [Marcuse 1972: 5]. It would be equally possible to consider the amenities and possessions for which the couples in our sample were striving as representing something like the minimum material basis on which they and their children might be able to develop a more individuated style of life, with a wider range of choices, than has hitherto been possible for the mass of the manual labour force.
>
> (ibid.: 183–184)

The idea of false needs also seems to rest on the assumption that if people were not engrossed in satisfying these false needs, say watching television (for which they will have more time if they own washing machines), they would be doing something more worthwhile, satisfying their real needs. But what would this entail? What would the fulfilment of real needs involve? Would it necessarily exclude owning washing machines and watching television? It is as if Frankfurt School theorists know what people should and should not be doing on the basis of their own ideological preferences. This is linked to their definition of real needs, which raises problems of its own. The idea of what people should and should not be doing, and what they should really want, although couched in vague and abstract terms, actually assumes a particular model of cultural activity, one influenced by the example of art (e.g. classical music) and the social position of the elite intellectual, to which all people should aspire.

This argument can be extended to the School's understanding of the fate of the working class in western capitalist societies. For the School, this class's real need lay in the revolutionary overthrow of capitalism and its replacement by socialism. The fact that this revolution failed to materialise did not lead the Frankfurt School theorists to question the basis upon which it had been predicted in the first place. What they did was to assume that it should have happened, and then tried to work out why it had failed to materialise, a characteristic of much Marxist thinking in the twentieth century. They appeared to accept that a specifically working-class revolution was no longer possible, and accounted for this by means of the distinction between false and true needs, although the latter was expressed in abstract and universal terms. They argued that the dominance of false needs for the products of the culture industry securely incorporated the working class into the major institutions of capitalist societies, thereby suppressing its real need.

In this picture, true needs are seen as abstract, ahistorical and utopian aspects of human nature, and yet always have to be achieved in specific, historical and social circumstances. This means that the attempt to distinguish between false and true needs in a way which has empirical relevance is never considered. Similarly, the difficulties involved in trying to define true needs in ahistorical terms are rarely raised. How can needs be defined without reference to their social definition, historical transformation and practical fulfilment (or non-fulfilment)? It is difficult to define needs in ways which do not refer to their historical, social and cultural characteristics. Even if needs may be generally determined in some manner, they have to be socially recognised to be fulfilled or for their non-fulfilment to be understood. For these and other reasons, questions can be raised about the extent to which the work of the Frankfurt School can develop a sociological analysis of popular culture.

Benjamin and the critique of the Frankfurt School

Another way of critically assessing the Frankfurt School's ideas is to look at the writings of Walter Benjamin, who for a time was involved in the intellectual activities of the School, but whose cultural analyses appear to differ from those offered by Adorno.[11] For a while before the Frankfurt School was exiled from Germany in the 1930s by the Nazis' seizure of power, Benjamin was a member of the Institute, although one of its more marginal intellectual participants. In the mid-1930s he wrote what some regard as one of the most seminal essays on the popular arts in the twentieth century, 'The work of art in the age of mechanical reproduction' (1973; originally published in 1936).

In this essay, Benjamin aims to assess the effects of mass production and consumption, and modern technology, upon the status of the work of art, as well as their implications for contemporary popular arts or popular culture. Benjamin argues that the work of art acquired an 'aura' which attested to its authority and uniqueness, its singularity in time and space, as a result of its original immersion in religious rituals and ceremonies. The work of art was placed at the centre of religious practices which culturally legitimated and socially integrated the prevailing order. Through this ritual function it gained the aura associated with religion.

Once embedded in this fabric of tradition, art retained its aura independently of its ritual role in religious ceremonies. This process was hastened by the changes associated with the Renaissance which extended the secularisation of the work of art and its subject matter. The focus of artistic attention began to shift from religious to secular subjects. The Renaissance initiated the struggle for artistic autonomy. This struggle involved the ideas that the work of art was unique in its own right, irrespective of any religious considerations, and that being an artist was a unique vocation, guided by a privileged insight into the truths of human existence, a transcendent knowledge founded in the aura of the work of art.

These ideas received their extreme expression in the 'art for art's sake' movement in the mid- to late nineteenth century.

This was a reaction to the emergence of capitalist industrialisation and the commercialisation of culture, and the threats they posed to the aura of the work of art. It is these effects of 'the age of mechanical reproduction' with which Benjamin is most concerned.

The examples of photography and the sound film may help us understand Benjamin's argument. He writes:

> that which withers in the age of mechanical reproduction is the aura of the work of art . . . the technique of reproduction detaches the reproduced object from the domain of tradition. By making many reproductions it substitutes a plurality of copies for a unique existence. And in permitting the reproduction to meet the beholder or listener in his own particular situation, it reactivates the object reproduced. These two processes lead to a tremendous shattering of tradition . . . their most powerful agent is the film
>
> (ibid.: 223)

Likewise, 'from a photographic negative, for example, one can make any number of prints; to ask for the "authentic" print makes no sense' (ibid.: 226).

In effect, art, as visualised by Adorno, has now 'left the realm of the "beautiful semblance"' (ibid.: 232). However, Benjamin views these developments in a positive manner. The work of art which is reproducible has lost its aura and autonomy, but has become more available to more people. The ritual value of the work of art is replaced by its exhibition value. Not only do film and photography show us things we may never have seen before or realised existed (ibid.: 239), they also change the conditions in which they are received. 'Mechanical reproduction of art changes the reaction of the masses toward art' (ibid.: 236) by allowing them to participate in its reception and appreciation. The new popular arts are more accessible to more people and afford them a role in their critical evaluation.

In contrast to painting (ibid.: 237), the sound film is 'superior' in 'capturing reality', and in giving the masses the opportunity to consider what it has captured. Benjamin argues:

> behaviour items shown in a movie can be analysed much more precisely and from more points of view than those presented on paintings or on the stage . . . the film, on the one hand, extends our comprehension of the necessities which rule our lives; on the other hand, it manages to assure us of an immense and unexpected field of action . . . with the close-up, space expands; with slow motion, movement is extended. . . . Let us compare the screen on which a film unfolds with the canvas of a painting. The painting invites the spectator to contemplation; before it the spectator can abandon himself to his associations. Before the movie frame he cannot do so. No sooner has his eye grasped a scene than it is already changed. It cannot be arrested. . . . The mass is a matrix from which all traditional behaviour towards works of art issues today in a new form. Quantity has been transmuted into quality. The greatly increased mass of participants has produced a change in the mode of participation.
> (ibid.: 237–238, 240, 241)

Therefore Benjamin stresses the democratic and participatory rather than the authoritarian and repressive potential of contemporary popular culture. This position is not, of course, without problems of its own, which include the relationship between power and the new popular arts, historical accuracy and an exaggerated technological optimism.[12] But we are not concerned with a detailed assessment of Benjamin's essay. Instead it is presented here as a useful critical footnote to the work of the Frankfurt School.

Further reading

Adorno, T. (1991) *The Culture Industry*, London, Routledge.

Benjamin, W. [1936] (1973) 'The work of art in the age of mechanical reproduction', in *Illuminations*, London, Fontana.

Bennett, T. (1982) 'Theories of the media, theories of society', in M. Gurevitch *et al*. (eds), *Culture, Society and the Media*, London, Methuen.

Bottomore, T. (1989) *The Frankfurt School*, London, Routledge.
Craib, I. (1984) *Modern Social Theory*, London and New York, Harvester Wheatsheaf (chapter 11).
Gendron, B. (1986) 'Theodor Adorno meets the Cadillacs', in T. Modleski (ed.), *Studies in Entertainment*, Bloomington, Indiana, Indiana University Press.
Jay, M. (1973) *The Dialectical Imagination*, London, Heinemann.
Marcuse, H. (1972) *One Dimensional Man*, London, Abacus.
Wolin, R. (1994) *Walter Benjamin*, Berkeley and Los Angeles, University of California Press (chapter 6).

Chapter 3

Structuralism, semiology and popular culture

THIS CHAPTER PRESENTS A discussion of structuralism and semiology. Since their emergence they have had an important effect upon the study of popular culture, and have influenced other seemingly distinct perspectives such as feminism and Marxism. Also, their concepts, such as binary oppositions, signs, signifiers, signifieds and decoding, have continued to be used in the analysis of popular culture. Unlike mass culture theory or the Frankfurt School, their legacy appears to be secure and wide ranging. Given their continued prominence it may even be premature to talk about their legacy (particularly that of semiology). They benefited from the increasing interest in theory taken by social science in the 1960s, and their reputation is said to owe something to their concern with societies which are increasingly inundated with popular culture. Here we shall outline their basic ideas, illustrate them empirically and indicate some of their limitations. However, one question which needs to be dealt with first is: What is the difference, if any, between semiology and structuralism?

If one reads the literature extensively, it becomes apparent that these terms are often used interchangeably. This suggests there is no problem because they mean the same thing. However, things are not so simple. Structuralism has been defined as a theoretical and philosophical framework relevant to the social sciences as a whole, which stresses the universal, causal character of structures. Semiology has been defined as the scientific study of sign systems such as cultures. The *Fontana Dictionary of Modern Thought* defines structuralism as 'a movement characterized by a preoccupation not simply with structures but with such structures as can be held to underlie and generate the phenomena that come under observation . . . with deep structures rather than surface structures . . . referable [according to Lévi-Strauss] to basic characteristics of the mind'. Semiology is defined as 'the general (if tentative) science of signs: systems of signification, means by which human beings –

individually or in groups – communicate or attempt to communicate by signal: gestures, advertisements, language itself, food, objects, clothes, music, and the many other things that qualify' (Bullock and Stallybrass 1977: 566 and 607). Structuralism claims that mental and cultural structures are universal, and that their causal effects give rise to observable social phenomena. However, semiology need not be associated with either of these claims. This is roughly the usage that will be followed in this chapter. It is not totally satisfactory because structuralism and semiology have studied the same things in similar ways. But it does suggest that semiology can be used as a method which does not endorse the universal and causal claims of structuralism.

Structural linguistics and the ideas of Saussure

The Swiss linguist Ferdinand de Saussure (1857–1913) attempted to establish and develop the discipline of structural linguistics. On the basis of this he suggested it was possible to found a science of signs.[1] In these respects, his ideas played a crucial role in the emergence of structuralism and semiology. Discussing his ideas should therefore help clarify their intentions and methods, and their relevance for studying contemporary popular culture.

Saussure is concerned with establishing linguistics as a science. To do this he makes a number of distinctions and definitions which have become familiar to anyone acquainted with the academic study of culture. Saussure's starting-point is the need to define the object of structural linguistics. For this reason, he draws a distinction between *langue* and *parole*, between language as an internally related set of differentiated signs governed by a system of rules (language as a structure) and language as used in speech or writing (language as an accomplished fact of communication between human beings). Langue is, according to Saussure, the object which linguists should study for it is the focus of their analyses and their principle of relevance.

Langue is the overall system or structure of a language (its words, syntax, rules, conventions and meanings). It makes the use of language (parole) possible and is given or taken for granted by any individual speaker. Langue allows people to produce speech and writing, including words and phrases which may be completely new. This idea of langue has proved influential because it makes it relatively easy to infer that all cultural systems, such as myths, national cultures or ideologies, may be described and understood in the same way.

Parole is defined and determined by langue. It is the use of language made possible by, and deriving from, langue. Parole is the sum of the linguistic units involved in speaking and writing. These cannot be studied in and of themselves as single and separate historical items. Instead, they provide evidence about the underlying structure of langue. The aim of linguistics is to use speaking and writing to reveal the underlying structure of the language, the object of linguistics. The rules and relations of this structure can then be used to account for the particular uses people make of their language. Linguistics, therefore, involves the study of langue as a system or structure.

Structural linguistics aims to discover and scrutinise the system of grammatical rules governing the construction of meaningful sentences. These rules are not usually apparent to the users of the language who none the less can still utter or write meaningful sentences. As Saussure himself argues: 'In separating language from speaking, we are at the same time separating: (1) what is social from what is individual; and (2) what is essential from what is accessory and more or less accidental' (1974: 14). From a sociological point of view it is absurd to regard speaking as an individual, non-social act. But for structural linguistics and its subsequent followers, Saussure is distinguishing between fundamental and contingent social and cultural structures, between those structures which provide the explanation and those which need to be explained.

The second distinction Saussure introduces is that between the signifier and the signified. According to Saussure, any linguistic sign, such as a word or phrase, can be broken down into these two elements of which it is composed. It is a distinction which can only be recognised analytically, not empirically, and is a function of langue rather than parole. It accounts for the capacity of language to confer meaning, a feature which has made it attractive for analysing cultural structures other than language (see, for example, Barthes's semiology below). For Saussure, the meaning of particular linguistic units is not determined by an external material reality which imposes itself upon language. These units do not have a direct referent in the external, material world. This world exists but the meanings which are conferred upon it by language are determined by the meanings inherent in language as an objective structure of rules and relations. The meanings conferred by language arise from the differences between linguistic units which are determined by the overall system of language.

The linguistic sign is made up of the signifier and the signified. Words such as 'dog' or 'god' do not acquire their meaning from their equivalents in the world outside language but from the way language contrasts them through its ordering of the letters. In the linguistic sign, the signifier is the 'sound image', the word as it is spoken or written down, and the signified is the concept of the object or idea which is being referred to by the sign. With the examples of 'dog' and 'god', the letters you see or the sounds you hear are the signifiers, and the object and idea evoked by these sounds and words are the signifieds. A letter change can therefore give us an entirely different concept. Language confers meaning on both of the examples through their linguistic differences and their place in the differentiated categories of animals and supernatural beings.

Since the meanings of particular linguistic signs are not externally determined but derive from their place in the overall relational structure of language, it follows that the relationship between the signifier and signified is a purely arbitrary one. There is no necessary reason as to why the notation 'dog' should refer to that specific animal nor 'god' to a supernatural deity. There is no intrinsic, natural or essential reason why a particular concept should be linked with one sound image rather than another. Therefore, it is not possible to understand individual linguistic signs in a piecemeal, ad hoc or empiricist fashion. They have, rather, to be explained by showing how they fit together as arbitrary signs in an internally coherent system or structure of rules and conventions. These signs cease to be arbitrary and become meaningful once they are located within the general structure of the language. They are only properly understood when placed in this structure. This structure is what Saussure calls langue, and it is not given but has to be reconstructed analytically.

These ideas are fundamental to the development of semiology as a way of studying popular culture. However, the relationship between signifiers and signifieds is not arbitrary in culture as it is in language. According to semiology and structuralism, there are necessary factors linking conventions, codes and ideologies which ensure the association of specific signifiers with specific signifieds.

Saussure argues that if languages are seen as systems, they can only be studied and understood in relational terms. The same argument applies to cultures if they are seen as systems. For structural linguistics, structuralism and semiology, meaning can only be derived from a general objective structure of rules in which particular units are differentiated from each other, and derive their meaningful character from their place in this structure. This structure is not given empirically but has to be discovered and defined in relational terms.

Langue can be discovered and defined as a system, for Saussure, if the linguistic signs of parole are studied, not as distinct, individual items, but as signs of the structure of langue. There are two types of relationship within this system which Saussure considers important: syntagmatic relationships between units in a linguistic sequence, say words following each other in a sentence; and paradigmatic relationships between units which might replace each other in a sequence, say substituting one word for another in a sentence. To define any unit or sign in this manner is to specify its relation to other units or signs which can be combined with it to form a sequence, or which are different from it and can replace it in sequences. In either case, it is the relational character of the structure which enables the unit or sign to acquire meaning. This helps explain why structural linguistics has been influential because it suggests that other cultural systems can be analysed in the way Saussure analyses language.

The final distinction Saussure makes is between synchronic and diachronic analysis. He argues that if the task of linguistics is to reconstruct the langue which makes speech and writing possible at any particular point in time, then synchronic analysis has to be kept separate from diachronic analysis. Synchronic analysis refers to the study of structures or systems at a particular point in time, while diachronic analysis involves the study of structures or systems over time. In Saussure's linguistics, synchronic analysis entails the reconstruction of the system of language as a relational whole which is distinguished from, but not necessarily subordinated to, the diachronic study of the historical evolution and structural changes of particular linguistic units and signs. To mix the two would undermine the attempt to define the relational structure of a language. Language is seen as a system of interrelated signs which are made meaningful by their place in the system rather than by their place in history. Freezing the system assimilated by speakers and writers at one point in time allows its structural and relational character to be clearly identified without being obscured by contingent and incidental historical circumstances. Saussure seems to suggest that the structure of langue can be more easily established if synchronic and diachronic analyses are kept separate. But he has been criticised, as have structuralism and semiology, for emphasising synchronic analysis and neglecting historical and social change.

Saussure regards linguistics as a sub-branch of semiology. He suggests that semiology is a science which studies the life of signs within society, shows what they are composed of, and discovers the laws which govern them. Language can be studied as a semiological system of signs which make communication possible and meaningful. It can be clarified further by being compared with other systems of signs. Structural linguistics is one of the first stages in the development of semiology. In making his case, Saussure laid the foundations for later attempts to use structuralism and semiology to study other systems such as popular culture.

Structuralism, culture and myth

The type of linguistics developed by Saussure has not gone unchallenged, and it is not the only way that language has subsequently been studied. Saussure's ideas are important because, as we shall see, they have influenced the development of structuralism and semiology. However, they have attracted a number of criticisms.[2] For example, his definition of parole has been rejected for a number of reasons. Speech and writing are social rather than individual activities, langue is only ever apparent in parole anyway, and the social nature of speech and writing makes them change, unlike langue. Only the latter is social, and change a relatively minor detail in Saussure's theory. He also tends to regard human beings as little more than mouthpieces for the rules of language which govern their speech and writing. Fairclough notes that 'language varies according to the social identities of people in interactions, their socially defined purposes, social setting, and so on. So Saussure's individualistic notion of parole is unsatisfactory' (1989: 21).

Fairclough criticises Saussure's theory by stressing the links between language and power. He asks if there is such a thing as language in the 'unitary and homogeneous sense' which Saussure says it possesses. According to Fairclough, the English language in the United Kingdom, for example, usually means 'British standard English', which resulted from 'the economic, political, and cultural unification of modern Britain'. Despite Saussure's argument, languages, including English, 'appear to be the products of social conditions specific to a particular historical epoch' (ibid.). Langue may be studied for its formal properties but cannot be understood apart from its particular uses, independently of parole. If this is so, it questions the distinction Saussure draws between them. Notwithstanding these criticisms, Saussure's work has significantly influenced the development of structuralism and semiology. Fairclough himself retains a distinction of sorts between langue and parole when he refers to the 'underlying social conventions' and the 'actual use' of language (ibid.: 22).

Our discussion of structuralism will begin with Lévi-Strauss's concept of structure.[3] The French social anthropologist Claude

Lévi-Strauss (b. 1908) is well known for introducing the concepts and methods of structuralism into anthropology, and using them for studying the myths circulating in pre-industrial societies. His version of structuralism is concerned with uncovering the common structural principles underlying specific and historically variable cultures and myths. These structural principles involve the logical and universal characteristics of the human mind which lie behind, classify and produce the empirical examples of cultural myths which can be discovered. This idea of structure is theoretical and explanatory. In the first instance, it has little to do with empirical reality, but it causes the things we can see. It is not directly available to observation, and lies behind, while producing, what we can view. The relationship pictured here by Lévi-Strauss is similar to the one Saussure draws between langue and parole.

This structure is unobservable and causal, which means its power must be unconscious. Human beings subject to this structure and its power are unaware or unconscious of its influences; in much the same way, the speakers or writers of a language are unaware or unconscious of its rules but can still use them correctly. Moreover, consciousness often involves the misrecognition of underlying structural causes and is a poor guide to their defining characteristics. The perceptions of human beings are as likely to misconceive as reveal these characteristics, and it falls to structuralist analysis to say what they are.

Structuralism can do this because it is able to construct a relational model of what this underlying structure is like, even if it cannot be verified directly by empirical observation. According to structuralist analysis, a model of the underlying reality has to be constructed in which all the parts of this structure are systematically related to each other in the same way that all the units of a language are related to each other. In both cases, parts and units acquire their distinctive meanings as a result of their position in a relational whole. For structuralism, structures such as language and culture are more than the sum of their parts. It thus argues that things cannot be studied in their empirical isolation but only in their structural unity.

Structuralism's picture of this is of an underlying, unobservable, unconscious, universal, relational, but real and causal structure. It is defined more precisely by Lévi-Strauss as a logical grid of binary oppositions, combining rational modes of classification. It consists of a determinable number of related elements or oppositions which can be combined or classified in a finite number of ways. All types of culture represent different empirical combinations or symbolic reconciliations of inherent logical oppositions. Empirical cases are secondary expressions or temporary reconciliations of basic structural oppositions; they represent the logical transformations of the structure of oppositions inherent in the human mind. Lévi-Strauss argues that:

> If the general characteristics of the kinship systems of given geographical areas, which we have tried to bring into juxtaposition with equally general characteristics of the linguistic structures of those areas, are recognised by linguistics as an approach to equivalences of their own observations, then it will be apparent . . . that we are much closer to understanding the fundamental characteristics of social life than we have been accustomed to think. . . . We shall be in a position to understand basic similarities between forms of social life, such as language, art, law, and religion, that on the surface seem to differ greatly. At the same time, we shall have the hope of overcoming the opposition between the collective nature of culture and its manifestations in the individual, since the so-called 'collective consciousness' would, in the final analysis, be no more than the expression, on the level of individual thought and behaviour, of certain time and space modalities of the universal laws which make up the unconscious activity of the mind.
>
> (1963: 65 and 21)

A few examples may help clarify this argument. In his study of totemism (1969), Lévi-Strauss spells out his method of working. Totemism refers to the use of types of animals or other 'natural' phenomena to represent a specific social group, say a clan or a tribe. According to Lévi-Strauss, totemism cannot be explained by any particular example since there is no necessary reason why certain totems should represent certain groups. He rejects utilitarian and functional explanations and says that the relationship between the group, the signified and the totem, the signifier, is arbitrary. What he argues instead is that the empirically observable phenomenon is only one possible combination which exists alongside other logical possibilities. These can be discovered if the overall relational structure of possibilities and transformations is constructed. By following this procedure, totemism becomes intelligible.

The theory presumes that totemism is an empirical sign of the fundamental and universal tendency of societies to classify socio-cultural things, such as groups or tribes, by means of things which are natural, such as animals or plants. Lévi-Strauss constructs a grid of binary oppositions and possible permutations based on two assumptions: that totemism provides a non-social (natural) representation of the social (cultural) which is both individual and collective; and that the natural consists of categories and particulars, and the cultural of groups and persons. As a result, totemism is located within the possible combinations of the logically related oppositions between collective and individual existence, and culture and nature. It is intelligible as one way of transforming the elements contained in the following grid (Lévi-Strauss 1969: 84–85):

Nature	Category	Particular
Culture	Group	Person

These collective and individual expressions of the binary opposition between culture and nature can be combined and transformed into a number of distinct relational types as follows (ibid.):

	1	2	3	4
Nature	Category	Category	Particular	Particular
Culture	Group	Person	Person	Group

Totemism is thus understood, not as a distinct empirical phenomenon to be found only in certain cultures, but as a number of different types which stem from this classificatory structure of logical oppositions and possible transformations. Lévi-Strauss identifies totemism empirically with types 1 and 2, and says it is only indirectly related to types 3 and 4. It consists of certain relations and types which can be explained only when the complete structure, of which they are among the other possible combinations, has been reconstructed. It is this universal and underlying structure, organising the opposition between culture and nature, which gives rise to totemism, and allows other possible transformations to occur.

Totemism also provides a symbolic reconciliation of the opposition between culture and nature because they are united by the totem which represents them both. It is an empirical symbol through which societies and their cultures mediate the universal relationship between culture and nature. Other symbols can be analysed by other universal oppositions, such as those between good and evil, and the sacred and the profane.[4]

Another helpful example of structuralism is Lévi-Strauss's study of myths. In *Structural Anthropology*, Lévi-Strauss mentions a myth to be found among the Iroquois and Algonquin indians of North America which, he suggests, closely resembles the Oedipus legend. The story concerns incest between brother and sister rather than mother and son, and murder, although not the unwitting slaying by a son of his father; however, it does contain the moral that attempts to prevent incest make it inevitable. In looking at elements of these two myths he asks the questions: 'Is this a simple coincidence – different causes explaining that, here and there, the same motifs are arbitrarily found together? Or are there deeper reasons for the analogy? In making the comparison, have we not put our finger on a fragment of a meaningful whole?' (1977: 21). His answer to the last question is yes. However, he provides a test of his theory based on the observation that the native north American myth lacks the riddle to be found in the Oedipus legend. If these myths are fragments of a meaningful whole, an underlying, logical and causal structure, then a riddle, suitably transformed, should also be found in north American myth.

This is indeed what Lévi-Strauss discovers. He points out that riddles, such as that associated with the Sphinx episode in the Oedipus myth, are almost entirely absent among the 'North

American Indians'. So if such a riddle could be found it would show he has uncovered 'a fragment of a meaningful whole' that was not 'the effect of chance, but proof of necessity' (ibid.: 22). He says that among native north American myths only two types of riddles can be found: one where they are told to audiences by clowns whose birth is the result of incest; and one, to be found among the Algonquins, where owls ask riddles 'which the hero must answer under pain of death' (ibid.; this is the dilemma Oedipus finds himself in when confronted by the Sphinx). In the myth Lévi-Strauss started with, the incestuous brother, the hero of the myth, murders his double whose mother is a sorceress, a mistress of the owls. This means that we have a transformation of both the incestuous relationships, sister–brother, mother–son, and of the riddle which 'present a double Oedipal character, by way of incest on the one hand, and on the other hand, by way of the owl in which we are led to see, in a transposed form, an American Sphinx' (ibid.).

Again Lévi-Strauss has discovered meaningful relations between elements and oppositions – incest and riddles – which are transformed from one myth to another. These, in turn, suggest other possible relations, arising as they do from an underlying and universal mental structure which 'thinks' these relations and oppositions. He pursues, for example, the possible permutations of riddles with each other, those questions which have no answer and those answers which have no question. This takes him on to the death of Buddha and the Holy Grail cycle, where questions which should be asked are not. He also looks at the relations between sexuality represented by incest, and chastity represented by the heroes of myths, and tries to locate Oedipal type myths within a wider structure of possibilities. The point of these examples is to unravel the meaningful and logically based mental whole which lies behind them.

This argument is given additional force since it uncovers a structure which manages to prevail irrespective of the influences exerted by specific historical, social or cultural conditions. As Lévi-Strauss concludes: 'it seems that the same correlation between riddles and incest exists among peoples separated by history, geography, language and culture' (ibid.: 24). Comparable transformations of myth can be found in societies as far apart from each other, and as structurally distinct, as native north American tribes and the city states of ancient Greece. If this is so, the specific features of these societies cannot explain the character of myths. Instead, they are explained by the logical structure of the human mind which accounts for the similarities and transformations detected by structuralism in cultural myths. In a fitting conclusion to his discussion of these myths, Lévi-Strauss writes:

> we have only sketched here the broad outlines of a demonstration . . . to illustrate the problem of invariance which, like other sciences, social anthropology attempts to resolve, but which it sees as the modern form of a question with which it has always been concerned – that of the universality of human nature.
>
> (ibid.)

He consequently argues that, as a science, structuralism investigates 'a system ruled by an internal cohesiveness' which is 'inaccessible to observation in an isolated system', but which is 'revealed in the study of transformations through which similar properties are recognized in apparently different systems' (ibid.: 18).

Structuralism and James Bond

Umberto Eco's study of the James Bond novels written by Ian Fleming provides a structuralist analysis of contemporary popular culture. While this does not share all the presuppositions held by Lévi-Strauss, its evaluation can show us how structuralism studies contemporary popular culture, and indicate some of the limitations it confronts. A leading contemporary Italian intellectual and semiologist, Eco (b. 1932) is well known as a popular novelist as well as for his studies of popular culture. His study of the Bond novels is perhaps the best known example of his attempt to apply the methods of structuralism to the study of popular culture.[5]

Eco's concern is to uncover the invariant rules governing the narrative structure of these novels. These rules ensure the popular success of the novels and their appeal to a cultural elite. As popular culture, the novels are based upon an underlying structure of rules which makes them popular. For Eco, these rules are comparable to 'a machine that functions basically on a set of precise units governed by rigorous combinational rules. The presence of these rules explains and determines the success of the "007" saga – a success which, singularly, has been due both to the mass consensus and to the appreciation of more sophisticated readers' (1979: 146). This 'narrative machine' presumably connects at some unconscious level with the desires and values of the popular audience, for each cog or 'structural element' of which this machine is composed, is assumed to be related to 'the reader's sensitivity' (ibid.).

Eco constructs the series of oppositions upon which the novels are based. These oppositions, which are very similar to Lévi-Strauss's binary oppositions, can be combined and recombined with each other, and are 'immediate and universal' (ibid.: 147). Their 'permutation and interaction' means that the combination, association and representation of each opposition can be varied, to some extent, from novel to novel. None the less, they form an invariant structure of oppositions which defines the narratives and ensures the popularity of the novels. These oppositions involve the relations between characters in the novels (for example, between Bond and the villain or the woman), the relations between ideologies (for example, between liberalism and totalitarianism, or the 'free world' and the 'Soviet Union') and a larger number of relations between distinct types of values (for example, 'cupidity–ideals, love–death, chance–planning . . . perversion–innocence, loyalty–disloyalty' (ibid.)). These relationships are worked out by particular characters, the relations between characters and the unravelling of the story as a whole. For example, Bond, in his relations with the villain, represents the ascendancy of the free world over the Soviet Union, and the victory of chance over planning. But whatever the specific transformation of relations between oppositions in particular novels, the underlying structure of oppositions remains the same. Eco traces the nature of this structure and its transformations across the stories to be found in the James Bond novels.

This argument is linked to the idea that there is an invariant sequential structure underlying the novels. Eco compares this to 'play situations' or 'games' in which each initial 'move' gives rise to a countermove and so on, pushing the story forward. The prevalence of games of chance in the novels occurs 'because they form a reduced and formalized model of the more general play situation that is the novel. The novel, given the rules of combination of oppositional couples, is fixed as a sequence of "moves" inspired by the code and constituted according to a perfectly prearranged scheme' (ibid.: 156). Abbreviating slightly, this 'invariable scheme' can be detailed as follows:

> A M moves and gives a task to Bond;
> B Villain moves and appears to Bond . . . ;
> C Bond moves and gives a first check to Villain or Villain gives first check to Bond;
> D Woman moves and shows herself to Bond;
> E Bond takes Woman . . . ;
> F Villain captures Bond . . . ;
> G Villain tortures Bond . . . ;
> H Bond beats Villain . . . ;
> I Bond, convalescing, enjoys Woman, whom he then loses.
> (ibid.)

This scheme is invariant in that each novel must contain all these elements or 'moves'. It is demanded by the narrative structure of the novels and explains their popular success. However, these basic elements need not appear in this sequence. In fact, Eco goes to great lengths to show the range of variations possible. In this sense, paradigmatic relations are more fundamental to the structure which articulates the novels than syntagmatic relations. The sequence may change but the structure remains the same. And it does so, as Eco tries to demonstrate, irrespective of the many 'side issues' or incidental features which may be introduced to add colour and variety to any particular novel.

According to Eco, the coming together of these two structures of binary oppositions and premeditated moves accounts for the popular attractions of the novels. The incidental features or 'collateral inventions' play their part in this success, especially among more 'sophisticated' readers. Eco suggests that 'the true and original story remains immutable, and suspense is stabilized curiously on the basis of a sequence of events that are entirely predetermined'. As such, 'there is no basic variation, but rather the repetition of a habitual scheme in which the reader can recognize something he has already seen and of which he has grown fond.' This means that 'the reader finds himself immersed in a game of which he knows the pieces and the rules – and perhaps the outcome – and draws pleasure simply from following the minimal variations by which the victor realizes his objective' (ibid.: 160).

This argument is interesting because it combines the concepts of structuralism with a picture of the audience consistent with that presented by the mass culture critics and the Frankfurt School. As Eco continues, 'the novels of Fleming exploit in exemplary manner that element of foregone play which is typical of the escape mechanism geared for the entertainment of the masses' (ibid.: 161). A theory which relies upon the concept of an underlying and unconscious structure for its explanatory power is clearly liable to underestimate the significance of the role of the audience in understanding popular culture.[6] This view is evident in Eco's account of Fleming's use of ideology. He argues that the ideologies to be found in the novels are determined by the demands of mass culture. Fleming's reliance on cold war ideology, for example, derives simply from his endorsement of 'the common opinions shared by the majority of his readers' (ibid.). Eco suggests that 'Fleming seeks elementary oppositions; to personify primitive and universal forces, he has recourse to popular standards' (ibid.: 162).

Another aspect of Eco's structuralism, one consistent with that of Lévi-Strauss, concerns the universal character of the structure which lies behind and explains the popularity of the Bond novels. Eco argues that the narrative structure of these novels represents a modern variation on the universal theme of the struggle between good and evil. This struggle, which for Eco defines Fleming's Manichaean ideology even if it is the result of opportunism, forms a fundamental binary opposition. The Bond novels are comparable to fairy tales in which a knight (Bond), under the orders of a king (M), goes on a mission to destroy the monster, such as a dragon (the villain), and rescue the lady (the woman). Both types of story involve transformations of the basic elements embodied in the binary opposition between good and evil. They express a universal structure of basic oppositions which, because it is universal, will ensure popular success. Both the Bond novels and fairy tales are successful because they are universal in their underlying connection with the eternal conflict between good and evil.

The popular success of the Bond novels is accounted for by the idea that the mass audience is unknowingly in tune with the universal themes which are evoked. For this mass readership, 'it is clear how the novels of Fleming have attained such a wide success: they build up a network of elementary associations to achieve something original and profound' (ibid.: 163). However, there are more discerning readers who are conscious of the mechanics of the novels, and capable of grasping the more subtle and esoteric allusions in Fleming's writing (ibid.). Eco is here identifying a culturally stratified audience for the Bond novels, one divided between the mass popular readership, and a cultural elite. He thus elaborates upon the references to be found in the novels which appeal to the tastes of the culturally literate reader. He notes, for example, the resemblance between the physical description of James Bond and that of a typical Byronic hero (ibid.: 171–172 and 169–170). Moreover, 'the sophisticated readers' can 'distinguish, with a feeling of aesthetic pleasure, the purity of the primitive epic impudently and maliciously translated into current terms'. They can also 'applaud in Fleming the cultured man, whom they recognize as one of themselves, naturally the most clever and broadminded' (ibid.: 163).

Eco's structuralism leads him to argue that the structure of the novels places particular types of readers, masses and elites, in particular types of attraction, elemental primitivism and cultural sophistication. In view of this, it is curious that Eco finally comes to recognise the importance of readers who are not determined in their reading by the structure of the text. He argues that 'since the decoding of a message cannot be established by its author, but depends on the concrete circumstances of reception, it is difficult to guess what Fleming is or will be for his readers' (ibid.: 172). But without this 'definitive verification' what is the point of the analysis Eco has carried out? If it is the reception of the novels by their readers which determines their meaning, then what is the point of uncovering their invariant structure of binary oppositions? What value do structuralist analyses have if cultural meanings are derived from the 'society that reads', from 'the concrete circumstances of reception'? These circumstances are socially and historically specific patterns of cultural production and consumption, not invariant narrative structures or binary oppositions. To suggest that the influence exerted by the universal structure does not determine how and why people read the texts which it generates, is to call into question the value of structuralist analyses. This is all the more surprising since Eco starts from the assumption that identifying this structure will account for the popularity of the texts being studied.

There is some confusion here over the role of readers or audiences. Are the 'readings' of audiences determined by a universal structure, or by social, cultural and historical conditions? Related questions raised by this point are: do audiences themselves decide upon their understandings of popular culture?; or does the analyst or theorist decide for them?; and, if so, do the latter take account of the former in arriving at their interpretations of popular culture?

This problem is intensified by the ahistorical nature of Eco's structuralist analysis. His explanatory principle is, after all, an invariant, static and eternal structure. As Bennett and Woollacott argue, there are no fixed, universal and ahistorical codes; 'readings' of popular culture are always organised in historically specific contexts. They point out how difficult it is to make sense of the James Bond novels without taking into consideration their 'intertextuality' (Bennett and Woollacott 1987: chapter 3). This means that the popular cultural phenomenon of James Bond has to be assessed in the context of the range of 'texts', or cultural forms and media outlets, in which it is to be found. These include, most significantly, the James Bond films as well as the novels. Bennett and Woollacott also argue that readers come to novels with some prior cultural knowledge, and suggest that the codes developed in reading the British imperialist spy thriller formed an important aspect of the cultural knowledge readers brought to their interpretations of the Bond novels. They even speculate that some working-class readers would have read them in terms of the codes associated with detective fiction. Similarly, Denning argues that the emergence of codes associated with tourism and pornography in the 1960s was a crucial reference point for audiences of both the novels and the films (Denning 1987: chapter 4).

Barthes, semiology and popular culture

The semiological study of popular culture probably owes much of its reputation and importance to the writings of the French critic and semiologist Roland Barthes (1915–1980), and in particular to his book *Mythologies* (originally published in 1957). In the studies and theoretical arguments which make up this book, Barthes sets out a way of interpreting popular culture which has, with some notable revisions, been highly influential and extensively discussed ever since.[7] Before we consider this work, some general points about Barthes's semiology and his book *Writing Degree Zero* (written before he wrote *Mythologies*) need to be considered in order to clarify his subsequent work.

Barthes, structuralism and semiology

The general points made here are comparable to those made about structuralism, except that semiology does not assume there is a universal structure underlying sign systems. The signs and codes it refers to are meant to be historically and culturally specific. It does, however, insist that it is these codes and signs which make meaning possible and enable human beings to make their world intelligible.

The wider significance of semiology can perhaps be gauged by the way Barthes later clarified his aims in writing the pieces which make up his book *Mythologies*. He writes,

> I was dazzled by this hope: to give my denunciation of the self-proclaimed petit-bourgeois myths the means of developing scientifically; this means was semiology or the close analysis of the processes of meaning by which the bourgeoisie converts its historical class-culture into universal nature; semiology appeared to me, then, in its program and tasks, as the fundamental method of an ideological critique.
> (1988: 5)

This usefully indicates the intention of his book, even if it also hints at his subsequent reluctance to think of semiology as a systematic science.

As with structuralism, the first point which needs to be noted is that semiology is defined as a science of signs, in keeping with Saussure's original suggestion. It not only possesses a notion of ideology against which the truth of science can be measured, but it promises a scientific way of understanding popular culture. This allows it to be distinguished from the arbitrary and individualistic impressionism of liberal humanist studies of culture, as well as from those approaches which rely upon aesthetic discrimination and 'good taste'.

Semiology argues that material reality can never be taken for granted. It is always constructed and made intelligible to human understanding by culturally specific systems of meaning. This meaning is never 'innocent', but has some particular purpose or interest lying behind it, which semiology can uncover. Our experience of the world is never 'innocent' because systems of meaning make sure it is intelligible. There is no such thing as a pure, uncoded, objective experience of a real and objective world. The latter exists but its intelligibility depends upon codes of meaning or systems of signs, such as language.

These codes and signs are not universally given, but are historically and socially specific to the particular interests and purposes which lie behind them. It is in this sense that they are never innocent. Meaning is not something which is given or which can be taken for granted. It is manufactured out of historically shifting systems of codes, conventions and signs. Semiology is concerned with this production of meaning, with what Barthes calls 'the process of signification'. Cultural meanings are not universal, nor are they divorced from the social conditions in which they are to be found. Rather, they present themselves as universal when they are really historically and socially fixed. As Barthes writes in *Mythologies*, the function of myth is to 'transform history into nature' (1973: 140). This point will be clarifed by Barthes's analysis of specific myths; it is also an argument advanced in his book *Writing Degree Zero* (1967; originally published in 1953).

Writing Degree Zero

In this, his first book, Barthes was concerned with the French classical style of writing. This style, which emerged in court society in the seventeenth century, prided itself upon clarity and preciseness of expression, and set itself up as a universal model or standard for all writing. By the nineteenth century, the French classical style of writing was considered to be the only correct and rational way to write, an inevitable and 'natural' style which simply and unambiguously served to reflect reality. During this period, this model of lucidity came to be legitimised as a universal model of human communication.

However, Barthes understands it in a different way. For a start, despite its supposed universal and natural qualities, from the mid-nineteenth century onwards it begins to disintegrate. In this process, it is challenged by a growing number of styles, for example, writing as a craft or job, self-conscious literariness, and 'writing degree zero'. Barthes's critique of the French classical style is based upon the reasons for this disintegration. He argues that it is wider social forces and class interests which govern the formation and transformation of writing styles. The emergence of new class interests and conflicts in the nineteenth century results in the breakdown of the classical style. Barthes interprets this style, despite its pretensions, as an aspect of the rise of bourgeois hegemony, and thus as a 'class idiom'.

For Barthes, French classicism, irrespective of its pretensions, is neither neutral and universal nor natural and inevitable. Instead, it has to be located in its historical and social contexts. As such, it is central to the rise of bourgeois hegemony between the seventeenth and nineteenth centuries, and to the emergence of challenges to this hegemony from the 1850s onwards. According to Barthes, the classical style is rhetorical in character, motivated by the 'permanent intention to persuade'. It is the style of the law courts and the political campaign, aimed at changing opinions and ensuring the acceptance of the bourgeois view of the world. It has thus not simply been a reflection of reality but an attempt to shape conceptions of reality. It has not been neutral and universal, nor natural and inevitable, but historically specific and socially constructed, rooted in a particular set of class interests. Its meaning has not been given but produced, not 'innocent' but 'guilty'. French classicism is another 'myth', which tries to transform the historical into the natural in the interests of the bourgeois class.

This is, for Barthes, a feature of all writing. 'Writing degree zero' is a style developed in order to reject the idea of politically committed writing. It values writing which is colourless, transparent and neutral, blank and impersonal. It pretends to be as asocial and ahistorical as possible. In a way, it is not a style at all. But this is not possible according to Barthes. For him, all writing is a form of fabrication, a way of making things up, which therefore cannot avoid these signs of fabrication or style. Furthermore, all writing is ideological and cannot avoid being so. Writing is never just an instrument of communication, an open way of addressing people. It is rather a product of certain social and historical circumstances and certain power relations, and cannot escape their influence. Non-ideological writing, writing which presents itself as being beyond ideology, is for Barthes shown to be an illusion by his investigation of French classicism and 'writing degree zero'.

Myths and popular culture

Barthes carried these ideas further in his book *Mythologies*, which contains a series of short essays on various examples of popular culture, originally published in magazines, and an outline of the concepts and methods of semiology which he uses to analyse the examples. It is the latter we shall consider first. Myths are forms of popular culture, but they are also more than this, according to Barthes. We have to find out what is really going on, and to do this we have to turn to semiology.

'Myth is a system of communication, that is a message', Barthes writes, 'a mode of signification . . . a type of speech . . . conveyed by a discourse. Myth is not defined by the object of its message, but by the way in which it utters this message' (1973: 117). This means that the concepts and procedures of semiology can be applied to the study of myths. To understand this we need to remind ourselves of the claims semiology makes. Barthes notes that 'any semiology postulates a relation between two terms, a signifier and a signified' (ibid.: 121), a distinction elaborated by Saussure, as we have seen. There is also a third term in this, the sign itself (be it linguistic or mythological), which contains the signifier and the signified. Barthes wishes to use this argument to study myth, and he gives an initial and preliminary example of how this might be done.

The case he has in mind is a bunch of roses which can be used to signify passion. Barthes asks:

> Do we have here, then, only a signifier and a signified, the roses and my passion? Not even that: to put it accurately, there are here only 'passionified' roses. But on the plane of analysis, we do have three terms [even if empirically there is only one thing, the roses]; for these roses weighted with passion perfectly and correctly allow themselves to be decomposed into roses and passion: the former and the latter existed before uniting and forming this third object, which is the sign.
>
> (ibid.: 121–122)

In other words, the roses are a signifier of a signified, which is passion, something signified by the roses sent to a loved one. The bunch of roses can thus be analytically if not empirically broken down into a signifier, the roses, a signified, passion, and a sign which combines and is not separate from these two components, the roses as a sign of passion. Here, passion is the process of signification. This attribution of meaning – the roses signify passion and not, say, a joke or a farewell – cannot be understood simply in terms of the system of signs, but has to be located in the context of the social relationships in which the attribution of meaning occurs. However, this is a problem which semiology finds it difficult to deal with. It is similar to the problem Saussurian linguistics has in dealing with language independently of the contexts in which people actually use language.

Because the mythic process of signification is not totally comparable with that associated with language, Barthes uses other concepts to analyse myths. According to Barthes, myth 'is a second-order semiological system' (ibid.: 123). It relies upon signs in other first-order systems such as language (and horticulture, as with roses?) in order to engage in the process of signification. A sign in a first-order system, a word, a flower or a photograph, becomes a signifier in the second-order system of myth. Myth uses other systems, be they written or pictorial, to construct meanings. Myth thus becomes a metalanguage because it can refer to other languages, and requires the use of new if comparable concepts.

These concepts are established by Barthes through his most famous example. He writes:

> I am at the barber's, and a copy of *Paris-Match* is offered to me. On the cover, a young Negro in a French uniform is saluting, with his eyes uplifted, probably fixed on a fold of the tricolour. All this is the meaning of the picture. But . . . I see very well what it signifies to me: that France is a great Empire, that all her sons, without any colour discrimination, faithfully serve under her flag, and that there is no better answer to the detractors of an alleged colonialism than

> the zeal shown by this Negro in serving his so-called oppressors. I am therefore . . . faced with a greater semiological system: there is a signifier, itself already formed within a previous system (a black soldier is giving the French salute); there is a signified (it is here a purposeful mixture of Frenchness and militariness); finally, there is a presence of the signified through the signifier. . . . French imperiality.
>
> (ibid.: 125–126 and 128)

While retaining the analytical value of the distinctions made by structural linguistics, Barthes suggests that the study of myths needs to avoid confusion. Therefore, the signifier becomes 'form', the signified 'concept' and the sign 'signification'. In the example just mentioned, we have the form of the black soldier saluting the French flag, the concept of French military strength and the signification of the grandeur and impartiality of French imperialism. All of this is in the photograph, but has to be revealed by semiological analysis.

Using these concepts and this example, Barthes argues that myth works through the relationships between form, concept and signification. The form of this specific myth of French imperiality, the black soldier, is taken from one system, his real history, which gave him his meaning, and placed in another system, that of the myth, which denies his history and culture, and thus the real history of French colonial exploitation. What motivates this 'impoverishment of meaning' is the concept of French imperiality, which gives another history to the soldier, that of the grandeur and impartiality of French colonialism. The soldier is now made to function as a sign of French imperiality. As Barthes puts it, emphasising the process of signification: 'The French Empire? It's just a fact: look at this good Negro who salutes just like one of our boys' (ibid.: 134).

For Barthes, 'signification is the myth itself' (ibid.: 131), the coming together of form and concept in the cultural sign. But the form does not hide the concept, or make it disappear as some theories of ideology tend to insist. Barthes writes: 'myth hides nothing: its function is to distort, not to make disappear . . . there is no need of an unconscious in order to explain myth . . . the relation which unites the concept of the myth to its meaning is essentially a relation of deformation . . . in myth the meaning is distorted by the concept' (ibid.: 131–132). Unlike the linguistic sign, the 'mythical signification . . . is never arbitrary; it is always in part motivated' (ibid.: 136). This motivation of form by concept relates to the social and historical characteristics of myth.

Barthes notes that 'if one wishes to connect a mythical schema to a general history, to explain how it corresponds to the interests of a definite society – in short, to pass from semiology to ideology' (ibid.: 138), one has to become a semiologist and understand 'the very principle of myth: it transforms history into nature' (ibid.: 140). As with his analysis of French classical writing, Barthes argues that myth has to be understood by how it transforms the socially (the interests of the bourgeois class) and historically specific (the structure of capitalist societies) into something which is natural and inevitable; and which has to be accepted because it has always been the case and nothing can be done about it (for example, 'The French Empire? It's just a fact'), when it is really an historically specific structure of imperial power.

Barthes's idea that myth serves to naturalise history implies that this process influences consumers by naturalising their reactions to myth. He argues that the reader is allowed 'to consume myth innocently' because 'he does not see it as a semiological system but as an inductive one' since 'the signifier and the signified have, in his eyes, a natural relationship'. As such, 'the myth-consumer takes the signification for a system of facts: myth is read as a factual system, whereas it is but a semiological system' (ibid.: 142).

Myth is not an unconscious process, but, according to Barthes, its consumers take it at face value, and accept it as natural and inevitable. They need semiology to tell them that myth is a system of meaning which cannot be taken for granted. The semiological interpretation of myth assumes readers will understand myth in the way the theory predicts. It does not therefore take account of how people actually interpret myth, for if myths are so effectively mystifying, how can they be so easily demystified?

Bourgeois men and women novelists

In a later work, *Elements of Semiology*,[8] Barthes refined his understanding of the relationship between the signifier, the signified and myth by drawing a distinction between denotation and connotation. On one level, the meaning of popular cultural signs is self-evident. They are what they are or what they appear to be, an advert, a photo of a black soldier, a bunch of roses and so on. They denote something to us, they present it to us as a matter of fact: this is a photo of a soldier, an advert, a bunch of roses. Denotation refers to those things which appear to us as natural and which we can take for granted.

But the task of semiology is to go beyond these denotations to get to the connotations of the sign. Doing this reveals how myth works through particular signs, and shows how the constructed, manufactured and historical location of the myth can be discovered. The connotations of myths can thus be identified: this may appear to be a bunch of roses but it connotes passion; or this may appear to be a photo of a black soldier saluting the French flag, but it really connotes the grandeur and impartiality of French imperialism. The methods of semiology reveal the ideologies contained in cultural myths.

Barthes is concerned with the role of myth in modern society, how it is constructed and sustains meaning as a systematic force. His intention is to get behind the process of mythical construction to reveal the real meanings which are distorted by myth. This involves moving from meanings that are taken for granted, which make things appear natural and inevitable, to meanings that are rooted in historical circumstances and class interests, moving, as he puts it, 'from semiology to ideology' (1968: 139). Although there is some novelty and interest in Barthes's semiology, his theory of ideology seems more in tune with crude Marxist versions of the concept in that the myths of popular culture are viewed as serving the interests of a bourgeois class.

According to Barthes, bourgeois ideology characteristically denies the existence of a bourgeois class. He writes: 'as an ideological fact, it completely disappears: the bourgeoisie has obliterated its name in passing from reality to representation, from economic man to mental man' (1973: 150). This is a class with no name because myth functions as ideology to ensure that it is not named. For example, the myth of the nation guarantees the anonymity of the bourgeoisie by representing everyone as citizens. More generally, bourgeois ideology focuses upon the figure of universal 'man', thereby dissolving the reality of social classes. He argues that 'the fact of the bourgeoisie becomes absorbed into an amorphous universe, whose sole inhabitant is Eternal Man, who is neither proletarian nor bourgeois.' He continues, 'the whole of France is steeped in this anonymous ideology . . . dependent on the representations which the bourgeoisie has and makes us have of the relations between man and the world' (ibid.: 153 and 152).

Barthes is therefore led to the conclusion that bourgeois ideology lies at the very heart of myth in modern society. 'The flight from the name "bourgeois"', Barthes insists, 'is not therefore an illusory, accidental, secondary, natural or insignificant phenomenon.' Rather, 'it is bourgeois ideology itself, the process through which the bourgeoisie transforms the reality of the world into an image of the world, History into Nature.' He concludes that 'this image has a remarkable feature: it is upside down. The status of the bourgeoisie is particular, historical: man as represented by it is universal, eternal' (ibid.: 154). This is how Barthes understands myth. Myth transforms history into nature, which is exactly the function of bourgeois ideology. Myth thus facilitates the tasks of bourgeois ideology and represents the interests of the bourgeois class.

Barthes conducts a similar analysis of gender, and we can use this example to conclude our outline of semiology. Yet again he takes a photo in a magazine as an example. Since the signs of popular culture are, at first sight, self-evident and all around us, we don't have to look very far for examples of how myths work. For Barthes, it is partly because modern bourgeois society is flooded with cultural signs that semiology is so important. This time his example is of a photo of seventy women novelists. From Barthes's point of view, what is interesting is that these women are also identified by the number of children they have. The photograph and its caption denote a group of women writers who are also mothers. The connotation is, however, what interests Barthes. He identifies this as the attempt, by the sign of women as novelists and mothers, to make the role of women as mothers appear to be primary, natural and inevitable, whereas it is really historically and culturally specific. Women may succeed in being novelists, but the connotations of the photo and caption distort this to imply that women are more naturally concerned with motherhood. The photo and caption together form the signifier, the signified of which is the natural role of women to be mothers, irrespective of whatever else they do or aspire to do, such as being novelists.

'The eternal statute of womanhood' is used by Barthes to interpret this myth. He suggests this means that 'women are on the earth to give children to men.' They can 'write as much as they like', they can 'decorate their condition, but above all', they cannot 'depart from it'. They can 'acquire self-confidence' and 'can very well have access, like men, to the superior status of creation'. However, men need to 'be quickly reassured: women will not be taken from them for all that, they will remain no less available for motherhood by nature' (ibid.: 56–57).

Myth is again seen by Barthes to transform history into nature. This time the role of women as mothers is made to appear natural and inevitable, the related connotation being that the power and dominance of men is equally natural and inevitable. The myth exhorts women as follows: 'Love, work, write, be business-women or women of letters, but always remember that man exists, and that you are not made like him; your order is free on condition that it depends on his; your freedom is a luxury, it is possible only if you first acknowledge the obligations of your nature' (ibid.: p. 58).

Structuralism and semiology: some key problems

We can now clarify and add to the problems which have already been raised about the perspectives discussed in this chapter. We can therefore look at some of the criticisms which can be made of Lévi-Strauss's structuralism and Barthes's semiology.

Lévi-Strauss's structuralism

A familiar complaint about Lévi-Strauss's ideas is that they lack empirical validity.[9] A number of related criticisms can be made here. It can be claimed that Lévi-Strauss's theories are supported by a highly selective and very partial use of examples, that they are simply not based upon sufficient evidence or that they are so constructed as to be resistant to any kind of empirical refutation. These claims may appear strange in that Lévi-Strauss's work is full of examples, but critics insist that these are only admitted if they are favourable to his case and divert attention away from cases which might refute his theories. For example, his analysis of totemism is only possible because he confines it to the study of myth, and does not consider how it works in relation to kinship systems. His analysis of Oedipal myths is only successful because he selects those features of the stories which suit his case, and ignores others which contradict the idea that they are expressions of a universal mental structure. Also, the myths he refers to may not be interpreted in the logical manner he suggests, but may be better understood by how they function in specific historical societies.

The argument that Lévi-Strauss ensures his theories are closed to empirical refutation is closely linked to the criticism that his ideas are too abstract and theoretical. His concern with the mental structure which lies behind the myths he studies leads him to engage in cerebral exercises rather than empirical research. His notion of structure can be regarded as so abstract that it allows him to reach the conclusions he does. The more abstract an idea is, the more vague it is, and thus the more closed it is to empirical refutation. This is closely linked to his definition of structure as a mental or psychic phenomenon. Lévi-Strauss's structuralism is marked by idealism and reductionism in that the variety and complexity of myths are reduced to the mental structure of the human mind. There are said to be two problems with this argument. First, it neglects the material processes of production whereby societies reproduce themselves, and thereby reproduce their cultures. Second, it reduces culture to a mental structure and so neglects its complexity and its historical and social specificity. It thus fails to provide an adequate explanation of this complexity and specificity, and cannot account for the things which it is trying to explain except by ignoring their specific character.

Another way of appreciating this problem is to look at the claim that structuralism presents an ahistorical approach to the study of culture. We have already seen how Saussure distinguishes between synchronic and diachronic analysis. We have also seen how difficult it is to maintain this distinction in practice. It is difficult to disentangle the uses of language over time from the formal rules which are used by speakers at any particular point in time, and it is misleading to treat such rules as simply static and fixed norms. With Lévi-Strauss's work we confront this problem more directly in that he does not appear to recognise this distinction. His almost exclusive concern appears to be with synchronic analysis, uncovering the hidden and unconscious mental structure which gives rise to the myths we can observe. Insofar as his work dispenses with history, it confronts the same kind of difficulties experienced by Saussurian linguistics. Downplaying the importance of history means that the problems posed for any analysis of popular culture by historical variations in societies and cultures are simply not addressed. Indeed, it could be argued that it is impossible to understand the formal structures of language or myth outside of their social and historical contexts.

These problems are linked to the deterministic view structuralism has of the subject or human agency. The major determinant of cultural myths is the logical structure of the human mind, and this exerts its power irrespective of any particular social or historical context. It also exerts its power irrespective of the efforts of human subjects to impose their meanings on their social world, and to attempt to alter them in different ways. However, culture needs to be explained by human agency just as much as it needs to be explained by history. For example, the variations in meaning entailed in the production and consumption of culture tend not to support the contention that fixed and immutable universal oppositions make cultural myths possible. If meanings can be contested, human agency cannot be easily ignored.

The problems structuralism has in dealing with human agency can also be seen in the explanatory importance Lévi-Strauss attaches to the unconscious. As we have seen, the mental structure exerts its power irrespective of the role of subjects who are unaware of what is happening. Questions can be raised about the empirical validity of this argument. How is it possible to validate the causal influence of something which is unconscious? If the mental structure remains unconscious we must presumably remain unaware of it, and cannot therefore talk about it in any meaningful empirical sense. Alternatively, if we can claim to demonstrate its existence how can it be unconscious?

Lastly, we can look at the difficulties associated with Lévi-Strauss's understanding of the binary opposition between nature and culture. He sees this as a basic logical opposition lying behind, and causing, the temporary reconciliations between nature and culture to be found in myths such as totemism. Yet how clear and basic is this opposition? How can it be conceived of as a component of a universal mental structure lying outside specific societies and cultures, when it can only be defined in cultural terms? The concept of nature within particular societies is not 'natural' but culturally defined. Lévi-Strauss does refer to the ways in which the distinction between nature and culture varies between societies, for example with respect to definitions of edible and inedible food (1970). However, rather than trying to account for this historically and sociologically, he reduces it to an invariant mental structure. Clearly all societies are confronted by a nature which they have to deal with. Therefore their cultural definitions of nature can be seen as the ways they understand nature and make it meaningful. Nature can never therefore be 'innocent'; it exists as a reality which is interpreted by a society's culture. This idea is in keeping with the arguments of semiology, which does not appear to deny the importance of culturally specific definitions of categories such as nature and culture.

Roland Barthes's semiology

Some might suggest that the semiology developed by Barthes is preferable to structuralism because it is historical and relates the signs of popular culture to social forces and class interests.

Barthes's approach has had a major influence upon studies of popular culture, but it faces certain problems which will be considered in closing this chapter.[10]

For a start, it is hard to say whether Barthes's analyses of myth fare any better than those of Lévi-Strauss when it comes to the problem of empirical validation. While semiology, like structuralism, is presented in principle (at least in Barthes's earlier work) as a rigorous scientific method, this is not carried over into its practice. What validity does Barthes's interpretation of a particular cultural item possess? He does not attempt to indicate why his interpretation is to be preferred to others.

For example, he suggests that roses signify passion. But how can he validate this conclusion, and say they should be understood in this way, and not as a way of signifying a joke, a farewell, or a platonic thank you? How do we discriminate between these interpretations? What evidence could a semiologist call upon to back up Barthes's interpretation? Similarly, semiologists are fond of referring to the codes which lie behind, or are embodied in, a particular sign or myth, but rarely if ever produce evidence of this code independently of the sign or myth under consideration. The fact that, later on, Barthes argues that texts are polysemic in being open to different interpretations hardly gets us very far.[11] Presumably, he is not arguing that texts are open to an infinite number of interpretations, nor that all interpretations are equally accceptable. So why should one interpretation be preferred to another? And why should some interpretations of signs be rejected?

This lack of attention to empirical validation is also evident in the problem semiology has in attributing meaning to myths. One of the aims of semiology is to show how the meaning attributed to a particular myth is systematic and not arbitrary. But it can be argued that the opposite is the case. Semiology wants to demonstrate that the meanings uncovered by its approach are systematic in that they possess a comprehensive structure and are prevalent within the society in which the myth is found. However, if the analysis is confined to the sign itself and the problem of empirical validation is ignored, it is difficult to see how this claim can be substantiated. How do we know, for example, that the conclusions offered by semiology are not the result of the subjective impressions of the analyst but an objective uncovering of the systematic structure of meaning? Indeed, is semiology better viewed as a type of textual appreciation or literary criticism than as an objective social science?

A brief example will hopefully clarify this point. Williamson has tried to apply semiology to the analysis of magazine advertisements, and in her first analysis of an advert in her book, one for car tyres showing a car on a jetty, she writes:

> the jetty is supposedly here as a test of braking power; it provides an element of risk. . . . However, the significance of the jetty is actually the opposite of risk and danger . . . the outside of the jetty resembles the outside of a tyre and the curve is suggestive of its shape . . . the jetty is tough and strong . . . because of the visual resemblance, we assume that this is true of the tyre as well. In the picture, the jetty actually encloses the car, protectively surrounding it with solidity in the middle of dangerous water; similarly, the whole safety of the car and driver is wrapped up in the tyre, which stands up to the elements and supports the car.
>
> (Williamson 1978: 18)

This analysis is dependent upon the idea that the jetty represents a place which is strong and safe, and that this is an expression of a wider cultural code. How else could the signification of the jetty work? But why should we assume that people will regard a jetty as a place of safety no matter how strong and secure it may appear? In fact, Williamson's attribution of meaning, which equates the jetty with safety, is totally arbitrary. Accordingly, the implication that it is indicative of a cultural code is unfounded.

There are some related problems associated with the semiological analysis of popular culture. Much is made of Barthes's distinction between denotation and connotation. It is argued that myth works because we see the denotations of a particular sign or myth but its connotations remain hidden until they are revealed to us by a semiologist. Yet is there such a thing as pure denotation? Are not the connotations of a sign as clear as, if not sometimes more clear than, its denotations? Moreover, insofar as signs are interpreted by their connotations, without being backed up by independent evidence, there is no reason why the connotations of a particular sign should not be readily apparent. After all, Barthes sits down in the hairdresser's, sees the photo of the soldier on the cover of a magazine and quickly works out its connotations. How difficult is it then to make up the connotations of a myth on the spot? Can it be the case that connotations may not be so hidden or as difficult to see as semiologists argue?

As noted above, a major problem with the semiological study of signs is that it neglects the contexts in which signs are used to communicate. The question here is: Can signs be adequately understood if they are divorced from the contexts in which they are used and interpreted? For example, how can we know that a bunch of roses signifies passion unless we also know the intention of the sender and the reaction of the receiver, and the kind of relationship they are involved in? If they are lovers and accept the conventions of giving and receiving flowers as an aspect of romantic, sexual love, then we might accept Barthes's interpretation. But if we do this, we do so on the basis not of the sign but of the social relationships in which we can locate the sign. Moreover, if we accept the interpretation of the sign Barthes proposes (and he makes no attempt to indicate the social relationships in which it is to be found) how do we know that intentions and relationships are involved which are not about passion? The roses may also be sent as a joke, an insult, a sign of gratitude, and so on. They may indicate passion on the part of the sender but repulsion on the part of the receiver; they may signify family relations between grandparents and grandchildren rather than relations between lovers, and so on. They might even connote sexual harrassment. The point here is that it is impossible to interpret signs adequately unless their contexts of use, and the social relationships which confer meaning upon them, are taken into consideration. Semiology does not recognise that meaning is not a quality of the sign itself but of the social relationships in which it can be located.

This point can be taken further. Signs are implicated in social relationships in that they have to be produced in order to be culturally available as signs. (The use of roses to signify passion might be better understood as an example of how much 'love' has been commercialised.) A familiar complaint is that semiology ignores the context of production. Cultural signs, such as magazines, are produced by industries because of their marketability and profitability. They are among the commodities which are produced, circulated and consumed in a capitalist society. However, the semiological decoding of signs tends to ignore the context of industrial production.

This, in turn, raises the problem of the consumption of signs, the interpretations made of signs by the people at which they are directed. The key question here is, Why should the interpretation of signs and myths offered by semiology be accepted if they take no account of the interpretations placed upon them by their audiences? On what grounds can semiologists argue that their understanding of popular cultural signs is adequate if it neglects those groups who consume these signs? In part, this relates back to the fact that semiology fails to tackle the problem of justifying empirically its interpretations. In part, it also relates to the way semiology neglects the social relationships in which signs are produced and consumed. But it equally concerns how the meaningful character of popular culture can be determined. It would seem that this cannot be done without researching the part audiences play in arriving at interpretations of popular culture.

We have seen how Barthes has a fairly crude view of ideology. He sees it as working in the interests of the bourgeoisie. It is this theory which introduces the concept of ideology into semiological analysis, since the connotations and signifieds of signs are, in the end, reduced to bourgeois ideology.[12] To appreciate the dubious nature of this theory of ideology it is necessary to take into consideration the arguments of the next chapter.

Further reading

Barker, M. (1989) *Comics: Ideology, Power and the Critics*, Manchester, Manchester University Press (chapters 6 and 7).

Barthes, R. (1968) *Elements of Semiology*, New York, Hill and Wang.
—— (1973) *Mythologies*, London, Paladin Books.
Craib, I. (1984) *Modern Social Theory*, London and New York, Harvester Wheatsheaf (chapter 7).
Culler, J. (1983) *Barthes*, London, Fontana.
Dyer, G. (1982) *Advertising as Communication*, London and New York, Methuen (chapter 6).
Fiske, J. and Hartley, J. (1978) *Reading Television*, London and New York, Methuen.
Leach, E. (1970) *Lévi-Strauss*, London, Fontana.
Lévi-Strauss, C. (1969) *Totemism*, Harmondsworth, Penguin.
Sturrock, J. (ed.) (1979) *Structuralism and Since*, Oxford, Oxford University Press.
Woollacott, J. (1982) 'Messages and meanings', in M. Gurevitch *et al.* (eds), *Culture, Society and the Media*, London, Methuen.

Chapter 4

Marxism, political economy and ideology

THIS CHAPTER WILL critically assess contemporary Marxism's analysis of popular culture.[1] It will consider, in particular, approaches to the study of popular culture which have emerged from within the Marxist tradition in the last thirty years or so. These involve the Marxist theory of political economy, the Marxist structuralist theory of ideology associated with the work of Althusser, and the concept of hegemony derived from the writings of Gramsci.

A few words about Marx's thoughts on ideology may be useful before we look at these approaches.[2] They will help us recognise the influential aspects of Marx's work, for it is through the idea of ideology that subsequent Marxism has usually tried to understand popular culture.

Marx and ideology

Karl Marx (1818–1883) does not appear to have clearly defined ideology, any more than he clearly defined social class. He, in fact, appears to have had different views on ideology as his thoughts progressed and changed. One of these views is based on the theory of commodity fetishism, already outlined in the chapter on the Frankfurt School. The first approach to be considered here argues that the dominant ideas in any society are those which are drawn up, distributed and imposed by the ruling class to secure and perpetuate its rule.

In one of his earliest discussions of ideology (in *The German Ideology*, originally published in 1845/46), Marx argued that 'the ideas of the ruling class are, in every age, the ruling ideas: i.e. the class, which is the dominant material force in society, is at the same time its dominant intellectual force'. This is because 'the class which has the means of material production at its disposal, has control at the same time over the means of mental production.' As a result, 'the ideas of those who lack the means of mental production are, in general, subject to' the ruling ideas, while 'the individuals composing the ruling class . . . rule also as thinkers, as producers of ideas, and regulate the production and distribution of the ideas of their age. Consequently their ideas are the ruling ideas of the age' (1963: 93).

This clearly suggests that the predominant ideas common to a capitalist society, including its popular culture, are those of the ruling class. They are produced and spread by the ruling class or its intellectual representatives, and they dominate the consciousness and actions of those classes outside the ruling class. Whatever other ideas the latter may have, it is the ideas of the ruling class which are the ruling ideas, although they may not be the only ideas in circulation. It is also suggested that if the working class is to oppose the ruling capitalist class successfully it must develop its own ideas and its own means of producing and distributing them. This will enable it to struggle with and combat the ideas of the ruling class, an idea consistent with the concept of hegemony.

This perspective on ideology stresses the role of human agency and struggle. The ruling class constructs and circulates ideas which secure its power because they dominate the minds of the working class. However, the material conditions of exploitation and oppression experienced by the working class make it oppose and struggle against the ruling class by producing its own ideas, together with its own industrial and political organisations. Therefore a dominant ideology, the ideology of the ruling class, enables the ruling class to rule by controlling this emergent consciousness of the working class and other groups who are outside the ruling class but who are subject to its ideas.

Murdock and Golding attempt to adapt Marx's view of ideology for a political economy approach to the analysis of the mass media (1977). They argue that Marx's statement in *The German Ideology* entails three empirical propositions which they argue can be successfully validated: that the production and distribution of ideas is concentrated in the hands of the capitalist owners of the means of production; that therefore their ideas receive much greater prominence and hence dominate the thoughts of subordinate groups; and that this ideological domination serves to maintain the prevailing system of class inequalities which benefits the ruling class and exploits the subordinate classes.

However, apart from the theory of commodity fetishism, Marx appears to have had a further and more deterministic theory about the place of ideology in the structure of capitalist societies. This is commonly known as the base–superstructure model. The base of a society is its mode of material production, the economic system by which it reproduces itself, and the source of exploitative class relations. It determines the superstructure of a society, its political and ideological institutions, the social relations and sets of ideas that lie outside the base such as the family, the state, religion, education and culture.

As Marx explains:

> In the social production which men carry on they enter into definite relations that are indispensable and independent of their will; these relations of production correspond to a definite stage of development of their material powers of production. The totality of these relations of production constitutes the economic structure of society – the real foundation, on which legal and political superstructures arise and to which definite forms of social consciousness correspond. The mode of production of material life determines the general character of the social, political and spiritual processes of life. It is not the consciousness of men that determines their being, but, on the contrary, their social being determines their consciousness. At a certain stage of their development, the material forces of production come in conflict with the existing relations of production, or . . . with the property relations within which they had been at work before. . . . Then occurs a period of social revolution. With the change of the economic foundation the entire immense superstructure is more or less

> rapidly transformed . . . the legal, political, religious, aesthetic or philosophical – in short, ideological – forms in which men become conscious of this conflict and fight it out.
>
> (1963: 67–68; originally published 1859)

Despite differences between this perspective on ideology and that offered in *The German Ideology*, Murdock and Golding incorporate it into their conception of a political economy of the mass media. Since Marx offers this statement as an outline of a political economy of civil society, it can be taken to include the modern media. Murdock and Golding combine Marx's ruling ideas and base–superstructure models of ideology. In referring to the passage just cited, they argue:

> Marx is concerned to emphasize the fact that the system of class control over the production and distribution outlined in *The German Ideology* is itself embedded in and conditioned by the fundamental dynamics underpinning the capitalist economy. Hence, an adequate analysis of cultural production needs to examine not only the class base of control, but also the general economic context within which this control is exercised.
>
> (1977: 16)

They take the view that Marx is not an economic determinist. They suggest, first, that his sense of causation is not rigidly deterministic but one 'of setting limits, exerting pressures and closing off options', allowing for autonomy within the general limits set by 'the economic relations of capitalism'. Second, they argue that for Marx the relation between the base and superstructure is a dynamic one, necessitating concrete and historical analyses of capitalism (ibid.: 16–17).

However, these points may themselves be questioned. To say the relation between base and superstructure is dynamic does not prevent it from being defined in rigid and deterministic terms: the dynamic is continually determined by the economic base. Also, if the historical nature of capitalism cannot be theorised in advance of its concrete examination, how can we know that cultural autonomy must always be limited by the economic base? Equally, how can the base–superstructure distinction be accepted in advance of historical research?

As Murdock and Golding note, there is clear evidence that Marx may not have wished to put forward an over-deterministic view of the relation between the economic base of societies and their political and ideological superstructures. Compare the above statement from Marx, for example, with this one taken from the third volume of *Capital*:

> The specific economic form in which unpaid surplus labour is pumped out of the direct producers, determines the relation of domination and servitude, as it emerges directly out of production itself and in turn reacts upon production. . . . It is always the direct relation between the masters of the conditions of production and the direct producers which reveals the innermost secret, the hidden foundation of the entire social edifice. . . . This does not prevent an economic basis, which in its principal characteristics is the same, from manifesting infinite variations and gradations, owing to the effect of innumerable external circumstances, climatic and geographical influences, racial peculiarities, historical influences from the outside, etc. These variations can only be discovered by analysing these empirically given circumstances.
>
> (1963: 113)

This passage clearly adds substance to Murdock and Golding's interpretation of Marx's theory, but it also indicates some of the difficulties it confronts. It argues that the economic relations of capitalism determine the other social relations to be found in these societies. They provide the foundations or the base for the rest of society. Yet innumerable, incidental and small-scale influences can give rise to 'infinite variations and gradations' while economic relations remain the same. This questions the rigour of the base–superstructure model. The superstructure, assuming it includes 'innumerable, external circumstances', is now argued to be subject to infinite variations which do not derive from the base. The last statement cited is not even talking about 'autonomy within limits', since the possibilities for superstructural variations with the same economic base are seemingly infinite.

The base–superstructure model argues that the limits set by the base must affect and constrain the superstructure it gives rise to. This means that superstructural variations must be limited and finite, otherwise why argue that they are determined by the economic base? However, this defence demands rather than denies economic determinism. If the economic base does not determine the superstructure then what significance can the distinction have? Even if the relationship is defined by the limits the economic base sets upon the superstructure, how can the same economic base be associated with innumerable and infinite variations in the superstructure? This argument must seriously undermine the theory's explanatory power.

This is probably one of Marxism's fundamental problems. On the one hand, it can adopt an economic determinist position with all the difficulties this entails. On the other hand, it can claim that the economic base sets limits to the superstructure; or it can even suggest that there is 'reciprocal interaction' between the two. The problem with the latter two responses is that they do not really need the ideas of base and superstructure, and tend to rob Marxism of its theoretical distinctiveness in this area (cf. Williams 1977: 80).

Marxism and political economy

Despite misgivings about Marx's ideas, his work can be used to develop a political economy approach to the analysis of the mass media and popular culture. One example, which will be considered in this chapter, is the political economy perspective put forward by Murdock and Golding.[3] As we have seen, they try to combine the ruling ideas and base–superstructure models with empirical research in arguing a case for this perspective.

One of their starting-points is the claim that the sociology of class has failed to recognise the importance of the mass media.

Sociology is concerned with the persistence of class inequalities but does not realise how significant the mass media are in legitimating inequalities in wealth, power and privilege. The media make inequalities appear natural and inevitable to those who suffer the deprivation and oppression they entail. The subordinate classes gain most of their knowledge of the world from the mass media. Since control of this flow of knowledge, information and social imagery is concentrated in the hands of those who share in the power, wealth and privilege of the dominant class, this ruling class will ensure that what is socially circulated through the mass media is in its interests and serves to reproduce the system of class inequalities from which it benefits. The mass media are of crucial importance in relaying information, knowledge and imagery throughout contemporary capitalist societies. Their structure of ownership and control is thus equally important.

Murdock and Golding are critical of those approaches, such as the Frankfurt School or semiology, which exaggerate the autonomy of culture, since they consequently neglect the fundamental influence of the material production of popular culture, and the economic relations within which this takes place. They argue that these approaches analyse cultural forms in isolation from the social relations in which they operate, and so fail to carry out concrete historical analyses of the economic production of culture. One example they cite is Adorno's assumption that the popular music industry in America can be studied and understood simply by investigating its products, without looking at how music is produced industrially (Murdock and Golding 1977: 18–19). However, Murdock and Golding to some extent share Adorno's view that the ideology spread by the mass media ensures social and political acquiescence, and so holds capitalist societies together and secures the dominance of their ruling classes.

One of the primary concerns of Murdock and Golding's approach is the ownership and control of the mass media and cultural production. They start from the questions raised by Marx and conduct a 'concrete analysis of the economic formations and process that underpin the contemporary communications industry' (ibid.: 20). The mass media reproduce class inequalities. If it can be shown that the ownership and control of the mass media are concentrated in the hands of a ruling class, this point can be substantiated. They argue that empirical research shows that the ownership and control of the mass communication industries is indeed concentrated in the hands of relatively small groups of powerful economic and financial interests. This finding supports the ruling-class ideas model put forward by Marx in *The German Ideology*.

Murdock and Golding empirically examine and support Marx's ruling-class ideas model, but they are also critical of tendencies within Marxist and radical theory. In particular, they oppose what they see as 'crude and oversimplified' accounts of the relationship between the ruling class's ideology, the ideas and values of the owners and controllers of the mass communications industries, and what appears in the products of the mass media, that is, the ideas and values that circulate as popular culture. Crude and simplistic versions tend to view this relationship as a very direct and immediate one. They assert that the mass media are simply conduits or outlets for a ruling class ideology which automatically ensures the desired acquiescence of subordinate groups to ruling-class domination. This theory is usually supported by evidence based either on ownership and control or textual analyses of media output. However, Murdock and Golding wish to see the relationship between ownership and control, and mass media output, that is between class power and popular culture, between ruling-class ideas and the dominant ideology, as an indirect and mediated one. Mass media 'institutions do play important roles in legitimizing an inequalitarian social order, but their relationship to that order is complex and variable and it is necessary to analyse what they do as well as what they are' (ibid.: 34).

> By concentrating on the economic base', Murdock and Golding argue, 'we are suggesting that control over material resources and their changing distribution are ultimately the most powerful of the many levers operating in cultural production. But clearly such control is not always exercised directly, nor does the economic state of media organizations always have an immediate impact on their output.
>
> (ibid.: 20)

With the aim of avoiding a crude and simplistic economic determinism, the case for a political economy of the media and culture is advanced in three main ways: by looking at instances in which, at first glance, the logic of economic determinism does not appear to be important, but in which it can be shown to be crucial; by demonstrating empirically the extent to which the ownership and control of the mass communication industries has become concentrated in the hands of a capitalist class; and by assessing the consequences of this for the consumer markets in media and cultural products. Let us take each of these in turn.

One type of media institution which does not appear to obey the logic of economic determinism is public sector broadcasting. This is represented in Britain by the BBC, which is supposed to provide a media culture which enlightens and educates as well as entertains. Because this service is funded primarily by a licence fee and not by the prices its products can command on the market, it is not obviously subject to capitalist pressures. Public service, not private profit, is said to determine what gets produced. However, Murdock and Golding argue that state media institutions such as the BBC have in practice to operate as if they were commercial enterprises and not public services. The BBC has to persuade governments to maintain or raise its licence fee. To do this, it has to be able to demonstrate that it is being run efficiently. In the absence of evidence on profits or markets, it has to show it is cost effective and does not have huge deficits or waste money. It also has to prove it is providing a service which people want, while catering for various minority interests. Like commercial television and radio, it has to compete for audiences and become involved in ratings wars. For Murdock and Golding, this underlines 'the importance for an understanding of cultural production of its material base and economic context' (ibid.: 22–23).

They go on to argue that the ownership and control of the means of production have become concentrated in the hands of a relatively small number of very large corporations. The evidence on this supports Marx's ruling-class ideas theory. The increasing level of concentration is demonstrated empirically by the proportion of the market controlled by the largest five firms in different industrial sectors, including the communication and leisure industries. This concentration also occurs across sectors, in that the largest concerns hold controlling positions in several sectors of the culture industry simultaneously. Increasing concentration therefore occurs alongside increasing conglomeration. Murdock and Golding argue that this evidence indicates that the owners of the means of production continue to exercise high degrees of control over both production and distribution. The culture industry conglomerates are found to be associated with wider industrial and financial concerns, and they contend that these groups form a coherent class with common interests. They conclude that their approach and the theory put forward by Marx in *The German Ideology* are substantiated:

> *The German Ideology* continues not only to pose relevant questions but also to provide a pertinent general framework within which to begin looking for answers . . . Marx's propositions have . . . been rendered more relevant by recent developments in the structure of capitalism.
>
> (ibid.: 32–33)

This is finally related to a brief account of cultural production which stresses the use of a 'sequential logic' to investigate 'economic structures prior to their cultural products' (ibid.: 36). They note the lack of studies which use an analysis of economic forces to examine the dominant ideology lying behind media imagery, and argue that the emphasis upon consumerism within popular culture tends to mask the realm of production and class inequalities. Their own analysis of changes in the structure of ownership and control identifies three consequences for cultural production, distribution and consumption:

1 'The range of material available will tend to decline as market forces exclude all but the commercially successful' (ibid.: 37);
2 This exclusion will be systematic since it will cover those 'voices lacking economic power or resources' (ibid.). Those with most economic power will be able to improve their market position, and ensure that media products endorsing and legitimating the class structure will be circulated and

consumed, while those most critical of the prevailing system will not;

3 This will make it more difficult for alternative viewpoints, politics and cultures to enter the market because they will lack the necessary economic resources. The pressure of rising costs means that all media have to try to reach as large an audience as possible. They can do this by aiming at a large mass audience, or at smaller but affluent groups, but they cannot afford to lose audiences. It therefore becomes necessary to rely upon tried and tested formulae, rather than trying to be different and innovative. Popular culture which has proved successful in the past, and which embodies those 'values and assumptions which are most familiar and most widely legitimated' (ibid.: 37), will be encouraged at the expense of that which does not have these features.

Thus, Murdock and Golding conclude that

> the determining context for production is always that of the market. In seeking to maximize this market, products must draw on the most widely legitimated central core values while rejecting the dissenting voice or the incompatible objection to a ruling myth. The need for easily understood, popular, formulated, undisturbing, assimilable fictional material is at once a commercial imperative and an aesthetic recipe.
>
> (ibid.: 40)

The limits of political economy

Unlike political economy, a number of the other theories considered in this book ignore how popular culture is shaped by the commodity form, and disregard the importance of the production, circulation and consumption of ideas, knowledge and culture, and how they are bounded by systems of class power and control. As we have seen, there are approaches which neglect both the production of popular culture and the economic constraints under which it occurs. The political economy approach highlights some of the structural conditions under which popular culture is

of the dominant class. Equally, they wish to stress the autonomy that professionals working in media organizations exercise in producing culture within the limits set by class power, the profit motive and the economic structure of ownership and control. Arguably, they might want to accord the same degree of autonomy to 'professionals' working in universities dominated by 'income streams'. Political economy does not want to see the mass media as agents in a ruling-class conspiracy, but neither does it want to accord them too much autonomy from economic and class power (1991: 25). However, it is difficult to see how far this argument can be taken and still remain committed to the ruling-class ideas model. The mass media propagate ideas which underpin the power of the ruling class, and yet the organisations and groups which do this can act with a certain level of autonomy. How then can the propagation of ruling-class ideas be ensured if media organisations and professionals are not mere mouthpieces for these ideas? Political economy wants to study media organisations as institutions which mediate between the economic structure of the media and their cultural output, but finds it difficult to square this with its claim that what they do is highly restricted by the need to produce and disseminate ruling-class ideology.

Althusser's theory of ideology and structuralist Marxism

The emergence of a political economy perspective on the mass media can be seen as a polemical response to other developments within modern Marxism. The political economy approach accepts some idea of economic determinism in the sense that the economy sets limits upon all other forms of social relations. It does not directly analyse culture in isolation from these limits, nor does it accord it much significance in its own right. In the rest of this chapter, some other developments within modern Marxism which have placed more emphasis upon the importance of culture and ideology will be considered. First, we shall look at Althusser's efforts to develop a theory of ideology on the basis of what could be termed a structuralist interpretation of Marxism.[5]

Louis Althusser (1918–1990) was a French philosopher whose major work was published in the 1960s and 1970s, at a time when there was widespread intellectual interest in Marxism and structuralism. In keeping with the conventions of academic theory in France, Althusser himself denied he was a structuralist in the same way that more contemporary theorists deny they are post-structuralists or postmodernists. Althusser is concerned with Marxist theory, and the need to secure its philosophical foundations. At their simplest, Althusser's objectives are to establish Marxism as a science and to rid it of economic determinism. In trying to attain them, Althusser develops a distinctive view of science which sees it as an abstract and logical system which proceeds from first principles, and works upon all kinds of empirical material to produce knowledge. For Althusser, the first principles of Marxism as a science are to be found in the works of Marx, Engels, Lenin and Gramsci; these are to be examined, clarified, refined and applied by the theorist in order to demonstrate their veracity. Althusser sees himself carrying on the tradition of Marxist science established by Marx, and trying to resolve theoretical problems Marx, in particular, left unresolved, such as the absence of a theory of ideology. The solutions for these problems are to be found in the Marxist classics even if they are undeveloped or barely recognised. The classics contain the solutions to problems thrown up by the development of Marxist theory and the history of capitalism, but much theoretical labour has to be expended before they can be discovered and explained. Consequently, Althusser presents his arguments in an abstract and assertive manner: this makes sense if you feel that the texts you rely on contain the truth, but can be difficult to accept if you do not.

While we do not want to dwell for long over Althusser's definition of science and of Marxism as a science, it is useful to note their importance in his development of concepts and theories. This can be seen, for example, in how his theory of ideology (which has influenced some subsequent analyses of popular culture) is asserted to be a logical resolution of a theoretical problem which Marx himself chose not to address in a systematic or rigorous manner. Althusser's idea of science is equally one of the guiding assumptions in his critique of the economic determinism to be found within Marxism.

We have seen that while political economy rejects crudely reductionist theories, it does argue for economic determinism in that the economy is the most fundamental constraint upon other types of social activity. Economic determinism likewise entails empirical propositions which can be tested by empirical research. According to Althusser, economism is a problem whch has to be eradicated from Marxist theory because it represents a type of 'essentialism'. The economy is an essence which gives rise to and shapes all other social institutions; these thereby merely express this inner essence; and this is not how a science should proceed. Fortunately for Althusser, Marx's position is open to a non-essentialist interpretation, and this confirms its scientific status.

According to Althusser, economic determinism is not a problem which can be resolved empirically, despite his references to the material history of societies and to the class struggle. Real scientific solutions must be theoretical. Althusser knows that Marxism was and is a theory of economic determinism. However, he insists that, scientifically speaking, economic determinism works only in 'the last instance'. The meaning of this idea is central to Althusser's theory of ideology: he wants to argue that ideology is a force within societies in its own right, but retain Marx's emphasis upon economic determinism.

Althusser's point is that societies have to be thought of as relations between structures rather than essences and their expressions. The economic base or mode of production, and the superstructure or politics and ideology, form structures which are related to each other in definite ways. The political and ideological superstructures are not mere expressions of the essence of the economic base. 'In the last instance' (a logical not a chronological concept), the economic base will be the decisive factor due to its effects upon both other structures and the dynamics of the society overall. But this does not prevent superstructures from being 'relatively autonomous' from the base, or from exercising power and influence upon the base, and upon the pace and direction of social change. In the real world, economic determinism never exists in a pure form, so its existence and effects are always difficult to disentangle from other influences, and determine in their own right. This is how Althusser interprets Marx's claim that the superstructure is not only determined by the base but by numerous secondary, incidental and contingent factors.

Marxism has to take account of these possibilities while retaining its logical coherence as a theory which stresses economic determinism. In the last instance, the economy reigns supreme. It limits, influences and shapes the other structural levels of societies such as ideology. These other levels, however, are not completely determined by the base; they are only determined by the economy in the last instance. They are autonomous from or independent of the base, even if this autonomy or independence is relative. They have some influence over the economic base and how it changes no matter how much they are limited by it. Althusser argues that Marxist science is not subject to economism, and that ideology is 'relatively autonomous' and exercises its own 'specific effectivity'. This means that ideology needs to have its own theory.

Althusser makes clear how important the theory of ideology is for Marxist science in his essay 'Ideology and ideological state apparatuses'. In this piece, Althusser tries to develop this theory by building on Marx's concept of the reproduction of the social relations of production. In arguing for such a theory, Althusser makes clear his view of the base–superstructure model:

> Marx conceived the structure of every society as constituted by 'levels' or 'instances' articulated by a specific determination: the infrastructure, or the economic base (the 'unity' of the productive forces and the relations of production) and the superstructure, which itself contains two 'levels' or 'instances': the politico-legal (law and the State) and ideology (the different ideologies, religious, ethical, legal, political, etc.).
>
> (1971: 129)

This formulation allows the specific powers of the superstructure, as well as the base, to be defined. It suggests a 'metaphor' in which the base provides the foundation on which rest the 'floors' or 'levels' of the superstructure. In this sense, the base determines the superstructure: 'in the last instance' it is the foundation which keeps the superstructure 'up in the air'. The theory suggests that the superstructure possesses 'relative autonomy' from the base, and can reciprocally influence it. For Althusser:

> the great theoretical advantage of the Marxist . . . spatial metaphor of the . . . base and superstructure is . . . that it reveals that questions of determination are crucial; . . . that it is the base which in the last instance determines the whole edifice . . . [this] . . . obliges us to think what the Marxist tradition calls conjointly the relative autonomy of the superstructure and the reciprocal action of the superstructure on the base.
>
> (ibid.: 130)

To 'think' about this relative autonomy and reciprocal action, Althusser uses the idea of reproduction to pursue his theoretical analysis of ideology.

Althusser's essay starts with the problem of how the social relations of production are reproduced. Particularly instructive from our point of view is what Althusser has to say about the reproduction of labour power. This is, in part, ensured by the payment of wages, but the worker has to be 'competent' in the work tasks he or she performs. This competence is both technical – about having and being able to use the right skills required by the work task – and cultural – about 'good behaviour', the 'right attitude', being respectful of authority, a diligent and conscientious worker, etc. Under capitalism, these technical and cultural skills are acquired through the school system. As Althusser argues:

> To put this more scientifically, I shall say that the reproduction of labour power requires not only a reproduction of its skills, but also . . . a reproduction of its submission to the rules of the established order, i.e. a reproduction of submission to the ruling ideology for the workers, and a reproduction of the ability to manipulate the ruling ideology

> correctly for the agents of exploitation and repression, so that they, too, will provide for the domination of the ruling class 'in words' . . . the school (but also other State institutions . . .) teaches 'know-how', but in forms which ensure subjection to the ruling ideology or the mastery of its 'practice'. All the agents of production, exploitation and repression, not to speak of the 'professionals of ideology' (Marx), must in one way or another be 'steeped' in this ideology in order to perform their tasks 'conscientiously'.
> (ibid.: 127–128)

This understanding invokes a 'new reality', that of ideology, and suggests that the problem of reproduction can be theorised in terms of 'forms of ideological subjection' (ibid.).

This line of reasoning leads to the claim that the superstructure secures the reproduction of the relations of production, the social relations between capital and labour in the capitalist mode of production. Althusser identifies certain agencies of the state whose work is ideological and which perform this task. He calls them ideological state apparatuses; they 'function massively and predominantly by ideology' (ibid.: 141), by the ruling ideology, the ideology of the ruling class. They are distinguished from repressive state apparatuses which function 'massively and predominantly by repression' (ibid.; cf. Gramsci's distinction between coercion and hegemony, see below). Examples of repressive agencies are the military, the police, the prisons and the courts, while ideological agencies include religion, education, the family, trade unions, the mass media and popular culture. For Althusser, the reproduction of the relations of production are secured by the superstructure: the repressive state apparatuses do this by the use of force or coercion, and the ideological state apparatuses by the use of ideology. It is worth stressing here that he sees the mass media, education and popular culture as ideological state apparatuses which secure the reproduction of the relations of production.

Althusser rarely refers to empirical or historical phenomena except in the most vague and abstract terms, and he barely recognises popular culture and the mass media. But we can gauge what he thinks about them through his discussion of education, which he argues is the dominant ideological state agency in modern capitalism. It is the school which instils into people the technical and cultural skills required by their work in the relations of production. It:

> takes children from every class at infant-school age, and then for years, the years in which the child is most 'vulnerable', squeezed between the family State apparatus and the educational State apparatus, it drums into them . . . a certain amount of 'know-how' wrapped in the ruling ideology . . . it is by an apprenticeship in a variety of know-how wrapped up in the massive inculcation of the ideology of the ruling class that the relations of production in a capitalist social formation [society], i.e. the relations of exploited to exploiters and exploiters to exploited, are largely reproduced.
>
> (ibid.: 148)

So far we have seen that, for Althusser, ideology functions to secure the reproduction of capitalist relations of production by instilling the necessary skills into the minds and behaviour of the population. This is a function of the state which is performed, in the modern era, by its educational agencies, primarily by the school. But what is ideology? We do not have much sense of what ideology actually is apart from the ruling ideas (the know-how wrapped up in ruling-class ideas) which ensure the continuity of capitalism. This may partly be a result of Althusser's tendency to define ideology by its functions, which makes it difficult to understand what its content might be except for that which can be guaranteed to be functional.

However, Althusser does provide an abstract account of ideology which, for our concerns here, involves three related points: that 'ideology is a "representation" of the imaginary relationship of individuals to their real conditions of existence' (ibid.: 152); that it is a material force in societies; and that it 'interpellates' individuals as subjects within particular ideologies.

The first point is probably the most difficult to grasp. It is raised in his ideology essay, but he also presents a similar definition in his glossary of useful terms for Marxists of his persuasion, which is included at the end of his book *For Marx*: 'Ideology is the "lived" relation between men and their world, or a reflected form of this unconscious relation' (1969: 251). In his essay, he distinguishes his position from those which either see ideology as something directly imposed upon the powerless by powerful groups in order to maintain their power, or as a reflection of the alienation prevailing in the wider society. For Althusser, what people represent to themselves in ideology is not their real world as such but their relationship to the real world. This relationship is an imaginary one and

> underlies all the imaginary distortion that we can observe . . . in all ideology: what is represented in ideology is therefore not the system of the real relations which govern the existence of individuals, but the imaginary relation of those individuals to the real relations in which they live.
>
> (1971: 155)

It is Marxist science which reveals 'the system of real relations'.

Althusser's second point suggests that 'ideology has a material existence.' Again he is distinguishing his position from those which argue that ideology exists merely as an illusory set of ideas in people's minds, and is thus less real than society's material base and its associated class power and alienation. The imaginary relation Althusser refers to is a material relation. Ideology is not just about ideas or a question of mental states or consciousness, but a material practice carried out by groups and institutions. The school, for example, cannot be understood as a set of illusory ideas. It has to be analysed as a form of institutional practice. Ideology entails actions by people living the imaginary relation it defines for them (for example, praying or voting). These actions are practices

> governed by the rituals in which . . . [they] . . . are inscribed, within the material existence of an ideological apparatus, be

> it only a small part of that apparatus: a small mass in a small church, a funeral, a minor match at a sports' club, a school day, a political party meeting, etc.
>
> (ibid.: 158)

This leads to the third point, Althusser's main point, which claims that 'ideology interpellates individuals as subjects' (ibid.: 162–163). As a state institution which reproduces capitalism, ideology is a material force which embodies people's imaginary relationship to their real world. It ensures that people live an imaginary relation to reality because it forms them as subjects. For Althusser, people have little control over this process, and no chance of avoiding it. One way to understand this idea is to think of what sociologists call socialisation, the process by which individuals gradually learn to think and behave in ways common to the society in which they are brought up.

For Althusser, the subject is the defining feature of all ideology, and all ideology works by taking individuals and placing them, that is interpellating them, as subjects within the framework of ideology. For example, a religion will place all individuals who participate in its material practices as subjects – believers – who are subject to one subject, God. Similarly, the ideology of political democracy will place individuals as citizens, that is subjects, who are subject to the sovereignty of parliament. Patriarchal ideology will interpellate individuals as more powerful men or less powerful women. Popular culture in contemporary societies might be argued to function by taking individuals and placing them as consumers, their subject status being defined by their consumption patterns. Likewise, it could be argued that the educational system serves first to place individuals as students in order to place them as workers and as members of social classes. Not all of these examples are cited by Althusser himself but hopefully they indicate the point he is trying to make, that ideology functions by turning individuals into subjects.

Althusser's Marxism: economic determinism and ideology

Althusser's work can be seen as an attempt to establish Marxism as a science on the basis of the revolution in knowledge ushered in by Marx's writings. This work involves both the eradication of errors from the Marxist canon and the development of new theories to deal with outstanding problems. Althusser's argument represents a major effort to outline a Marxist theory of ideology, one which is relevant to the analysis of popular culture and the mass media even if it does not touch directly on these areas. Nowadays, the academic consensus tends to reject Althusser's ideas, but – as we have seen – his work does confront the problem of economic determinism head on, recognises what he calls the 'specific effectivity' of ideology and tries to find a place for it within Marxist theory.

Althusser does not rid Marxism of its dogmatism since he is prone to assert – rather than argue – his case in terms of the authority conferred by the Marxist canon. However, in dealing with the problem of economic determinism, he does show the limitations as well as the potential offered by a Marxist analysis of the mass media and popular culture as ideology. Althusser, along with Gramsci (see page 142), helps us identify the critical limits of this perspective, although no account of popular culture could do without some of its insights concerning cultural production, the ideological nature of social struggles, and the role of theory in providing deterministic explanations.

The importance of Althusser also lies in the influence he has had on the development of the academic study of ideas, knowledge and culture. This in part derives from the association of his work with structuralism, semiology and 'French theory' more generally. But equally Althusser's work at one point seemed to promise to resolve the problem of economic determinism through the construction of a new Marxist theory of ideology. An indication of this is the significance of Althusser for the work of the Centre for Contemporary Cultural Studies at Birmingham University and the theoretical output of cultural theory and film studies journals such as *Screen* in the 1970s.[6] In this context, Althusser's work helped foster the growing interest in Gramsci's ideas on which he drew himself for his own distinctive theory.

Despite this, there are some major problems with Althusser's approach to the study of ideas and culture.[7] The most intractable seems to be the problem of developing a Marxist theory of ideology which does not rely upon economic determinism. This is a key issue for Althusser, but not one he manages to resolve. The question is this: How can the ideas which predominate in a particular society be determined by its economic base, and yet be able to influence, in a relatively independent way, the structure and direction of the society, including its economic base? Althusser's claim that the base (the economy) itself determines the power and autonomy exercised by the superstructure (ideology), while interesting, seems to restate rather than resolve the problem. In fact, it is a stronger version of economic determinism, because it says that the base determines the superstructure and its relative autonomy. Is ideology economically determined; or is it determined by economic processes which, because it is a material force, it can in turn determine?

The idea that they influence each other reciprocally is no answer since, as Althusser recognises, it ignores the issue of determination which is central to Marxist theory, though it is also significant for scientific theory more generally. If everything determines everything else there is no point in theory, for developing theoretical explanations is precisely about evaluating, against the empirical evidence, the greater causal importance of certain factors as against others. To say that one factor causes another is to say that it determines it in definite ways. From this point of view, the problem of economic determinism is an empirical problem, one relevant to sociological theory.

Althusser does not pursue this type of argument. He is therefore still faced with the question: if ideology can have a causal impact upon the economic base then how tenable is a theory based upon economic determinism? Another answer is to say that the latter sets limits upon the former rather than directly shaping it. But this does not help much. Defining these limits would be difficult empirically, while it could no longer be assumed that the base is determinant in the first or last instance. The influence ideology could have would always be limited, but this would none the less qualify the extent to which economic determinism prevails. We are still left with a theory which is neither one thing or the other and again restates but does not solve the problem. We might also ask: Why are these limits never transgressed by ideological forces?

These criticisms can be made clearer by Althusser's own example of education. He wants to develop a theory of ideology which recognises its 'relatively autonomous effects' and does not rely upon economic determinism. Yet what he has to say about education, which is very vague and sketchy anyway, is not consistent with either of these conditions. The function of ideology arises from the mode of production: ideology secures the reproduction of the relations of production. This means that ideology is accounted for by the economic base; and has what autonomy it is assumed to have by virtue of its function which is determined by the mode of production. The concept of relative autonomy does not resolve the problem of economic determinism. Likewise, we learn very little about education aside from the hypothetical function it performs for the mode of production. Education is reduced to a mechanism for the enforced indoctrination of technical skills and respectful attitudes, the imposition of the dominant ideology, and for distributing people into the realm of production. This may not present that accurate an account of the educational systems of specific capitalist societies, and it means here that the relative autonomy of education gets lost in the tasks it is constrained to perform for the mode of production.

Althusser's theory of ideology not only fails to deal with the problem of economic determinism, but also encounters the problem of functionalism. The basic criticism of functionalist explanations is that they mistake the consequences of social phenomena for their causes. For example, a theorist may decide that a specific institution, such as education, functions to distribute people into the mode of production, and may therefore conclude that this explains the emergence of education as well as its continued existence. The functional consequence thus becomes the causal explanation although they should logically be independent of each other. Even if we assumed for the sake of argument that education had such a function, this could not explain why a particular system of education emerged in the first place. At the very least, causal and functional explanations need to be kept separate from each other. With Althusser's theory of ideology, an historical account of the emergence of a system of education is ruled out because we know what its functions are, and need not take account of its origins. Ideology – more specifically, the 'educational state apparatus' – is defined solely by the functions it performs for the mode of production, and there is not much else that can be said about it.

The functionalism and economic determinism in Althusser's theory of ideology mean that it cannot visualize education as a 'relatively autonomous' institution with its own 'specific effectivity'. Furthermore, the function of education as ideology seems capable of ensuring the indefinite perpetuation of capitalism. Functionalist arguments do often seem to imply the eternally guaranteed continuation of the system for which an institution is functional. What is surprising is that a Marxist, which is what Althusser claims to be, should think like this. Marxism is not necessarily hostile to functionalist explanations (these explanations easily find their place in Marxist theories of the superstructure); nor is it the case that functionalist explanations are inherently wrong. But it is hardly characteristic of Marxism as it stands to argue that capitalism will go on forever.

Those who choose to defend Althusser can say his main explanatory theory is the class struggle. Marxism itself is often seen as a theory which explains societies and social change by their historically specific class struggles. However, this theory is difficult to reconcile with a simple-minded functionalism. The functions of an institution – the mass media, popular culture, education or whatever – cannot be performed efficiently or persist undisturbed if continually confronted by wide-ranging and deep-seated class struggles. Such struggles, especially if they are important, must be capable of undermining functions at some point, no matter how powerful the functional institution.

Admittedly, Althusser does try to pay due attention to class struggles, mentioning them profusely in his short postscript to his ideology essay (1971: 170–173). He incorporates the idea of class struggles into his discussion of education as an ideological state apparatus, by arguing that education arises as a result of class struggles (no historical evidence of this is provided), and that the educational apparatus is internally riven by class struggles. These comments sit uneasily with his functionalist theory of ideology, and look more like vague gestures rather than reasoned arguments. If ideological institutions such as education or the mass media are riven by internal class struggles, how are they able to perform efficiently and consistently the functions entrusted to them by the mode of production? These struggles must introduce elements of indeterminacy and contingency into the way these institutions operate, limiting if not undermining their supposedly smooth and efficient performance of their functions. If these institutions are the result of class struggles over their structure and direction, where have these struggles, and the interests, aspirations and issues they entailed, actually gone? Tracing the origins of these institutions to the effects of class struggles may appear to offer a non-functionalist understanding of their causes. But Althusser does not relate these struggles to his account of ideology except to imply that education, the ideological state apparatus, has resolved the problem of the class struggle by instilling in the dominated classes the ideology of the ruling class, '"know-how" wrapped up in the ruling ideology'. It is no wonder that the significance of all kinds of social conflicts are lost sight of in Althusser's theory. They are buried by the functional operations of ideological institutions. However, if Althusser does not frame his theory of ideology on the basis of class struggles, it has been suggested that such a Marxist theory can be found in Gramsci's writings.

Gramsci, Marxism and popular culture

As we have seen, Althusser's theory encounters critical problems which limit its application to the study of popular culture. These include its abstractness, its functionalism, its determinism and its neglect of conflict. In the end, they restrict its potential as a Marxist analysis of ideology. More recently, Gramsci's work has been seen as a way of overcoming some of these problems; and, as a result, his ideas have become more influential. Indeed, the critique within cultural studies of Althusser and structuralist Marxism is made that much easier if Gramsci is fixed upon as the star for the Marxist analysis of popular culture to follow.[8]

The major reason for Gramsci's importance is his development of the concept of hegemony, and his influence is indicated by how extensively it has been used. Now it even defines a particular approach to the study of popular culture, though it, or sometimes his name, usually attracts the prefix 'neo' to suggest that they not be used uncritically. Bennett (1986), for example, introduces a reader on popular culture, arising from the research and teaching of the Centre for Contemporary Cultural Studies at Birmingham University, by underlining what he calls 'the turn to Gramsci', and firmly locates the progress of the study of popular culture in Gramsci's ideas. The analysis of 'Thatcherism' and its fortunes during the 1980s by members of this centre clearly owes a great deal to Gramsci's notions of hegemonic and counter-hegemonic struggles, and of the role played in them by 'intellectuals'.[9]

These examples show how Gramsci's ideas have defined a particular perspective on popular culture. In a paper calling attention to what its author sees as the absence of a guiding theory in cultural studies, McRobbie (1991b) argues that what is needed to resolve this situation is a neo-Gramscian theory of hegemony. The idea that Gramsci shows the way forward for cultural studies is also aired in a recent book surveying a wide range of cultural theories. Its author, Storey, says that on the whole he supports McRobbie's position:

> McRobbie's response to the so-called paradigm crisis in contemporary cultural studies is to argue for a return to neo-Gramscian hegemony theory. This is more or less my own position. . . . I still want to believe that hegemony

> theory is adequate to most of the tasks of cultural studies and the study of popular culture.
>
> (1993: 199–200)

Storey, however, qualifies this conclusion by saying that he is equally attracted by the idea of 'the critical plurality of cultural studies'. By this, he means taking 'the different ways of working, the different contexts, the different conclusions – as equally valid (if differently weighted) contributions to the multidisciplinary field of cultural studies and the study of popular culture' (ibid.: 200). The value of these conclusions will have to be left for the moment. We have first to determine what Gramsci's arguments amount to: then we can assess whether his work deserves the importance it is given.

We can introduce his main ideas and begin to determine their significance by looking at Gramsci's relation to Marxism. It is not possible here to deal in any depth with either Gramsci's other theories or his political activism, though they cannot pass without comment.[10] Born in Sardinia, Antonio Gramsci (1891–1937) went to Turin in 1911 as a student and was eventually engaged in journalism and political activism before his arrest by the fascist state in 1926. He worked on radical and socialist newspapers in close association with the militant working-class movement in Turin, which was centred on the Fiat car factories. He was an active member of the Italian Socialist Party, and became one of the founder members of the Italian Communist Party. He was imprisoned in 1926, and died in prison. It was during this eleven-year period that most of the work for which he is now famous was written, often when he was ill, and always under the vigilant and censorious eye of the prison authorities. He therefore had to write in a way which would escape the notice of the prison censors. These conditions meant it took much longer for his writings to reach the outside world, and to be translated into foreign languages. Thus, Althusser influenced cultural studies before Gramsci did, although the latter was an important influence on the former.

This career of political activity and struggle, as Anderson (1979: 50 and 45) has noted, makes Gramsci something of a unique figure as a theorist. Usually the writers, including Marxists, whose work is assessed for its theoretical importance are based in universities and follow intellectual careers, although they sometimes dabble in a bit of political journalism. But Gramsci is very different, even if he, too, saw himself as an intellectual, an 'organic intellectual' of the working class. Gramsci's politics shaped his ideas directly in that they grew out of his political experiences and the political repression and hardship he suffered. For Gramsci, Marxism is not simply a science whose concepts have to be defined and developed in a rigorous and logical manner, nor merely a perspective well equipped to make sense of the world, but a political theory focused upon the emancipation of the working class. Marxism in this sense is a theory which guides, motivates and inspires, while monitoring and building, the socialist working-class revolution.

Like Althusser, Gramsci wants to eradicate economic determinism from Marxist theory and to improve its explanations of the superstructure. However, Gramsci is more interested in Marxism's significance as a theory of political struggle than in its scientific credentials. In fact, Gramsci is opposed to scientistic and deterministic interpretations of Marxism. Instead, he prefers an interpretation which stresses the fundamental role performed in historical change by human agency in the shape of class and other social struggles. The concept of hegemony and related ideas are designed precisely to advance this interpretation. Gramsci is opposed to economic determinism because it reduces the superstructure to the economy, and involves a strict determinism; Althusser, on the other hand, is prepared to accept some variant of determinism because it is scientific (Gramsci 1971: 378–419).

A couple of brief examples should make this clear. The theory of class consciousness and political action characteristic of some schools of Marxism uses the 'class in itself, class for itself' distinction to trace the history of the working class within capitalism. This argues that the working class is first formed objectively in the mode of production because it is exploited, excluded from property rights and coerced to perform wage labour. Gradually, as a result of its objective class situation, it begins to develop class consciousness and forms its own industrial and political organisations, and its own ideology and culture. These institutions enable it to eventually seize state power, and usher in the socialist overthrow of capitalism.

Gramsci's critical argument is that this scenario ignores the uneven and contingent nature of class struggle, tracing its emergence directly to the economic base. This means it neglects the fact that class struggle is subject to reversals and setbacks as well as victories, and is not a smooth evolutionary process. Neither is it possible, according to Gramsci, to see class struggle as a purely objective or economic struggle, since it must inevitably involve ideas and ideologies.

A similar case is made by Gramsci about the French Revolution. He argues that Marxist interpretations of this revolution rely too heavily on the significance of the economic class struggle between the aristocracy and the bourgeoisie, and underestimate the significance of the role of ideas and intellectuals in ensuring the bourgeoisie's success in the revolution. For Gramsci, the same point can be made about the Marxist theory of the socialist, working-class revolution: that it should not devalue the importance of the role of ideas and culture in the making of this revolution, any more than it should underestimate the importance of the role of bourgeois ideas and culture in preventing it from happening. This role of ideas and culture is what Gramsci understands as hegemony, which is produced by the activity of intellectuals, and feeds into the class struggle (ibid.: 5–7, 77–82 and 452–453).

During his imprisonment, Gramsci began to understand his own political experiences in these terms (Anderson 1979; Buci-Glucksmann 1980). During and after the First World War, capitalism, as he saw it, experienced profound and severe economic and political crises. The bolshevik revolution had occurred in Russia, and working-class insurrections had broken out in various parts of Europe, where governments faced hostile political opposition on several fronts. In Turin, for example, there had been a series of factory occupations, while the national government appeared corrupt and unstable. This situation would have seemed ripe for socialist revolutions, yet, apart from the Soviet Union, it resulted in either fascist seizures of power or the retrenchment of liberal democracy. Gramsci's response was partly to stress the need to build a Marxist political party directly involved in the struggles of the working class. He wanted to translate Lenin into Italian, and argued that one reason the factory occupations failed was because they lacked political direction.

He similarly noted the failure of economic crises to lead to political and ideological crises favourable to the cause of socialism and the working class. This suggested two things: that economic crises by themselves could not subvert capitalism; and that it was crucial that class struggles be political and cultural, struggles over hegemony, as well as economic and industrial. According to Gramsci, the working-class insurrections failed because bourgeois hegemony remained intact, which was another way of saying that socialism's counter-hegemony was not strong enough to transform the economic crises into political and ideological crises. There are thus two related aims in Gramsci's theoretical writings which derive from his political experiences and which inform his development of Marxism as the political theory of working-class emancipation: to combat economism and determinism in Marxist theory; and to provide a theory of the significance and autonomy of the superstructure, most notably of its culture and ideology.

Gramsci's concept of hegemony

Most commentators on Gramsci's work tend to talk about his variable use of the concept of hegemony, tracing its history and noting its importance in different areas of his work.[11] This type of exercise need not concern us here. Our interest lies in Gramsci's Marxist analysis of the mass media and popular culture which is focused upon his understanding of hegemony. He defines hegemony as a cultural and ideological means whereby the dominant groups in society, including fundamentally but not exclusively the ruling class, maintain their dominance by securing the 'spontaneous consent' of subordinate groups, including the working class. This is achieved by the negotiated construction of a political and ideological consensus which incorporates both dominant and dominated groups.

An early exposition of Gramsci's ideas says that:

> the hegemony of a political class meant for Gramsci that that class had succeeded in persuading the other classes of society to accept its own moral, political and cultural values. If the ruling class is successful, then this will involve the minimum use of force, as was the case with the successful liberal regimes of the nineteenth century.
>
> (Joll 1977: 99)

A more recent interpretation, which usefully outlines variations in the meaning of the concept, says:

> Gramsci uses the concept of hegemony to describe the various modes of social control available to the dominant social group. He distinguishes between coercive control which is manifest through direct force or the threat of force, and consensual control which arises when individuals 'willingly' or 'voluntarily' assimilate the world-view or hegemony of the dominant group; an assimilation which allows that group to be hegemonic.
>
> (Ransome 1992: 150)

This argument means that the prevailing culture in a society at any point in time is an outcome and embodiment of hegemony, of the 'consensual' acceptance by subordinate groups of the ideas, values and leadership of the dominant groups. The extent to which the subordinate groups genuinely consent to the hegemony of the dominant group is open to question. However, Gramsci does contrast hegemony with coercion, thereby stressing, unlike most Marxist theories of ideology, their mutual importance. In Gramsci's theory, subordinate groups accept the ideas, values and leadership of the dominant group not because they are physically forced to, nor because they are ideologically indoctrinated, but because they have reasons of their own. For example, hegemony is secured because concessions are made by dominant to subordinate groups and its cultural expression will reflect this.

For reasons already stated, Gramsci's arguments are not always clear, but they can still be elucidated. He sees hegemony as one aspect of social control arising out of social conflict. It is not a functional imperative of capitalism, but a set of consensual ideas arising out of, and serving to shape, class and other social conflicts. He argues that 'the supremacy of a social group manifests itself in two ways', as 'domination' and as 'intellectual and moral leadership'. A social group dominates antagonistic groups, which it tends to 'liquidate', or subjugate perhaps even by armed force; it leads kindred and allied groups. A social group can, and indeed must, already exercise 'leadership' before winning governmental power (this indeed is one of the principal conditions for the winning of such power); it subsequently becomes dominant when it exercises power, but even if it holds it firmly in its grasp, it must continue to 'lead' as well' (1971: 57–58). Hegemony is a type of social control distinct from coercion, and leadership is crucial to the way it is exercised. It expresses subordinate consent to the authority of the dominant group in society, and to its ideas and values.

Hegemony is accepted and works because it relies upon the granting of concessions to subordinate groups which do not pose a threat to the overall framework of domination. As Gramsci makes this point:

> the fact of hegemony presupposes that account be taken of the interests and the tendencies of the groups over which hegemony is to be exercised, and that a certain compromise equilibrium should be formed – in other words, that the leading group should make sacrifices of an economic-corporate kind. But there is also no doubt that such sacrifices and such a compromise cannot touch the essential; for though hegemony is ethical-political, it must also be economic, must necessarily be based on the decisive function exercised by the leading group in the decisive nucleus of economic activity.
>
> (ibid.: 161)

Gramsci here suggests that the power of the dominant group ultimately derives from its position in the economy (its cornerstone is the bourgeois class), and that concessions which underlie hegemony are primarily economic in character, for example welfare provisions or wage rises. But if hegemony is also a struggle over ideas and the consent to dominant ideas, then it must equally include concessions to the ideas and values of subordinate groups. Far from merely colluding with dominant ideas, the latter must find their own ideas recognised in the prevailing hegemony. (How it is possible for subordinate classes to have their own ideas in a hegemonic system is another matter.) Hegemony arises out of conflict, and the compromises which resolve it, express, however provisional and momentary they may be, the issues, interests and ideas at stake in the conflict.

This can be illustrated by the example of the police and crime series on British television in the mid-1970s.[12] It has been argued that these series formed part of an attempt by dominant groups to re-establish their hegemonic position through a 'law and order' moral panic. The prevailing and dominant hegemony of social-democratic reformism was breaking down under the strain of class, industrial and racial conflicts. As a result, dominant groups engaged in political, ideological and cultural struggles to restore their hegemony. This restoration took a more authoritarian and populist direction, which was reflected in popular culture. For example, police and crime series, such as *The Sweeney* (1975–1978) or *The Professionals* (1977–1983), began to recognise popular concerns about increasing crime, and the threat posed to social order (populism), while urging that order and law be vigorously reasserted in society (authoritarianism). In this and other ways, authoritarian-populist hegemony restored the leadership of the dominant groups by reacting to the popular aspirations of subordinate groups to secure their consent.

Hegemony is formed by certain institutions and groups within capitalist societies, what Gramsci calls civil society, which produces, reproduces and changes hegemony, while the state is responsible for the use of coercion. This is a fairly simple and direct equation whereby the state exercises repression and civil society exercises hegemony. While this distinction has been hotly debated, its influence on Althusser's distinction between repressive and ideological state apparatuses is fairly obvious. For Gramsci, popular culture and the mass media are places where hegemony is produced, reproduced and transformed; they are institutions of civil society which involve cultural production and consumption. Hegemony operates through the institutions of civil society which characterise mature liberal-democratic, capitalist societies. These institutions include education, the family, the church, the mass media, popular culture, etc. Civil society is where Gramsci places culture and ideology within societies, and hegemony is the concept he uses to understand how they work. For him, popular culture and the mass media are accounted for by the concept of hegemony.

Another way of understanding this argument is via Gramsci's discussion of political strategy. Using a comparison with military strategy, he draws a distinction between war of manoeuvre or movement and war of position. War of movement refers to a swift, frontal and direct attack on the enemy with the aim of winning quickly and decisively. This is comparable to insurrectionary political action. It describes the bolshevik revolution of 1917 in Russia, which involved a war of movement against the political target provided by a centralised and dominant state power left unprotected by civil society. Hegemony in civil society was weak while the state was strong and highly visible, so a revolutionary war of movement against the state could be mounted and concluded successfully.

According to Gramsci, the liberal, democratic societies of western capitalism are different in that they have relatively weaker states but stronger and more complex civil societies which reinforce the hegemony of the dominant group. In this situation, a war of position, rather than a war of movement, is the strategy revolutionary socialist forces should adopt. A war of position involves a long, protracted and uneven struggle over the hegemony of the dominant group, and its eventual replacement by the hegemony of the subordinate groups fighting for power and the revolutionary transformation of society. This is a war of retrenchment waged primarily through the institutions of civil society. It is a strategy which: (1) faces up to the long and drawn out nature of the struggle; (2) is resigned to the likelihood of defeats and reversals; and (3) recognises that the struggle is cultural and ideological as well as economic, political and 'military', the war of movement being delayed until the battle for hegemony has begun to succeed. The revolutionary forces have to take civil society before they take the state; they therefore have to build a coalition of oppositional groups united by an hegemony which usurps the dominant and prevailing one. Without this struggle for hegemony, all attempts to seize state power will be futile. The maze-like and 'complex structure' of the civil society of 'the most advanced states' makes sure of this. In this perspective, popular culture is explained by the struggles over hegemony carried on within the institutions of civil society.

A few more points need to be made to finish this outline. The first is that, for Gramsci, hegemony is not a fixed and finite set of ideas which have a constant function to perform. Clearly hegemony secures the dominance of the most powerful classes and groups in society, and does so by even determining what is called 'common sense'. None the less, it emerges from social and class struggles which it, in turn, shapes and influences; and its hold over subordinate groups can never be fully guaranteed. The concept of hegemony is capable of becoming a version of the dominant ideology thesis, which would bring it closer to the theories of both Althusser and the Frankfurt School. A charitable view of Gramsci's argument would suggest that hegemony is a contested and shifting set of ideas by means of which dominant groups strive to secure the consent of subordinate groups to their leadership, and not a functional ideology consistently serving the interests of dominant groups by indoctrinating subordinate groups.

The last point to note is that Gramsci sees hegemony as something that is produced by intellectuals. His theory suggests that the producers, distributors and interpreters of popular media culture, within the institutions of civil society, are intellectuals engaged in forming and contesting the prevailing hegemony. Gramsci is using the term 'intellectuals' not in its restricted elitist sense of great artists, major writers or renowned academics, but in a much broader occupational sense to refer to those employed in the production and dissemination of ideas and knowledge in general: 'all men are intellectuals . . . but not all men have in society the function of intellectuals' (ibid.: 9). The function of intellectuals is defined – albeit not exclusively – by occupational positions in the institutions of civil society; those concerned with the production, distribution and interpretation of culture, ideas, knowledge, discourses, etc., all of which are related to hegemony. Not all intellectuals have the same power, nor are all intellectual tasks of equal weight. Some intellectuals may directly produce hegemonic ideas, others may merely elaborate them, while some others will carry out delegated tasks laid down by those with authority. But all those whose function is in some way intellectual, that is to say those who work with ideas (even if all work involves some intellectual activity), are involved with hegemony in the institutions in civil society. This is how a Gramscian perspective would understand the particular roles associated with the production, distribution, consumption and interpretation of popular culture within the modern mass media.

Conclusions: Marxism, Gramscian Marxism and popular culture

Let us return to the point at which we began our discussion of Gramsci. The theory offered by Gramsci may prove a useful way forward for the study of popular culture, but it needs to recognise the importance of economic constraints. This is particularly true if the intention is to remain within a general Marxist framework while avoiding economic determinism. Storey puts it like this: 'neo-Gramscian hegemony theory at its best insists that there is a dialectic between the processes of production and the activities of consumption' (1993: 200). For this point of view, neo-Gramscian theory has the potential to pursue this analysis without the determinism and economism of other variants of Marxist theory; and it would appear to offer an approach grounded in concrete historical realities rather than speculative theoretical abstractions.

However, Gramsci's theory confronts problems which suggest it may be more limited than its supporters realise, and which raise questions about its relevance to Marxism.[13] There are a number of secondary but still significant problems with Gramsci's theory. For example, there is the difficulty with separating hegemony from coercion, since hegemony can itself be coercive. Hegemony is about domination, while coercion can be used in a hegemonic fashion. Force can be used against certain subordinate groups with the consent of other subordinate groups: a presumably hegemonic use of coercion. Likewise, coercion can be used in a legitimate or hegemonic way by agencies of the state. Moreover, is the fascist celebration of violence coercive or hegemonic, or indeed both? And does not the world of work, the sphere of economic production, rely upon both coercion and hegemony in order to operate effectively?

Linked to this is the problem of confining hegemony to civil society and coercion to the state. Gramsci may accept that institutions in civil society can also act coercively and that state institutions can act in a hegemonic manner. But how then can an institution like parliament be analysed, since it is central to liberal-democratic states and can order coercive acts to be performed, but equally works hegemonically through ceremonials and rituals, and the staging of democratic politics? Such an example questions the analytical and empirical usefulness of the distinction between state and civil society, and between hegemony and coercion.

There are also a number of more fundamental problems which need to be mentioned in closing this chapter. There is, first, the claim that Gramsci's theory represents merely another variant of the dominant ideology thesis (Abercrombie *et al*. 1980). Gramsci stresses the importance of conflict for the emergence of hegemony and historical changes. None the less, it is usual for dominant groups to assert hegemony to secure their rule. Hegemony is a consequence of class conflict, but it continually favours one side of the struggle rather than the other: the dominant group at the expense of the subordinate groups. The concept of hegemony seems sometimes to describe a series of football games in which both sides can play but only one side can win.

The dominant group invariably wins by gaining acceptance of a new hegemony, while the potential for change appears to be highly limited save for an increasingly distant revolutionary struggle. As the argument proceeds, the importance of conflict and change gives way to the stultifying hold of hegemony over subordinate social groups. If hegemony ends up being about the continually successful reassertion of the rule of the dominant groups in society, in which the ideas of the subordinate groups can make little headway, then we appear to have returned to a version of the ruling-class ideas model, a dominant ideology thesis.

This is clear in Gramsci's argument that social control and social order – and thus the continued dominance of the most powerful groups in society – can only be secured by a dominant ideology. Gramsci does recognise the importance of coercion, but he thinks that hegemony is a more potent type of social control. However, consent to a prevailing social order does not necessarily arise because people are indoctrinated or forced to acquiesce, nor because they spontaneously consent to, or believe in, a dominant ideology. People can accept the prevailing order because they are necessarily compelled to do so by the need to make a living; or because they cannot conceive of another way of organising society and fatalistically accept things as they are.[14] A theory such as Gramsci's assumes that the only relevant question is: Why should people accept a particular social order? Yet it is equally possible to ask: Why shouldn't they?

The concept of hegemony can be applied in the analysis of a wide range of social struggles. Although, in Gramsci's hands, the concept tends to be applied to class struggles, it has been welcomed because it can analyse other conflicts, and link together different types of struggle in a more general analysis. This analysis explains culture and ideology as hegemony and traces it back to its social roots in the class struggle. There is nothing wrong with identifying the social roots and contexts of ideas and culture; this is a key concern of the sociology of popular culture. But it becomes a problem if all culture is explained by its relation to class struggle. This class reductionism neglects the specific character and autonomous effects of culture and ideas. It also tends to treat them in an absolutist manner in that they must be seen to favour one class or another involved in struggle, usually the dominant one. It equally assumes that in principle all types of popular culture must have some form of functional relation to the class struggle.

However complicated and mediated the relationships between culture and class are argued to be, if culture is not accorded some autonomy from class struggles the analysis becomes reductionist. To argue that a class analysis of popular culture is important does not mean that class or some other social division is all we need to take into consideration. A reductionist analysis ignores not only crucial social factors other than the one it seeks to privilege, but also the independence and influence of the phenomenon it is seeking to explain. A class analysis of culture, such as that put forward by Gramsci, runs these risks with the concept of hegemony.

If Gramsci's theory relies on economic or class reductionism, then it would not appear to have found a new way forward for the Marxist theory of ideology. In the end, Gramsci's theory is limited because it fails to resolve the problem of economic determinism. Ironically enough, Gramsci and the Gramscians have been accused of not paying sufficient attention to the economy and material production as a result of their excessive concentration upon culture and ideas. In their haste to introduce ideology into Marxist theory, they have been found guilty of the charge of 'culturalism'. This means they have made the mistake of being too absorbed with the superstructure in their wish to avoid 'economism' and their desire to solve the problem of economic determinism.[15] While it does bring out the role that culture, ideas and ideology can play in the social production and consumption of popular culture, culturalism is said to be a problem because it loses sight of the distinctive Marxist emphasis upon the economy and the mode of production. However, if we want to move on from this impasse, we need to recognise how important it may be to develop a sociology of popular culture which can include both ideology and the economy in its explanations.

Further reading

Abercrombie, N., Hill, S. and Turner, B. S. (1980) *The Dominant Ideology Thesis*, London, Allen and Unwin.

Anderson, P. (1979) *Considerations on Western Marxism*, London, Verso.

Bennett, T. (1982) 'Theories of the media, theories of society', in M. Gurevitch *et al.* (eds), *Culture, Society and the Media*, London, Methuen.

—— (1986) 'Introduction: "the turn to Gramsci"', in T. Bennett, C. Mercer and J. Woollacott (eds), *Popular Culture and Social Relations*, Milton Keynes, Open University Press.

Elster, J. (1986) *An Introduction to Karl Marx*, Cambridge, Cambridge University Press (chapter 9).

Golding, P. and Murdock, G. (1991) 'Culture, communications and political economy', in J. Curran and M. Gurevitch (eds), *Mass Media and Society*, London, Edward Arnold.

Hall, S. and Jacques, M. (eds) (1983) *The Politics of Thatcherism*, London, Lawrence and Wishart.

Joll, J. (1977) *Gramsci*, London, Fontana.

McLellan, D. (1986) *Ideology*, Milton Keynes, Open University Press.

Murdock, G. (1993) 'Communications and the constitution of modernity', *Media, Culture and Society*, vol. 15.

Simon, R. (1982) *Gramsci's Political Thought: An Introduction*, London, Lawrence and Wishart.

Swingewood, A. (1991) *A Short History of Sociological Thought*, Basingstoke, Macmillan (second edition).

Chapter 5

Feminism and popular culture

THE RECENT AND GENERAL resurgence of feminism and feminist theory has been apparent in the growing interest shown by cultural studies and the sociology of culture in popular cultural representations of women. Feminism as an intellectual activity and a political strategy has a long history (Spender 1983). But for this book, there have been two important developments: the emergence of the modern women's movement from the late 1950s onwards; and the analysis and critique it has advanced of how and why popular culture and the mass media have dealt with women and their representations in an unfair, unjust and exploitative manner within the wider context of gender inequality and oppression.[1]

It is possible to argue that there have been at least three strands of feminism which have been significant: liberal feminism which criticises the unequal and exploitative employment and representation of women in the media and popular culture, and argues for remedial equal opportunities legislation to rectify this situation; radical feminism which sees the interests of men and women as being fundamentally and inevitably divergent, regards patriarchy or the control and repression of women by men as the most crucial historical form of social division and oppression, and argues for a strategy of female separatism; and socialist feminism which accepts this stress on patriarchy but tries to incorporate it into an analysis of capitalism, and argues for the radical transformation of the relations between the genders as an integral part of the emergence of a socialist society. More recently in the study of popular culture, these differences appear to have become blurred as attention has shifted away from radical feminism and towards other theories such as structuralism and postmodernism. Nowadays, feminism seems to consist of the argument that the inequalities in gender power relations are socially and culturally constructed; the development of a more populist but still feminist understanding of the female audiences for popular culture; and the search for a theoretical framework which incorporates class, race, ethnicity and other important social divisions.[2]

The theories and perspectives considered in this book tend to be specific to the study of culture, such as semiology or mass culture theory, or to be more general and wide ranging, such as structuralism or Marxism. Feminism is more like the latter in the scale and range of the themes and problems it addresses. Indeed, as we shall note, it contains an intellectual and critical history of the study of popular culture which can be seen in its assessment of cultural and media studies. In this chapter, feminism and popular culture will be considered in two related ways. First, we shall consider the feminist critique of both popular culture and the study of popular culture. Feminists have been critical of a number of things in these areas, but a few in particular stand out. These include popular cultural representations which marginalise or stereotype women, the relative absence of women involved in cultural production and the relative neglect of women as audiences for popular culture. Feminists have been equally critical of how academic study has exacerbated these processes by failing to take seriously or consider more fully the position of women and gender oppression. Academic studies, as much as popular culture itself, have excluded, ignored or trivialised women as a social category. They have, as a result, been opposed by feminists on political and intellectual grounds.

The feminist critique has targeted theories and perspectives which have colluded in this sexism even though it has found some of them important and influential. Gamman and Marshment make the point in these terms:

> since the late seventies feminists have . . . suggested that women's experience is subordinate to the categories and codes through which it is articulated. Here, feminist appropriations of Continental Marxism have been of particular significance: the work on 'common sense' and 'ideology' by Gramsci and Althusser, and psychoanalytic work on the acquisition of gender, have been employed by feminists to

> 'politicise everyday life – culture in the anthropological sense of the lived practices of a society' – and to problematise the culture's definition of femininity and masculinity.
>
> (1988: 2; cf. Penley 1988)

But while many feminist studies and arguments have made use of insights, methods and concepts derived from these approaches, such as the semiological decoding of the sexism in apparently 'feminist' adverts, they have all been criticised for failing to come to terms with the analysis of women and gender. This critique has, in turn, led both to internal debates within feminism and to the development of feminist analyses of popular culture. This latter point – the feminist analysis of popular culture – is the second main area discussed in this chapter.

The feminist critique

A lot of the earlier work on women and popular culture concentrated upon what Tuchman has called the 'symbolic annihilation of women'.[3] This refers to the way cultural production and media representations ignore, exclude, marginalise or trivialise women and their interests. Women are either absent, or represented (and we have to remember that popular culture's concern with women is often devoted entirely to their representation, how they look) by stereotypes based upon sexual attractiveness and the performance of domestic labour. In short, women are 'symbolically annihilated' by the media through being absent, condemned or trivialised.

Cultural representations of women in the mass media, it is argued, support and perpetuate the prevailing sexual division of labour and orthodox conceptions of femininity and masculinity. The 'symbolic annihilation of women' practiced by the mass media confirms that the roles of wife, mother and housewife, etc., are the fate of women in a patriarchal society. Women are socialised into performing these roles by cultural representations which attempt to make them appear to be the natural prerogative of women.[4] Van Zoonen summarises these points as follows:

produced, distributed and consumed, and it has to play a key role in any adequate sociological analysis of popular culture.

In a more recent update of their position, Golding and Murdock argue that the distinguishing feature of their approach 'is precisely its focus on the interplay between the symbolic and economic dimensions of public communications'. It shows 'how different ways of financing and organizing cultural production have traceable consequences for the range of discourses and representations in the public domain and for audiences' access to them' (1991: 15). This point need not imply the economic determinism of orthodox Marxism. However, some might suggest that the difficulties it raises are similar to those associated with the base–superstructure model. The stress on the interplay between the economic and symbolic aspects of popular culture and the mass media, and the 'traceable consequences' of the former for the latter, need not be contentious; but does it necessarily imply that there are no 'traceable consequences' of 'discourses and representations' for the 'financing and organizing of cultural production'? Emphasising the interplay between economy and culture is not necessarily the same thing as emphasising the greater explanatory importance of the economy. The dilemma for political economy is that it has to treat both of these arguments as if they are the same. To choose between them would mean either losing its distinctiveness by stressing the relatively equal interplay between economy and culture, or arguing for economic determinism by stressing the greater importance of the economy.

In the end, political economy opts for the latter. As Golding and Murdock acknowledge, 'we can think of economic dynamics as defining the key features of the general environment within which communicative activity takes place, but not as a complete explanation of the nature of that activity' (ibid.: 19). This is not the same thing as arguing for the interplay between economic dynamics and communicative activity. It also seems to be assumed that the two exist in isolation from each other; that communication is never about economics, and that economic activity, including cultural production, is carried on without the intervention of communication.[4] Also, if economic dynamics cannot offer a complete explanation of communicative activity, then what other factors would need to be included to make it complete?

This point raises the question of whether political economy can tell us why popular culture is popular. Golding and Murdock refer to the tried and tested cultural formulae which media corporations produce in order to maximise their audiences, and their profits. The drive to maximise profits involves the drive to maximise audiences. The consumption of popular culture, the market, is crucial to the search for profits. But how can the profit motive account for the popularity of popular culture? What determines the tried and tested formulae which can be used to maximise audiences? How does the structure of ownership and control explain the popularity of popular culture? Is it the case that popular culture can be read off from the ideas of the ruling class which has the power to impose it on the rest of the population and so make it popular? Or are there other factors which can help account for the popularity of popular culture, but which are not defined by the political economy perspective?

The political economy perspective sees the mass media conveying dominant values and assumptions which derive from and serve the interests of the ruling class, and which reproduce the prevailing structure of class power. However, little or no direct evidence is presented to suggest that the ideologies broadcast by the mass media have these desired effects, though it has to be acknowledged, as we have seen, that ideology is a subsidiary consideration in the arguments of political economy. It seems to be assumed that if the power of the dominant ideology is asserted as the theory predicts, then its success in moulding the thoughts and actions of audiences is more or less automatically guaranteed. The political economy approach, therefore, does not fare much better than many other perspectives in providing the basis for an understanding of the audiences for popular culture. It does, however, provide the beginnings of a better understanding of the social and economic context within which audiences consume popular culture (cf. Murdock 1993: 525)

In making their general case, Golding and Murdock argue that the mass media are not mere conveyor belts for the interests

> Numerous quantitative content analyses have shown that women hardly appear in the mass media, be it depicted as wife, mother, daughter, girlfriend; as working in traditionally female jobs (secretary, nurse, receptionist); or as sex-object. Moreover, they are usually young and beautiful, but not very well educated. Experimental research done in the tradition of cognitive psychology tends to support the hypothesis that media act as socialization agents – along with the family – teaching children in particular their appropriate sex roles and symbolically rewarding them for appropriate behaviour. . . . It is thought that media perpetuate sex role stereotypes because they reflect dominant social values and also because male media producers are influenced by these stereotypes.
> (1991: 35–36)

This summary also neatly captures the similarities between this line of thinking and other conceptions of dominant ideology we have encountered elsewhere in this book.

One of the most extensive statements of the argument that the mass media 'symbolically annihilate' women has been made by Tuchmann. She relates this notion to the 'reflection hypothesis' which suggests that the mass media reflect the dominant social values in a society. These concern, not the society as it really is, but its 'symbolic representation', how it would like to see itself. Tuchmann argues that if something is not represented in this affirmative manner it implies 'symbolic annihilation': 'either condemnation, trivialization, or "absence means symbolic annihilation"' (1981: 169). With respect to the symbolic representation of women in the American media, she points out that although 'women are 51 per cent of the population and are well over 40 per cent of the labour force', 'relatively few women are portrayed' in this way: 'those working women who are portrayed are condemned. Others are trivialized: they are symbolized as child-like adornments who need to be protected or they are dismissed to the protective confines of the home. In sum, they are subject to symbolic annihilation' (ibid.: 169–170). The reflection hypothesis argues the media have to reflect social values in order to attract audiences. Therefore, their search for a 'common denominator' to maximise audiences means that they 'engage in the symbolic annihilation of women by ignoring women at work and trivializing women through banishment to hearth and home' (ibid.: 183).

Surveying the evidence on America between the 1950s and the mid- to late 1970s, Tuchmann finds this argument to be especially true of popular television and the press. With television, she discovers the following: that women are markedly underrepresented while men tend to dominate programmes: that the men represented tend to be shown pursuing an occupation; that the few women who are shown working are portrayed as being ineffectual, and certainly not as competent as their male counterparts; and that 'more generally, women do not appear in the same professions as men: men are doctors, women, nurses; men are lawyers, women, secretaries; men work in corporations, women tend boutiques' (ibid.: 173). She continues:

> the portrayal of incompetence extends from denigration through victimization and trivialization. When television women are involved in violence, unlike males, they are more likely to be victims than aggressors. Equally important, the pattern of women's involvement with television violence reveals approval of married women and condemnation of single and working women.
>
> (ibid.)

This symbolic annihilation of women is confirmed by the adverts shown on television.

> Analyses of television commercials support the reflection hypothesis. In voice-overs and one-sex (all-male or all-female) ads, commercials neglect or stereotype women. In their portrayal of women, the ads banish females to the role of housewife, mother, homemaker, and sex object, limiting the roles women may play in society.
>
> (ibid.: 175)

The press and women's magazines provide further evidence of the symbolic annihilation of women. However, women's magazines are not as directly responsible for this as most other areas of the media, because the more specialised and smaller scale of their audience means that the reflection hypothesis does not so readily fit their case. It is true that research on women's magazines has 'found an emphasis on hearth and home and a denigration of the working woman'. But it is equally the case that 'such differences as do exist between working-class and middle-class magazines remain interesting . . . for they indicate how much more the women's magazines may be responsive to their audience than television can be', the latter having to appeal to a much larger and more undifferentiated audience than the former (ibid.: 176, 178 and 179). Their smaller audience also suggests that these magazines may be more responsive than popular television to changes in the social situation of women generally, and their readership in particular. According to Tuchmann, research has shown that magazines aimed at a predominantly working-class readership are more likely to show women at work, and as being independent and effective, than magazines aimed at a more middle-class readership. However, she insists this argument cannot be taken too far, even if women's magazines (both middle class and working class) may be more likely to recognise the social changes experienced by women, including the emergence of the women's movement, than the other areas of the media she considers. She concludes:

> the image of women in the women's magazines is more responsive to change than is television's symbolic annihilation and rigid typecasting of women. The sex roles presented are less stereotyped, but a woman's role is still limited. A female child is always an eventual mother, not a future productive participant in the labour force.
>
> (ibid.: 181)

Therefore, in practice, this overall process has meant that men and women have been represented by the mass media in conformity with the cultural stereotypes which serve to reproduce traditional sex roles. Men are usually shown as being dominant, active, aggressive and authoritative, performing a variety of important and varied roles which often require professionalism, efficiency, rationality and strength to be carried out successfully. Women by contrast are usually shown as being subordinate, passive, submissive and marginal, performing a limited number of secondary and uninteresting tasks confined to their sexuality, their emotions and their domesticity. In portraying the sexes in these ways, the mass media confirm the natural character of sex roles and gender inequalities. The concern being voiced here is that this 'symbolic annihilation' means that women, their lives and their interests are not being accurately reflected by the mass media. Popular media culture does not show us women's real lives. The counterparts to the absence, condemnation and trivialisation of women are omission, bias and distortion on the part of the mass media. Popular culture offers a fantasy, surrogate world to its consumers, not the real world they actually live in. In order for the mass media to socialise people successfully into the reality of their sex roles it must not show them what these sex roles are really like. A number of critical questions are raised by this. If people are not shown the reality of their gender roles how can they be successfully performed in society? Why don't people conform to their stereotypes? And if they don't, what use are the stereotypes? What harm would be done if the reality of women's lives were reflected by the media? After all, women are presumably aware that their lives are different from those portrayed in popular culture, so what would be the problem in showing their lives as they really are? Or is the argument that women are being duped by their representations? These questions indicate the confusion which can arise with this approach.

Women and advertising

Advertising and its representation of women are areas of popular culture which have attracted the attention of feminists. Baehr comments: 'from its very beginnings the Women's movement has responded critically, often angrily, to what it has rather loosely called "sexism in the media". Advertisements were an obvious first target and Betty Friedan devoted a large part of *The Feminine Mystique* to a content analysis of women's magazines and to a critique of advertising and market research techniques' (1981: 141). This critical analysis has unearthed the gender stereotypes mentioned above. As Dyer notes: 'analysis of ads suggests that gender is routinely portrayed according to traditional cultural stereotypes: women are shown as very feminine, as "sex objects", as housewives, mothers, homemakers; and men in situations of authority and dominance over women' (1982: 97–98).

A look at some studies of the representation of women in advertising can help clarify these issues: these suggest they may not have changed that much since some of the earlier studies were carried out. Dyer cites a study from 1981 which surveyed 170 different television adverts. It

> found that 66 per cent of the central figures in financial ads . . . were men or 'voiced-over' by men. In all ads men were depicted as independent, whereas women were shown as dependent. Men were typically portrayed as 'having expertise and authority', as being objective and knowledgeable about the product; females were typically shown as consumers of products. Of the central figures shown in the home, 73 per cent were women and of the people who voiced no argument about the product, 63 per cent were women. . . . Male voice-overs were used in 94 per cent of the sample of ads for body products, 83 per cent of home products and 80 per cent of food products. These figures confirm similar content analyses of ads on American TV. . . . TV commercials clearly portray sex-role stereotypes, and according to some researchers repeated exposure to such stereotypes must influence the learning of sex-role stereotypes. The British research suggests that advertisements are not even approximately accurate in reflecting the real nature of sex roles. In 1978, for instance, 41 per cent of all employees in the UK were women. In the sample of British ads women comprised a mere 13 per cent of central characters portrayed in paid employment.
>
> (ibid.: 108–109)

Dyer therefore concludes:

> the treatment of women in ads amounts to what an American researcher has called the 'symbolic annihilation' of women.

> In other words, ads reflect the dominant social values; women are not important, except in the home, and even there men know best, as the male voice-over for female products suggests.
>
> (ibid.: 109)

These findings can be compared with those from a more recent study which comes to similar conclusions. This is a content analysis study of sexual stereotyping in British television advertising, based on a sample of 500 prime-time television adverts, and carried out by Cumberbatch for the Broadcasting Standards Council in 1990.[5] It shows the continuation of the stereotyping we have already come across. There were twice as many men as women in the adverts studied; 89 per cent of the adverts used a male voice-over, even if women were featured most prominently in the advert itself; the women featured in the adverts were usually younger and more attractive than the men – 34 per cent as against 11 per cent – while 1 in 3 of the women were judged to have 'model looks' as compared with 1 in 10 of the men; 50 per cent of the women were between 21 and 50 years of age compared with 30 per cent of the men, while 25 per cent of the women were over 30 years of age compared with 75 per cent of the men. Men were twice as likely as women to be shown in paid employment, and when shown at work it was depicted as being crucial to men's lives whereas 'relationships' were shown to be more important for women. Only 7 per cent of the sample showed women doing housework, but they were twice as likely to be shown washing and cleaning than men. Men were more likely to be shown cooking than women – 32 per cent as against 24 per cent – but in these cases the cooking was for a special occasion and/or demanded the use of particular skills, and was not portrayed as a domestic chore. In the 31 per cent of cases in which men were shown doing housework, it was usually seen as being performed for friends, whereas when women did housework it was usually seen as being for their family, their partner or for themselves. Last, women were twice as likely to be depicted as being married and receiving some type of sexual advance (presumably not in the same adverts) as compared with men.

This particular perspective (together with its use of content analysis as a research method) is associated by some feminist writers with what has come to be called liberal feminism. This type of feminism is said to be concerned with the way sex role stereotyping in the media reinforces it in the wider society. It argues that people are socialised into sex roles by such agencies as the mass media and the family. It demonstrates its case through content analyses, and demands more realistic representations of women in popular culture, as well as greater employment opportunities for women in the media industries. Van Zoonen describes it as follows: 'in liberal feminist discourse irrational prejudice and stereotypes about the supposedly natural role of women as wives and mothers account for the unequal position of women in society. General liberal principles of liberty and equality should apply to women as well' (1991: 35). Feminists have themselves become critical of this approach while not forgetting the advances it has made. There appear to be three major reasons why some schools of feminist thought have moved away from this position: the inadequacies of content analysis; the relative neglect of wider structures of economic, political and cultural power; and the absence of explanatory theories which can account for sex role stereotyping. As a result, feminists have turned to theories such as semiology, structuralism, Marxism and psychoanalysis, as well as to theories of patriarchy.

We can illustrate these developments by remaining with the example of advertising. One of the apparently most significant changes noted in this area has been the incorporation of 'feminist' demands and 'women's liberation politics' into advertising itself. This is something which, it is argued, a liberal feminism equipped only with a content analysis methodology, and the politics of equal opportunities, cannot adequately explain. Dyer notes this trend, which she sees as an aspect of the protective way advertising deals with criticism:

> some advertisers, aware of the objections of the feminist movement to traditional images of women in ads, have incorporated the criticism into their ads, many of which now present an alternative stereotype of the cool, professional,

> liberated women. . . . Some agencies trying to accommodate new attitudes in their campaigns, often miss the point and equate 'liberation' with a type of aggressive sexuality and very unliberated coy sexiness.
>
> (1982: 185–186)

Similarly, Gill has shown how an advert which uses a demand raised by the feminist movement in abortion campaigns ('a woman's right to choose') as a slogan for a holiday for young people ('club 18–30') would have to be judged to be 'feminist' by an atheoretical approach which relied upon content analysis. She argues that a more theoretically informed and qualitative approach, making use of ideas drawn from Marxism, structuralism and semiology, would readily reveal how the advert was really still rooted in a sexist conception of the role of women. She writes accordingly about her chosen example:

> the language of the advert is militant and demanding, in keeping with the slogan. Traditional content analysis would register this, noting words like 'rights', 'choose', 'freedom', 'express herself' and 'without constraint'. A feminist researcher using content analysis may then conclude that this is an advert which affirms feminist ideas, one which embodies a 'positive image' of women. However, the advert might be interpreted quite differently by someone using a more qualitative and interpretive method of analysis. Looking at the text we can see that in this advert a woman's right to choose is being limited to choices about her individual style which, in turn, are reduced to a choice about what to consume (i.e. what holiday to book). The meaning of the slogan has been changed: what was essentially a collective political demand is reduced to an individual personal one, concerning which of the 51 18–30 resorts to visit. This transformation of meaning has turned the feminist idea that the 'personal is political' on its head – by reducing the political to personal choices. . . . Further detailed examination of the language used by the advert and the way the message is structured might lead us to believe that it is an example of . . . the

> co-option or incorporation of feminist images – which are used in such a way as to empty them of their progressive meaning.
>
> (1988: 36)

This brief discussion of women and advertising has been intended to illustrate the feminist critique of popular culture, and some of the points at issue between different feminist approaches to its study. We now need to consider these arguments in more general terms.

The feminist analysis of popular culture

Feminism and mass culture

One way of appreciating the difference between the feminism we have looked at so far and the ones we shall discuss below, and the transition between feminist critiques and analyses of popular culture, is provided by Modleski's account of the relationship between gender and mass culture. Her account is a radical one since it goes beyond saying women have been 'annihilated' by popular culture and cultural studies to question the very language and assumptions in terms of which popular culture has been assessed.

Modleski's general point is that gender has a fundamental relevance for the concept of mass culture and for the study of popular culture more generally. This might now seem uncontentious, but Modleski's argument is about the categories which are used to understand popular and mass culture. Her argument is highly critically of the view that gender is merely another aspect which needs to be included to make the picture of popular culture more complete and representative than it has been before. For Modleski, the matter goes much deeper. She argues that 'our ways of thinking and feeling about mass culture are so intricately bound up with notions of the feminine that the need for a feminist critique becomes obvious at every level of the debate' (1986a: 38). Her concern is that women have been held responsible for mass culture and its harmful effects, while men are privileged to have the responsibility for high culture, or art, since mass culture is identified with femininity and high culture with masculinity.

The case Modleski has in mind is put forward by Ann Douglas. This suggests that the work of nineteenth-century women writers is inferior to that of their male contemporaries, and that women writers were responsible for the emergence of mass culture. She refers to Douglas, who is writing about Harriet Beecher Stowe's novel *Uncle Tom's Cabin* and her character Little Eva:

> Stowe's infantile heroine anticipates that exaltation of the average which is the trademark of mass culture . . . she is . . . the childish predecessor of Miss America, of 'Teen Angel', of the ubiquitous, everyday, wonderful girl about whom thousands of popular songs and movies have been made . . . in a sense, my introduction to Little Eva and to the Victorian scenes, objects and sensibility of which she is suggestive was my introduction to consumerism. The pleasure Little Eva gave me provided historical and practical preparation for the equally indispensable and disquieting comforts of mass culture.
>
> (ibid.: 40)

According to Modleski, the point should be to find out why consumption should be the concern of women within patriarchal societies, rather than blaming them for the rise of consumerism.

The argument of Douglas and others has, for Modleski, 'provided the historical preparation for the practice of countless critics who persist in equating femininity, consumption, and reading, on the one hand, and masculinity, production and writing on the other' (ibid.: 41). This equally exposes 'the masculinist bias of much politically-oriented criticism that adopts metaphors of production and consumption in order to differentiate between progressive and regressive activities of reading (or viewing, as the case may be)' (ibid.: 42).[6] Modleski shows how the very terms used to assess mass culture and define its inferiority to high culture are derived from, and refer back to, the sexist constructions of femininity and masculinity in the wider society. It is not merely a question of adding in gender as another feature of popular culture, but of understanding and challenging the hierarchy of categories which elevates the masculine and subordinates the feminine in examining popular culture. The perspective Modleski criticises has a set of oppositions which privilege masculinity and art at the expense of femininity and mass culture:

High culture (art)	**Mass culture (popular culture)**
Masculinity	Femininity
Production	Consumption
Work	Leisure
Intellect	Emotion
Activity	Passivity
Writing	Reading

Thus, for example, the fear expressed by high culture critics about how audiences are made passive, vulnerable and prone to consumerism by mass culture, is equally a fear about how audiences are becoming feminine, which suggests, for Modleski, how central gender is to our understanding of popular culture.

Feminist theory and the critique of content analysis

A key problem with the feminist perspective we considered in the first section arises from its view that the mass media should reflect reality, the reality of women's lives in a society which does not confer the same privileges upon women as it does upon men. But, as Van Zoonen asks, who can actually define this reality, since feminists themselves do not agree on its character for women (1991: 42)? The feminism she identifies as liberal feminism sees legislation and increased equality of opportunity as ways of undermining the 'unrealistic' portrayal of women in popular culture. Other feminist arguments take a different view. Van Zoonen refers us to radical and socialist feminist perspectives as well as what she sees as a cultural studies feminist approach (ibid.; cf. Baehr 1981: 47), which all argue that societies like our own are endemically sexist since they are rooted in patriarchal relations, and that remedial action, such as equal opportunities legislation, can at best only influence things at the margins. Gender inequalities and exploitation are much more systematic and qualitative than liberal feminism seems able to bargain for, and it is in these terms that the mass media have to be understood and explained. The media are not simply being devious in showing women in stereotypical roles, but have a far more basic role in helping to define and shape the fundamental meanings of femininity and masculinity. From this point of view, these are not identities which exist unambiguously elsewhere, and then come to be distorted by popular culture. They are, in part at least, constructed and reproduced through popular culture by mass media institutions. Liberal feminism fails to appreciate these points because it is atheoretical, neglects the wider structures of patriarchal power and sticks to the findings unearthed by content analysis.

An important prerequisite for the development of alternative feminist theories has therefore been the critique of content analysis. While this method obviously has general relevance for research in the social sciences, it has tended to occupy a significant if not unique place in media and cultural studies. It is usefully defined by Dyer in the following terms:

> the basic assumption of content analysis is that there is a relation between the frequency with which a certain item appears in a text/ad and the 'interest' or intentions of the producer on the one hand and on the other, the responses of the audience. What the text is all about or what the producer means by the text is 'hidden' in it and can be revealed by identifying and counting significant textual features. Content analysis is usually confined to large-scale, objective and systematic surveys of manifest content using the counting of content items as the basis for later interpretation.
>
> (1982: 108)

We have already seen the kind of results it can yield when used to analyse representations of women in advertising.

A number of feminist writers have been highly critical of this use of content analysis. These writers do not deny altogether its validity or the value of its findings, but are concerned to make its limitations clear.[7] There are a number of these criticisms. It is claimed that content analysis is atheoretical because it is not linked to an explanatory theoretical framework; instead, it is treated uncritically as a quantitative research method. The contrast being drawn here is with something like psychoanalysis in which a method (therapy) is linked to a theory of the human psyche (the Freudian notion of the subconscious). It is similarly thought to be atheoretical since it does not have an explanation of the relationship between the popular cultural text being analysed and the social structural context – including the underlying power relations – in which it can be located. According to Baehr, 'studies which describe sexist content cannot help us to understand the relationship between the content described and the social structures which produce it and within which it operates' (1981: 46).

The absence of theory is also evident in the way content analysis is said to emphasise quantity at the expense of quality, though this is not completely true. For example, the study of television advertisements by Cumberbatch cited above was able to discriminate between the quantitative fact of more men than women being portrayed cooking, and the qualitative fact that this cooking was shown to be a skilled accomplishment for special occasions. None the less, content analysis does concentrate upon the differing numbers of men and women represented performing particular roles rather than asking questions about how and why representations occur. Only a theoretically informed account of the structure of power relations between the genders can ask and answer such questions.

The lack of qualitative discrimination is bound up with the failure of studies using content analysis to distinguish between different levels of meaning. This criticism owes much to other theories such as semiology and Marxism which argue there are covert or hidden levels of meaning which lie behind and give rise to the overt or superficial meanings which content analysis deals with. The contrast between a quantitative method and the study of overt meanings on the one hand (content analysis) and a qualitative method and the study of covert meanings on the other (semiology or structuralist analysis) is brought out well by Baehr:

> for example, one woman newsreader reporting an item on 'militant bra-burning feminists' numerically equals one woman newsreader reporting on feminists' 'reasonable case for abortion on demand'. The method enumerates the visible form (i.e. both newsreaders are women) but leaves out the important question of the difference in the content presented. An increase in the number of female newsreaders here implies a change for the better. But as we already know that news coverage of women concentrates on their appearance, sexuality, etc. . . . more women reading the same old news simply reaffirms the very framework which reproduces sexism. That is not to say that more women should not be employed at all levels of media production, but it does suggest that content analysis as a methodology implicitly influences the kinds of questions asked and that the conclusions it draws may work against feminist interests.
>
> (1981: 147)

This more qualitative evaluation of newsreading and female representations, informed by theories which stress the basic importance of covert meanings, rests upon a critique of content analysis, its politics and its research agenda.

Not all feminists share Baehr's position. Muir argues, for example, that 'recent feminist debates have used psychoanalytic theory to explore why the "male gaze" is dominant in mainstream cinema. But there may be a more concrete (if related) explanation: that the masculine point of view is prevalent simply because men control the industry' (in Gamman and Marshment 1988: 143). Content analysis can therefore be mobilised to support this position by quantifying the prevalence of the masculine point of view in popular culture, just as other types of statistical evidence can identify male control over the media industries.

However, the feminist critique of content analysis has gone on to claim that it can only, at best, provide a static picture of social and gender relations and of representations of women and men. Content analysis can give some idea of what gender representations look like at particular points in time, but it cannot be more than descriptive. It is not explanatory and cannot answer questions such as where do cultural representations come from?; how do different types of representation in various areas of the media fit together?; and how and why do representations change over time? Without some kind of theory, it is difficult to answer these questions. Content analysis rests upon the claims that media representations are coherent and uniform, not ambiguous or contradictory, and that the sex role stereotypes presented by the media are clear and consistent, not complex and open to varying interpretations.

Content analysis also argues it is objective, though it relies upon categories it has defined to study media texts; these therefore may not be as objective as is claimed. For example, they may embody certain theoretical or political presuppositions which support its more general orientation but which, since they remain implicit and unstated, cannot be open to argument. The choice of the categories with which content analysis works involves theoretical and political decisions. If these were to be made apparent they would often undermine the claims made to objectivity. Last, as we have already seen in our discussion of women and advertising, content analysis is ill equipped to understand those instances in which popular media culture attempts to incorporate feminism, or to recognise the use of feminist arguments for purposes which are at odds with the interests of feminism.

Feminist theory, patriarchy and psychoanalysis

The capacity of the mass media to reflect the reality of women's lives in patriarchal, capitalist societies is something which is important to the liberal feminist viewpoint, and can clearly be examined by a content analysis methodology. Content analysis can be used to show how cultural representations of women, for example, in advertising, distort the reality of women's lives, portraying a fantasy world rather than the one women actually live in. But, as we have noted, feminists have questioned this view by asking who is to define the objective reality the media have to represent? They have pointed out that some cultural stereotypes may have their social equivalents or at least elements of them in the 'real' world (some advertisers, for example, aim their products at women because they are the main consumers of certain products), and have criticised the contention that cultural representations must either be real or unreal (the representations of women in soap operas, for example, might be difficult to understand if they are thought to be purely fictitious).

An important difference between theories lies behind these differing methodological and analytical assumptions: for there are theories which take for granted the media's ability to reflect reality if ideological distortions are removed, and theories which see the media and popular culture playing a crucial part in constructing reality. As we have seen, semiology, for example, does not necessarily deny that an objective reality exists, but it does insist that our knowledge of it is derived culturally by such things as language. This theoretical argument that reality is constructed has been used by feminists to criticise earlier feminist critiques and analyses (though it has not wished to deny their value), and to develop alternative theories and analyses of gender oppression and popular culture. For this feminist theory, reality cannot be taken for granted, but has to be understood as something which is, in important respects, culturally and ideologically constructed. It has therefore to be analysed by different theoretical perspectives drawn from structuralism, psychoanalysis and Marxism, and by more adequate concepts such as patriarchy.

Responding critically to the cultural representations of the 'liberated' woman in adverts and police series, Baehr provides a succinct summary of these points, and points towards the adoption of alternative theories:

> The fact that heroic women have supplemented heroic men on the screen involves us in more than just media head-counting. It brings us back to questions concerning the media's crucial role in the construction of meaning and in the re-construction and representation of feminism and feminist issues within patriarchal discourse. . . . The media are

> not transparent. They do not, and cannot, directly reflect the 'real' world any more than language can. To argue that they do . . . is to deny the whole process of mediation which comprises a set of structures and practices which produce an ideological effect on the material they organise. By relying on a behaviourist type of 'direct-effects' model of the media these studies present a simplistic, unidirectional and reductive connection between media and behaviour, by arguing that the media determine and directly affect how we see ourselves and how we behave 'as women' in society. . . . This approach mistakes the relationship between the media and their users as a causal one. It is not the media in themselves that determine what women are. Women are constructed outside the media as well, and it is their marginality in culture generally and in the media which contributes to their subordinated positions.
>
> (1981: 148–149)

Instead, attention needs to be given to 'the vital questions which explore the relationship between women's subordination in terms of their "economic" place in patriarchal relations under capitalism and the representation of those relations in the ideological domain which women inhabit and construct' (ibid.: 149).

This approach needs to recognise that 'much of the feminist contribution to the debate on the ideological role of the media in society draws its theoretical framework from the massive input of new theories from France', including semiology, structural linguistics, Althusser's Marxism and Lacanian psychoanalysis (ibid.: 145–146). Thus:

> a feminist analysis requires us to extend the study of the way the media operate in relation to the dominant bourgeois ideology to how they function within a patriarchal culture where 'preferred' meanings reside in a male discourse . . . the crucial question then becomes: how are media images and representations of 'femininity' constructed within patriarchal social and sexual relations of production and reproduction?
>
> (ibid.: 145)

This feminist analysis has developed a number of theoretical ideas which can be outlined briefly. The concept of patriarchy describes a social relationship in which men dominate, exploit and oppress women.[8] It defines the unequal relations between the genders, although it recognises that not all men or all women are equally advantaged or disadvantaged. Other structures of inequality, such as class and race, are also relevant. Hartman has suggested 'we can usefully define patriarchy as a set of social relations between men, which have a material base, and which, though hierarchical, establish or create interdependence and solidarity among men that enable them to dominate women' (1979: 11). Patriarchy refers to the unequal power relationship between men and women, which is very important in determining how women and men will be represented in popular culture, and how they will respond to those representations. Patriarchy clearly has a wider point of reference than this, and there is some debate about how it should be defined, and how important it is; but viewing it in the way we have helps to clarify its role in feminist analyses of the media and popular culture.

One example of the role it has played in the development of feminist theory and analysis is its use of psychoanalytic theory to analyse how and why men look at female representations in contemporary popular culture, and to assess the implications of this for the power men have over women. This argument is particularly identified with the work of Mulvey (1975). It is succinctly summarised by Gamman and Marshment:

> Mulvey's thesis states that visual pleasure in mainstream Hollywood cinema derives from and reproduces a structure of male looking/female to-be-looked-at-ness (whereby the spectator is invited to identify with a male gaze at an objectified female) which replicates the structure of unequal power relations between men and women. This pleasure, she concludes, must be disrupted in order to facilitate a feminist cinema.
>
> (1988: 5)

However, Mulvey herself (1981) has revised her argument in the light of criticism that it ignores both how women may subvert or negotiate the male gaze, and how popular culture offers opportunities for women to 'gaze' at female (and male?) protagonists. Moreover, the psychoanalytic approach reduces everything to gender, neglecting other aspects of power, such as class and race, which affect patriarchal relations and which subsequent feminist theorising has tried to take into consideration.

To some extent, the meaning of patriarchy will vary according to the theoretical framework within which it is used. Radical feminism sees it as the universal domination of women by men, whereas socialist feminism also stresses class and racial exploitation, though it values its explanatory power; a general concern of socialist feminism has been how to reconcile analyses of patriarchy with analyses of capitalism. Van Zoonen defines radical and socialist feminism in these terms (cf. McIntosh: 1978). For her, radical feminism not only views patriarchy as the most basic and universal structure of oppression, akin to the economy or mode of production in Marxism, but conceives of masculinity and femininity as innate biological characteristics of men and women. It argues that 'since mass media are in the hands of male owners and producers, they will operate to the benefit of patriarchal society . . . the power of the media to affect men's behaviour towards women and women's perception of themselves is beyond discussion' (1991: 37). Radical feminism has focused much of its empirical discussion of the media on the role of pornography, since some of its proponents regard this as the most graphic expression of the relation between patriarchy and popular culture.[9]

This theory is open to the criticisms we have already made of dominant ideology theories and ruling-class models of ideology. It obscures the complexity of the relations it analyses in three specific ways. First, there is no simple, direct and causal relationship between the media and their audience. Second, the media do not represent genders in a direct and uniform manner. And third, there is no necessary uniformity of interest among men on the one hand, and women on the other, towards what is represented by the media. Also, its exclusive concentration on patriarchy can be criticised because it ignores other significant structures of power such as class. These arguments have led to the development of socialist feminism, which has retained concepts of patriarchy and patriarchal ideology, while rejecting their association with biological definitions of gender. For this and other perspectives emerging within the area of cultural studies, gender is socially and culturally constructed rather than biologically conditioned.

> Unlike radical and liberal feminism, socialist feminism does not focus exclusively on gender to account for women's position, but attempts to incorporate an analysis of class and economic conditions of women as well . . . more recently, socialist feminism has tried to incorporate other social divisions along the lines of ethnicity, sexual preference, age, physical ability since the experience of, for example, black, lesbian and single women did not fit nicely in the biased gender/class earlier model.
>
> (Van Zoonen 1991: 38)

A problem for socialist feminism has been how to retain a theoretically coherent hold over all these crucial divisions; this goes back to the debates in the 1970s over how to reconcile feminist and Marxist theory.[10] The problem lies in developing a framework capable of intelligibly covering such a range of social inequalities. Also, this perspective is prone to either the economic reductionism of Marxism or the gender reductionism of patriarchal theories of society. Like liberal and radical feminism, it can see the mass media acting simply as a conveyor belt for patriarchal ideology, and the female audience as merely a mass of passive consumers imbued with false consciousness. Despite these and other difficulties, socialist feminism – and its critique – has laid the ground for further developments in feminism. Liberal feminism has been associated with a particular type of empirical study, and the turn to theory from continental Europe has been associated with important studies which have developed feminist theory and the feminist analysis of popular culture.

Feminist theory and the study of ideology

In view of what has been argued in the previous section, a good example to consider is McRobbie's work on female youth subcultures and popular culture. No doubt this work is by now a bit dated, and is no longer representative of feminist analyses of popular culture.[11] However, it is a useful example to discuss for a number of reasons. In developing its explanation, it uses a number of theoretical ideas, including semiology and concepts drawn from the work of Althusser and Gramsci. It is a familiar example, much discussed in the secondary literature. It brings out very clearly the limitations of some of the ideas and approaches it uses, a critique which can be developed below by looking at other empirical work and subsequent theoretical developments.

McRobbie's best known work has been about the subcultures of young working-class girls, and has concentrated in particular on the ideology of the teenage girls' magazine *Jackie*. Her position has shifted somewhat since the arguments were first published, but the original theoretical ideas which guided her research seem clear. Introducing her study of 'the way in which the girls experience the school, the family, and the youth club', she writes:

> the assumption upon which this is based, is that each of these institutions attempts to mould and shape their subjects' lives in particular ways. One of their central functions is to reproduce the sexual division of labour so that girls come willingly to accept their subordinate status in society. This work is done primarily through ideologies which are rooted in and carried out in, the material practices specific to each of these institutions.
>
> (1991a: 44)

This approach owes something to Althusser's theory of ideology, but even here McRobbie draws back from its full-blown determinism:

> from the evidence of this piece of work, it can be argued that there is no mechanical acceptance of these ideologies on the part of the girls . . . Althusser's claim that the ideological state apparatuses ensure 'subjection to the ruling ideology' is not so unproblematic . . . the girls' existence within them and experience of them, was clearly more a

> matter of 'gentle' undermining, subtle redefinition and occasionally of outright confrontation.
>
> (ibid.)

Of course, if ideologies do not work in the way they are supposed to, how can the sexual division of labour be reproduced? Despite this, McRobbie argues that her study shows how the specific effects of ideologies are a matter of empirical assessment as opposed to theoretical dogma.

McRobbie's study is an ideological analysis of *Jackie*. In keeping with what we have noted about her approach so far, McRobbie sees the function of the magazine as being to 'position' girls for their later roles as wives and mothers through the ideology of teenage or adolescent femininity it cultivates.[12] In contrast to the liberal feminist approach, the magazine is conceived of by her as a system of signs embodying this particular ideology which tries to secure the acceptance or 'consent' of young girls as individual 'subjects' to its specific codes and values. The magazine directly addresses a young female audience on the basis of a consumerism and a culture which defines female adolescence and which hides differences within this group arising from inequalities such as class and race. It does its work in the realm of leisure time, defined as free time, time away from work, which, for McRobbie, is part of 'civil society', 'the sphere of the personal or private'. It is here that hegemony is sought after and secured. 'Teenage girls are subjected to an explicit attempt to win consent to the dominant order – in terms of femininity, leisure and consumption, i.e. at the level of culture' (ibid.: 87).

To fill in the detail of the argument that the magazine acts as a powerful ideological force, McRobbie turns to semiology to unearth the codes which form the ideology of female adolescence. This method is preferred to content analysis on the basis of its critique described above. Despite it being new and hardly foolproof, semiology

> has more to offer than traditional content analysis, because it is not solely concerned with the numerative appearance of the content, but with the messages which such contents

> signify. Magazines are specific signifying systems where particular messages are produced and articulated. Quantification is therefore rejected and replaced with understanding media messages as structured wholes . . . semiological analysis proceeds by isolating sets of codes around which the message is constructed . . . these codes constitute the 'rules' by which different meanings are produced and it is the identification and consideration of these in detail that provides the basis to the analysis.
>
> (ibid.: 91)

This methodology, including its associated distinction between denotation and connotation, allows McRobbie to uncover the 'culture of femininity' which, 'as part of the dominant ideology', 'has saturated' the lives of young girls, 'colouring the way they dress, the way they act and the way they talk to each other. This ideology is predicated upon their future roles as wives and mothers' (ibid.: 93). While she does not wish to see these young girls as the passive victims of a dominant ideology or the capitalist and patriarchal quest for hegemony, it is difficult to make sense of her analysis if the ideology of *Jackie* does not have the specific effect of determining the beliefs and behaviour of its readers.

Semiological analysis is used by McRobbie, in combination with ideas drawn from Althusser and Gramsci about the prevalence of a dominant ideology, to discover a number of codes in *Jackie* which define its ideology of teenage femininity, and allow it to have a powerful influence over the lives of its readers. There are four such codes McRobbie identifies, although she is quick to point out that these are by no means the only ones which could be chosen.[13] The first, and perhaps the most important, is the code of romance, also termed 'the moment of bliss' (ibid.: 94). This code involves 'the individual girl looking for romance', finding the 'right' boy, although it has to confront the problem that romance may not last. Hence:

> the code of romance realises, but cannot accept, that the man can adore, love, 'cherish' and be sexually attracted to

> his girlfriend and simultaneously be 'aroused' by other girls. It is the recognition of this fact that sets all girls against each other, and forms the central theme in the picture stories. . . . No story ever ends with two girls alone together and enjoying each other's company. . . . They cancel out completely the possibility of any relationship other than the romantic one between girl and boy.
>
> (ibid.: 98–99, 101)

The second code is 'the code of personal life: the moments of anguish' which is about 'real life' difficulties and the 'problem' page in the magazine (ibid.: 108). The replies offered to readers tend to confirm and reinforce the ideology of adolescent femininity to be found elsewhere in the magazine (ibid.: 117). The third code is 'the fashion and beauty code' (ibid.); this teaches readers how to look and dress to meet the demands of this ideology, and instructs them in 'the sphere of feminine consumption' (ibid.: 125). Last, there is the code of pop music, which involves stars and fans (ibid.). After her survey of these codes McRobbie concludes:

> *Jackie* sets up, defines and focuses exclusively on 'the personal', locating it as the sphere of prime importance to the teenage girl. This world of the personal and of the emotions is an all-embracing totality, and by implication all else is of secondary interest. Romance, problems, fashion, beauty and pop all mark out the limits of the girl's feminine sphere. *Jackie* presents 'romantic individualism' as the ethos par excellence of the teenage girl. The *Jackie* girl is alone in her quest for love. . . . Female solidarity, or even just female friendship, has no real existence in the magazine. . . . This is . . . a double-edged kind of individualism since, in relation to her boyfriend . . . she has to be willing to give in to his demands, including his plans for the evening, and by implication, his plans for the rest of their lives.
>
> (ibid.: 131)

Despite her desire not to pre-empt questions about how such an ideology may actually influence the actions and values of the magazine's readers, about 'how girls read *Jackie* and encounter its ideological force' (ibid.: 131–132), McRobbie concludes with a view of the audience defined by the ideology of feminine adolescence. This ideology, 'as it takes shape through the pages of *Jackie* is immensely powerful, especially if we consider it being absorbed, in its codified form, each week for several years at a time' (ibid.: 131). The magazine's readers therefore succumb to the influence of the ideology it circulates.

Feminist analysis, semiology and ideology

Criticisms of McRobbie's and similar studies are relevant to critiques of semiological and Marxist theories of popular culture. They are also part of the critical debates within feminism about the use of these theories in empirical studies. This critical overview concentrates upon two particular themes: the argument over the relative merits of semiological or content-analysis approaches to the study of popular culture; and the relationship between ideology, popular culture and audiences.

It is clear that even in McRobbie's study it is not easy to dismiss the value of content analysis. At various points, the claims made are as consistent with content analysis as they are with semiology. McRobbie uses the latter rather than the former, but in talking about the problem page in *Jackie*, for example, she says 'it is boyfriend problems which occupy the dominant position', and that 'the stock response' of the advice offered by the writers of the page 'is to become more independent and thus more confident' (ibid.: 114). These conclusions are quantitative as well as qualitative. They could have been enumerated, and could perhaps have been defined more precisely if content analysis had not been so readily dismissed.

One of the critical comments made in Chapter 3 was that, despite its pretensions, semiology has often been arbitrary in the conclusions it reaches. This is true of McRobbie's analysis. She suggests, for example, that the magazine's focus on the personal, the emotional and the individual makes everything else appear to be of secondary importance. The young girls it addresses have to compromise their individuality and independence by giving in to the wishes of their boyfriends over where to go for a night out, and hence over the course of the rest of their lives. This last suggestion is, for McRobbie, made 'by implication'. It is not directly argued for in the text. Neither is it objectively validated by semiological analysis. But it is an inference drawn by the analyst as a result of her initial starting-point, and has to remain an arbitrary judgement, the result of the analyst's ideological position, unless and until some more objective basis, including some empirically plausible basis, can be established.

Semiology's claim that it distinguishes the latent meanings lying behind the surface qualities of the cultural text is particularly arbitrary. Arbitrariness here relates to two things: the validity of this distinction; and the exaggerated significance attached to latent or hidden meanings. First, if both kinds of meaning – overt and covert, or denotative and connotative – can in fact be determined, a number of questions are raised. Why privilege one set of meanings over another? Why should the surface meaning be dismissed if it is the one most people recognise? Why presume that there are no more meanings to be found which are even more 'hidden', once the 'preferred' meaning is discovered?[14] How can meanings which are covert have more impact upon people's consciousness than meanings which are overt? If people are only aware of the latter, why are they so likely to be influenced by the former? All sorts of assumptions about influence are made by semiologists which they never really try to decode.

Second, critical questions can be raised about the significance semiology attaches to the hidden meanings it uncovers and interprets. These are supposed to be explanatory and objective but often turn out, on inspection, to be arbitrary and subjective. Barker brings this out in his critique of McRobbie's study. He notes, for example, McRobbie's claim that to make its ideology acceptable to its readers, *Jackie* makes itself entertaining and pleasurable to read. The surface meaning in this instance is that the magazine is 'fun' to read, which is evident to McRobbie because of its 'lightness of tone . . . which holds true right through the magazine particularly in the use of colour, graphics and advertisements. It asks to be read at a leisurely pace indicating that its subject matter is not wholly serious, and is certainly not "news"' (ibid.: 90). This quality serves to obscure the ideology which is at work in the magazine (but which can be uncovered by the semiological analysis of its codes), while it ensures that the target audience will actually read the magazine. But this quality can be interpreted in another way. As Barker asks: 'why shouldn't we take this [*Jackie*'s lightness of tone] as a hint from *Jackie* not to become too engrossed, to take its pronouncements with a pinch of salt? In other words, why should it not be a modification of the message?' (1989: 158). He continues:

> this is a good example of semiology's becoming unassailable through making arbitrary distinctions, then declaring these arbitrary elements to have coded significance. Semiology requires this division of the surface features into those containing the ideology, and those which disguise it and act as transmission aids. There are no objective ways of deciding which is which. Therefore the method can only prove whatever the analyst 'knew in advance'. McRobbie knew that *Jackie* does not paint a feminist picture. Thus she was bound to discover in it an anti-feminist message.[15]
>
> (ibid.: 158–159)

Without some more objectively grounded arguments, semiology is prone to arbitrary interpretations.

Semiologists have responded to this with the idea that all cultural texts are polysemic.[16] This means that texts contain a number of different messages, and are open to a number of different interpretations. Semiological analyses are not intended to be objective, but merely try to tease out the variety of meanings to be discovered in the text. However, this undermines the validity of the conclusions semiology arrives at, and confronts the fact that texts do not contain an infinite number of meanings, and are not open to an infinite number of interpretations. Objective criteria are still needed to determine the limits which can be set on meanings and interpretations. In short, relativism is no answer. Nonetheless, semiological studies such as McRobbie's do still imply that their conclusions are valid and objective.

We have seen how semiology is open to the criticism that it is ahistorical. McRobbie's study is no exception, and this is so despite its use of Marxist theory, and the criticism made of content analysis's failure to study history. Barker's own study of *Jackie* suggests that there have been significant changes in its treatment of things like romance, but McRobbie's position cannot entertain this possibility since the ideological work performed by the magazine could not otherwise be guaranteed. According to Barker,

> from 1975 onwards there is a real decline in confidence in romance's possibilities . . . this poses real problems for McRobbie's account. Recall that she saw in Jackie a monolithic ideology of real power, trapping girls into a false sisterhood of jealousy. Her sample (scattered through 1974–75) was her evidence of this. Her sample, though drawn without any reference to the history of *Jackie*, had to be treated as 'typical'; how else could she justify drawing such large implications about *Jackie*'s role in selling young girls the 'appropriate ideology of consumerist capitalism'.
>
> (ibid.: 178–179)

This argument equally suggests that content analysis may have been rejected too quickly. Certainly, semiology no longer seems able to fulfil its promise of providing a usable alternative. We shall now look at criticisms which concern the feminist analysis of the relationship between ideology, popular culture and the audience.

Feminist analysis, ideology and audiences

Theories and studies which use methods such as semiology, or theories such as Althusser's on ideology, argue that ideology performs definite functions which clearly shape the attitudes and actions of those subject to its power. In McRobbie's study, ideology is seen to foster a culture of femininity among young working-class girls, which prepares them for their roles in later life as wives and mothers while encouraging their participation in consumer capitalism. This suggests that ideology will have the effects which the theory predicts. Otherwise, presumably, people will not do the things they are supposed to be forced to do by ideology, like becoming wives and mothers. Yet it is an argument which begs a number of critical questions about the indispensable nature of ideology, and its influence over its subjects.

For McRobbie, the ideology is necessary to explain subject positions taken by young girls, irrespective of whether or not a magazine like *Jackie* is published. What is important is that the function of ideology is performed: 'of course, *Jackie* is not solely responsible for nurturing this ideology of femininity. Nor would such an ideology cease to exist if *Jackie* disappeared' (1991a: 83). However, a number of problems arise from this argument. First, it is straightforwardly functionalist since it assumes that the function will inevitably be performed because it has to be performed. Second, it presumes that the ideology will find expression somewhere within popular culture because it is functionally necessary for its values to be implanted into its target population. But if this is so, why worry, as semiology does, about the structure of the specific forms in which it is expressed since these must merely act as outlets for their ideological content? Popular cultural forms can make no difference if the ideology must be expressed in order to do its work. If they do make a difference, and affect and shape their ideological contents, then the functional effects of ideology cannot be guaranteed. Third, this argument tends to proceed on the assumption that only ideology can influence the ways people think and act, and neglects other factors which can shape the course of people's lives. Last, returning to the problem of history, if the ideology fostered by *Jackie* is so important, why have the sales of the magazine declined dramatically since the late 1970s (ibid.: 170), and what other forms have been, and continue to be, capable of propagating this ideology?

As part of her general argument about the functional character of ideology and the usefulness of semiology, McRobbie extends her analysis of the ideological role of *Jackie* to the nature of its appearance for its readers and potential readers. If its ideology is to be effective, it has to have a distinctive appearance for its readers as well as being fun and entertaining. The magazine needs to appear as natural and given, not a result of commodity production and the quest for profit. This is reminiscent of Barthes's idea that myths work by making what is ideological and historical appear to be natural and inevitable. McRobbie writes:

> one of the most immediate and outstanding features of *Jackie* as it is displayed on bookstalls, newspaper stands and counters, up and down the country, is its ability to look 'natural'. It takes its place easily within that whole range of women's magazines which rarely change their format and which (despite new arrivals which quickly achieve this solidness if they are to succeed) always appear to have been there. Its existence is taken for granted. Yet this front obscures the 'artificiality' of the magazine, its 'productness' and its existence as a commodity.
>
> (ibid.: 92)

But as Barker asks, if this is the case, 'would it be hiding or revealing its existence-as-commodity more if the price were covered up?' (1989: 154). He argues that McRobbie mistakes the 'naturalness' of the magazine for its recognisable appearance which is not the same thing at all, and by no means hides the fact that the magazine is produced. Moreover, the magazine must find it difficult to hide its commodity status since at some point its readers must actually fork out their money to buy it. Yet again, as Frazer indicates, the process whereby the magazine is produced is hardly that hidden from its readers. One of the participants in the discussion groups on *Jackie* which she studied remarked, 'I wonder who takes the pictures and who are the people?' (1987: 407).

In fact, Frazer's study is highly relevant here since it provides a theoretical and empirical critique of McRobbie's study and the theory of ideology it relies upon.[17] It presents 'some empirical data – the transcripts of discussion among seven groups of girls about a photo-story from *Jackie* magazine, and about *Jackie* and other girls magazines like it', which are 'used to underpin an argument about the use of the concept of 'ideology' in social theory and research' (ibid.).

Theoretically, the use of ideology as an explanatory concept is challenged for a number of reasons. First of all, ideology is taken to refer to a set of ideas which are false, misleading or distorting, and which can be contrasted with science which reveals the truth. For example, Marxist theories, such as the one put forward by Althusser, see ideology as the means by which the capitalist relations of production are reproduced, and contrast it with the truth expressed by Marxist science. There ought therefore to be a way of clearly and convincingly distinguishing between ideology and science, but this is never made apparent. Second, in practice it is difficult to equate the varied ideas and values that people normally hold with the coherent and unitary system of beliefs predicted by theories of ideology. Third, it is assumed that ideology itself exists within societies as a unitary system of belief, but it is difficult, when the topic is researched, to find examples of ideas which conform to this expectation of theories of ideology. Fourth, empirical research is not encouraged by the claim that ideology is hidden behind, and gives rise to, the ideas which can be found in societies and the beliefs which people hold. If ideology is like this, its research becomes very difficult. This problem is not helped by the way theorists often seem able to discern, intuitively, the ideology in question without doing any research, and without outlining the criteria by which it may be recognised and distinguished from superficial, non-ideological phenomena.

Frazer herself has no objection to the use of concepts in science which refer to unobservable entities, but she argues that ideology as a concept is 'overly theoretical, in the sense that it is explanatorily unnecessary' (ibid.: 410). For her, the things that ideology is designed to explain, can be explained by 'concepts which are more concrete' (ibid.). At the heart of her critique of theories of ideology is her criticism of the claims that ideology actually makes people think and behave in definite and distinct ways; and that they would not think and behave in these ways unless compelled to do so by ideology. Theories which use the concept of ideology, according to Frazer, tend to operate with a fairly crude model of causality. In this model, ideology determines the general set of cultural beliefs in a society, which in turn determine the beliefs and attitudes of the members of the society, which in turn finally determine how these people actually behave. It is this model, she argues, which is questioned by the empirical evidence. Ideology does not make people do things in the way the theory expects them to: the theory 'predicts that people will be more, or differently, affected by "ideology" than evidence actually shows they are' (ibid.).

Among the best examples of this type of reasoning are approaches, such as semiology, which assume it is possible to infer the beliefs and actions of people from an analysis of the ideological content of the popular culture they consume. Once the analyst has determined the ideological meaning of a cultural 'text', it is believed it must have this effect on its readers. For Frazer, this claim can be criticised, first of all, by asking whether texts do possess one valid and unitary meaning. Clearly, if it is claimed that texts are polysemic, then this must limit their ideological effectiveness. Second, it can be criticised by empirical research designed to find out if texts (even if they can be given a unitary meaning) do have ideological effects upon their readers. What, then, do her findings tell us about the young girls she spoke to in her research discussions, and their reading of *Jackie*? And what does this tell us about the theory of ideology?

There are a number of points to be made here. First, Frazer argues that the young girls included in her research tended, on the whole, to read the magazine as fiction, distancing it from representations which might appear realistic. Second, these readers tended not to identify with the central characters in the stories, since 'these real readers were freer of the text than much theory implies' (ibid.: 417). Third, her analysis of the group discussions led her to the tentative conclusion that 'a self-conscious and reflexive approach to texts is a natural approach for teenage girls' (ibid.: 419). They were, after all, often highly critical of the magazine. Furthermore, they appreciated the type or genre of magazine in which *Jackie* could be placed, as well as its fictional character. And they were alive to the fact that it was a text which was produced, as the quote with which we introduced this study indicated, as opposed to a text which tried to appear natural (ibid.).

These findings lead Frazer to discount the value of the theory of ideology, and to suggest another way of understanding how readers relate to popular cultural texts. Even if it were possible to determine the ideological meanings residing in these texts, Frazer's research questions the extent to which readers are influenced by these meanings, and certainly casts doubt on the more deterministic uses of the concept of ideology. Instead, Frazer wishes to use the concept of a discourse register in order to make sense of the relationship between readers and texts, or between audiences and popular culture. A discourse register is 'an institutionalized, situationally specific, culturally familiar, public, way of talking'. Frazer continues: 'my data suggest that the notion of a "discourse register" is invaluable in analysing talk – the talk of all the girls' groups I worked with is marked by frequent and sometimes quite dramatic shifts in register' (ibid.: 420). These registers allow people to talk in specific situations and limit what they can say. They have legitimate and illegitimate areas or contexts of use. They are also wide ranging and diverse, and their use in social science does not aspire to realising the unitary coherence of ideology. She writes: 'it's very clear from the transcripts of the groups' discussions that all the girls have a multiplicity of discourse registers available to use' (ibid.: 422), ranging from the problem page of teenage magazines, the tabloid press and the small group discussion to feminism. Discourse registers, unlike ideology, can be researched directly to discover 'the power of concrete conventions and registers of discourse to constrain and determine what is said and how it is said', including the assessment of 'the influence of popular culture' (ibid.: 424).

This approach is useful for its critique of deterministic theories of ideology, and its attempt to conduct empirical research on audiences. However, it is less successful in rejecting some of the issues raised by theories of ideology, even if it can present a plausible challenge to their solutions. For a start, the use of the concept of discourse registers cannot really ignore the question of power. Its application may qualify the argument that the power of ideas comes from their combination into a unitary and coherent ideology which serves the interests of the most powerful groups in society, but it cannot exclude these considerations. For example, particular discourse registers may indicate the power of certain groups to make them publicly available. Likewise, the relative lack of power of subordinate groups may mean they have to resort to the discourses of others. Where, after all, do discourse registers come from? Where do their sources lie, and under what conditions do they continue to be used? Who propagates them and who resists their propagation? Are some discourse registers suppressed by others and are there those we never hear about? Do discourse registers allow certain groups to exercise power and if so how? Are all discourse registers equally important and powerful or are some more important and powerful than others? If it were possible to construct a hierarchy of discourse registers based upon their importance as publicly available discourses, would this not be highly significant for the analysis of power relations? Power is crucial for understanding the history of discourse registers, and for determining why some discourse registers may be more significant than others (cf. Barker 1989: 251–253).

Conclusion

This chapter has not presented an exhaustive discussion of the feminist analysis of popular culture. Rather some key theories and studies in its development have been highlighted in order to outline its arguments and demonstrate the influence it has had. This chapter has also shown how theories and perspectives discussed in previous ones have subsequently been used and criticised. At the moment, there is clearly a growing interest in the issues and work represented by Frazer's study. It is also clear that a great deal of work is focused upon the theoretical issues and empirical problems associated with the general turn from structuralism, semiology and Marxism, to neo-hegemony theory and postmodernism.[18] This is made apparent by Gamman and Marshment's definition of popular culture:

> Popular culture is a site of struggle, where many of these meanings [of the power struggles over the meanings which are formed and circulate in society] are determined and debated. It is not enough to dismiss popular culture as merely

> serving the complementary systems of capitalism and patriarchy, peddling 'false consciousness' to the duped masses. It can also be seen as a site where meanings are contested and where dominant ideologies can be disturbed. Between the market and the ideologues, the financiers and the producers, the directors and the actors, the publishers and the writers, capitalists and workers, women and men, heterosexual and homosexual, black and white, old and young – between what things mean, and how they mean, is a perpetual struggle for control.
>
> (1988: 2)

The immediate outcome of this is evident in a number of ways. There is the emergence of 'populist' analyses based upon the idea that the recipient of popular culture is an 'active reader' or 'subversive consumer'. There is the apparent move away from text-based to more ethnographic studies of popular culture (Moores: 1993; Stacey: 1994). There is the growing importance of the cultural studies approach to the analysis of gender which stresses the following: the socially and culturally constructed and contested character of gender; the more powerful role of producers as opposed to consumers in the making of popular culture; the combination of textual analyses with ideas about the negotiated meanings of gender they entail; and the active reception practices of men and women which are conducted with reference to the unequal power relations between them (Van Zoonen 1991: 44–51).

The growth of interest in consumption has also been a noticeable feature of recent feminist debates, and can be used to illustrate some of these points. In recent years, the view of women as passive consumers manipulated into desiring commodities and the luxuries of consumption by the culture industries has begun to be challenged by feminist theory and research. Within the context of the emergence of 'cultural populism', it has been argued that this notion of passive consumers undervalues the active role they play, the way their appreciation and interpretation of cultural consumption may diverge from that intended by the culture industries, and ignores how consumption cannot simply be understood as a process of subordination.

Consumption is a particularly important issue for feminists since women have often been defined as the main group of consumers by advertisers, by capitalist industries more generally and by much cultural theory. Challenges to this definition have thus been developed within cultural studies, though they do not necessarily share all the assumptions associated with cultural populism. Stacey, for example, in her study of the female audience for Hollywood cinema in Britain during the 1940s and 1950s, has no wish to underestimate the importance of cultural production. However, she presents a convincing argument to the effect that:

> the meaning of femininity within cultural production . . . is not synonymous with the uses and meanings of commodities to consumers. Following existing cultural studies work on consumption I shall suggest that women are subjects, as well as objects of cultural exchange, in ways that are not entirely reducible to subjection. . . . this work emphasises women's agency as consumers and highlights the contradictions of consumption for women.[19]
>
> (1994: 185; cf.: 176)

Consumption does not simply represent 'the power of hegemonic forces in the definition of woman's role as consumer', but rather 'is a site of negotiated meanings, of resistance and of appropriation as well as of subjection and exploitation' (ibid.: 187; cf.: 189 and 217–223).

Despite the surface temptations of neo-Gramscian theory, consumption itself is not primarily about hegemony. Hence, this interpretation of consumption can be criticised on a number of counts. First, it restricts consumption to cultural conflict, playing down its wider role as an economic process involved in realising the value of commodities. Second, it ignores the limits placed upon 'negotiated meanings', 'resistance' and 'appropriation' by such forces as income inequalities and the producers of commodities. Third, it fails to recognise that commodities must be purchased whatever conflict they attract. Fourth, it says nothing about the role of the production of commodities. And, last, it does not entertain the thought that such conflict does not affect or challenge the commodity form itself.

These criticisms can be charted further by noting some general problems with the feminist approach to the analysis of popular culture. First, it is not clear that the attempt to link gender with other types of social inequality within a unified theoretical framework has been that successful overall (but see Skeggs 1993 and 1997). This may partly explain the shift to such theories as postmodernism and discourse analysis (Gill 1993), which value diversity and difference rather than consistency and the search for more complete theories. But it still leaves open the question of how a feminist theory can integrate gender with such inequalities as social class or race; a point which also raises the thorny issue of whether some inequalities, such as class, are more deeply entrenched in contemporary capitalist societies than others, such as gender.

This is closely linked to a second problem, which concerns the extent to which gender can be studied in isolation from other social inequalities. The initial reason for doing this was part of the feminist critique insofar as it showed how so many areas of importance, such as women's impression on the class structure or their representations in popular culture, were missed if gender was not studied. However, although it may possibly be becoming less common, it is now much less clear that an exclusive focus on gender is that productive or useful for sociology. If, for example, it was a mistake to focus on class to the exclusion of gender in the analysis of social inequality, then presumably, it is mistaken, all other things being equal, to focus on gender to the exclusion of class. There may have been a need to redress the balance in the sense that its neglect had given rise to the need to concentrate more on gender than class, but there now seems to be a more pressing need to bring both types of analysis together, and to assess their relative sociological significance.

The last general problem which can be raised is how the competing feminist theories we discussed can be reconciled with each other. Is the postmodern critique to be accepted, the consequent 'cultural studies' perspective embraced, and previous feminist theorising rejected? If so, it will mean that many invaluable insights will be lost and many important arguments forgotten. Or is the problem of theoretical synthesis and development to be tackled and the resulting theoretical differences and difficulties confronted? If so, it will mean that the tricky and complex task of integrating liberal, radical and socialist feminism within a critique of postmodern theory will have to be undertaken. This involves a range of issues, from the persistence of patriarchy to the methodological assimilation of content and semiological analysis, some of which have been touched on in the preceding discussion. It may be that feminists would argue that such questions are no longer relevant if the claims of postmodern theory are pursued and endorsed instead. This option depends upon how useful postmodernism is as an approach to the analysis of popular culture, and it is to this that we shall now turn.

Further reading

Baehr, H. (1981) 'The impact of feminism on media studies – just another commercial break?', in D. Spender (ed.), *Men's Studies Modified*, Oxford, Pergamon Press.

Franklin, S., Lury, C. and Stacey, J. (eds) (1991) *Off-centre: Feminism and Cultural Studies*, London, HarperCollins (parts 1 and 2).

Frazer, E. (1987) 'Teenage girls reading Jackie', *Media, Culture and Society* vol. 9.

Gamman, L. and Marshment, M. (eds) (1988) *The Female Gaze: Women as Viewers of Popular Culture*, London, The Women's Press.

Gill, R. (1993) 'Ideology, gender and popular radio: a discourse analytic approach', *Innovation* vol. 6, no. 3.

McRobbie, A. (1991a) *Feminism and Youth Culture*, Basingstoke, Macmillan.

Skeggs, B. (1993) 'Two minute brother: contestation through gender, "race" and sexuality', *Innovation* vol. 6, no. 3.

Stacey, J. (1994) *Star Gazing: Hollywood Cinema and Female Spectatorship*, London, Routledge.

Tuchman, G., Daniels, A. Kaplan and Benet, J. (eds) (1978) *Hearth and Home: Images of Women in the Mass Media*, New York, Oxford University Press.

Van Zoonen, L. (1991) 'Feminist perspectives on the media', in J. Curran and M. Gurevitch (eds), *Mass Media and Society*, London, Edward Arnold.

Winship, J. (1992) 'The impossibility of Best: enterprise meets domesticity in the practical women's magazines of the 1980s', in D. Strinati and S. Wagg (eds), *Come On Down?: Popular Media Culture in Post-war Britain*, London, Routledge.

Chapter 6

Postmodernism, contemporary popular culture and recent theoretical developments

THIS CHAPTER WILL consider the postmodernist analysis of contemporary popular culture. Like the preceding chapters, it will assess critically the claims it makes. However, unlike them it will be even more concerned with the empirical arguments of postmodernism. One reason for this is that postmodern theory and post-structuralism, its theoretical and philosophical foundation, are relatively recent developments, and still less familiar than the other theories discussed: for example, there are few sources which present clear and readable accounts of postmodern theory. Compounding this problem, much of the debate about postmodernism has been too vague, abstract and difficult to understand. Compared with this theoretical output, relatively little has been said about postmodernism as an empirical or historical phenomenon.

Postmodernism has attracted increasing interest and attention in recent years. This can readily be seen by the book titles published using the term or its equivalents, or making clear their concern with postmodernism. The *Books in Print* index shows no book titles published on postmodernism between 1978 and 1981, but 14 published in 1988, 22 in 1989 and 29 in 1990. The *Humanities Index* shows no book titles or books on postmodernism published between 1980 and 1983, but a total of 241 appearing between 1987 and 1991.[1] This does not include books which are not specifically concerned with postmodernism but still discuss it, nor journal articles or coverage in the more popular media. Yet even here two major journals in the social and cultural sciences, *Theory, Culture and Society* and *Screen*, have devoted special issues to postmodernism,[2] while arts programmes have considered the major themes raised by the debate or looked at specific areas, such as architecture. Indeed, in the United Kingdom postmodernism is now a term commonly used about contemporary architecture.[3]

Despite this, relatively little has been said about whether postmodernism is on the rise in contemporary societies; if anything, it is assumed, almost without argument, to be already here. Most discussion seems more involved with the theory of postmodernism than with its empirical appearance. Relatively few contributors have asked the question: can we see postmodernism in the world around us? The tendency has been to assume rather than argue that it has become widespread in modern societies; and less attention has been devoted to showing this is the case.[4] In turn, this has been matched by the excessive attention given to the problem of defining the term itself.[5]

This chapter will look at postmodernist theory and the extent to which postmodernism can be identified empirically in modern societies, popular culture and the mass media being special areas of concern in the debate about postmodernism.[6] This focus on the empirical detection of postmodernism means that the chapter will answer the following questions: What is postmodernism? Can it be identified in contemporary popular media culture? What are some of the reasons advanced for its emergence? and What critique can be developed of its arguments?

What is postmodernism?

There are a number of points – those most heavily stressed in the literature – which can be used to define postmodernism.[7] This definition is something of a composite picture, but it is accurate enough for this chapter.

Culture and society

First, the argument is that postmodernism describes the emergence of a society in which the mass media and popular culture are the most important and powerful institutions, and control and shape all other types of social relationships. Popular cultural signs and media images increasingly dominate our sense of reality, and the way we define ourselves and the world around us. Postmodern theory is an attempt to understand a media-saturated society. For example, the mass media were once thought to hold a mirror up to a wider social reality, and thereby reflect it. Now reality can only be defined by the surface reflections of this mirror. Society has become subsumed within the mass media. It is no longer even a question of the media distorting reality, since this implies there is a reality, outside the surface simulations of the media, which can be distorted; and this is precisely what is at issue according to postmodern theory.

In a way, this idea comes from one of the directions taken by media and cultural theory. To put it simply, the liberal view argued that the media held up a mirror to, and thereby reflected in a fairly accurate manner, a wider social reality. The radical rejoinder to this insisted that this mirror distorted rather than reflected reality. Subsequently, a more abstract and conceptual media and cultural theory suggested that the media played some part in constructing our sense of social reality, and our sense of being a part of this reality (Curran *et al.* 1982; Bennett 1982). It is a relatively short step from this (and one which need not be taken) to the proposition that only the media can constitute our sense of reality. To return to the original metaphor, it is claimed that this mirror is now the only reality we have.

An aspect of this is the idea that in the postmodern condition it becomes more difficult to distinguish the economy from popular culture. Consumption – what we buy and what determines what we buy – is increasingly influenced by popular culture because popular culture increasingly determines consumption. For example, we watch more films because of the extended ownership of VCRs, while advertising, which makes increasing use of popular cultural references, plays a more important role in deciding what we will buy.

An emphasis on style at the expense of substance

A crucial implication of the first point is that in a postmodern world, surfaces and style become ever more important, producing and feeding off what is called a 'designer ideology'. Or as Harvey puts it: 'images dominate narrative' (1989: 347–348). The argument is that we increasingly consume images and signs for their own sake rather than for their 'usefulness' or for the deeper values they may represent. Images and signs are consumed precisely because they are images and signs, regardless of questions of utility and value. This is thought to be evident in popular culture itself where surface and style, playfulness and jokes, and what things look like, are said to predominate at the expense of content, substance and meaning. As a result, qualities such as artistic merit, integrity, seriousness, authenticity, realism, intellectual depth and strong narratives tend to be undermined. Moreover, virtual reality computer graphics can allow people to experience various forms of reality at second hand, potentially at least as surface simulations rather than real events.

Art and popular culture

If the first two points are accepted it follows that for postmodern culture anything can be turned into a joke, reference or quotation in its eclectic play of styles, simulations and surfaces. If popular cultural signs and media images are taking over in defining our sense of reality for us, and if this means that style takes precedence over content, then it becomes more difficult to maintain a meaningful distinction between art and popular culture. There are no longer any agreed and inviolable criteria which can serve to differentiate art from popular culture. Compare this with the fears of the mass culture critics that mass culture would eventually subvert high culture. The only difference seems to be that these critics were pessimistic about such developments, whereas some, but not all, postmodern theorists are by contrast optimistic.

A good example of what postmodernist theory is getting at is provided by Andy Warhol's multi-image print of Leonardo Da Vinci's famous painting, the *Mona Lisa*. This example of pop art echoes Walter Benjamin's (1973) argument (see above), as well as an earlier and similarly comical version of the same painting by Marcel Duchamp (McShine 1989). The print shows that the uniqueness, the artistic aura, of the *Mona Lisa* is destroyed by its infinite reproducibility through the silk-screen printing technique employed by Warhol. Instead, it is turned into a joke – the print's title is *Thirty are better than One*. This point is underlined by the fact that Warhol was renowned for his prints of famous popular cultural icons, such as Marilyn Monroe and Elvis Presley, and of everyday consumer items, such as tins of Campbell's soup, Coca-Cola bottles and dollar bills.

Another aspect of this process is that art becomes increasingly integrated into the economy because it is used to encourage people to consume through the expanded role it plays in advertising, and because it becomes a commercial good in its own right. Also, postmodern popular culture refuses to respect the pretensions and distinctiveness of art. Therefore, the breakdown of the distinction between art and popular culture, as well as crossovers between the two, become more prevalent.

Confusions over time and space

This point argues that present and future expansions, constrictions and concentrations of time and space have led to increasing confusion and incoherence in social senses of space and time, in our maps of the places where we live, and our ideas about the times by which we organise our lives. The title and narrative of the *Back to the Future* films capture this point fairly well. The growing immediacy of global space and time resulting from the dominance of the mass media means that previously unified and coherent ideas about space and time begin to be undermined, and become distorted and confused. Rapid international flows of capital, money, information and culture disrupt the linear unities of time, and the established distances of geographical space. Because of the speed and scope of modern mass communications, and the relative ease and rapidity with which people and information can travel, time and space become less stable and comprehensible, and more confused and incoherent (Harvey 1989: part 3).

Postmodern popular culture is seen to express these confusions and distortions. As such, it is less likely to reflect coherent senses of space or time. Some idea of this argument can be obtained by trying to identify the locations used in some pop videos, the narratives of some recent films, or the times and spaces crossed in a typical evening of television viewing. In short, postmodern popular culture is a culture *sans frontières*, outside history.

The decline of metanarratives

The loss of a sense of history as a continuous, linear narrative, a clear sequence of events, is indicative of the argument that metanarratives are in decline in the postmodern world. This point follows on from the previous arguments we have noted. Metanarratives are ideas such as religion, science, art, modernism and Marxism which make absolute, universal and all-embracing claims to knowledge and truth. Postmodern theory is highly sceptical about these metanarratives, and argues that they are disintegrating, losing their validity and legitimacy and increasingly prone to criticism. It is argued that it is becoming increasingly difficult for people to organise and interpret their lives in the light of metanarratives of whatever kind. This argument would therefore be relevant, for example, to the declining significance of religion as a metanarrative in postmodern societies. Postmodernism has been particularly critical of the metanarrative of Marxism and its claim to absolute truth, as it has been of any theory which tries to read a pattern of progress into history. In short, its argument is that metanarratives are in decline.[8]

The consequence of this is that postmodernism rejects the claim of any theory to absolute knowledge, or the demand of any social practice to universal validity. So, for example, on the one hand, there are movements in the natural or hard sciences away from deterministic and absolute metanarratives towards more contingent and probabilistic claims to the truth, while on the other hand people appear to be moving away from the metanarrative of life-long, monogamous marriage towards a series of discrete if still monogamous 'relationships' (Harvey 1989: 9; Lash and Urry 1987: 298). The diverse, iconoclastic, referential and collage-like character of postmodern popular culture clearly draws inspiration from the decline of metanarratives.

Contemporary popular culture and postmodernism

We now need to look more closely at some examples of popular culture to see if the existence of postmodernism can be detected. Clearly, what follows is by no means systematic or exhaustive. It is necessarily selective and designed to search for some elements and trends in popular culture in order to provide a preliminary assessment of the problems posed. It should help clarify the nature of postmodernism.

Architecture

This is a particularly appropriate example to use because, during the twentieth century, groups of architects have identified themselves as 'modernist' or 'postmodernist'. These terms have also been used to describe contemporary buildings.[9] The argument here is that modernism in architecture, which first came to prominence in the 1920s, based itself upon a radical rejection of all previous forms of architecture, and insisted that buildings and architecture have to be created anew according to rational and scientific principles. Functionality and efficiency, high rise, streamlined, glass and concrete structures, and a disregard for the past and for context, have all become its trademark. It has sought to reflect, celebrate and entrench the dynamism of industrial modernity through the rational, scientific and technical construction of built space.

Postmodernism in architecture rejects this metanarrative. Its hallmarks are: highly ornate, elaborately designed, contextualised and brightly coloured buildings; a stress on fictionality and playfulness; and the mixing of styles drawn from different historical periods in almost random and eclectic designs. Postmodernism turns buildings into celebrations of style and surface, using architecture to make jokes about built space. Examples of this include Philip Johnson's grandfather clock-shaped building for AT&T in New York, Charles Moore's Piazza Italia in New Orleans, or Richard Rogers's Lloyds building in the City of London. Rather than build or design according to rational, scientific principles, postmodern architecture is said to proceed according to the context in which the building is to be placed, and to mix together styles, for example classical (ancient Roman or Greek) with vernacular (popular cultural signs and icons). It embraces cultural definitions and the superiority of style, bringing together ideas and forms from different times and places. It also rejects the privileged metanarrative of modernist architecture, and the distinction drawn between classical and modernist architecture as art and vernacular architecture as popular culture. For example, Las Vegas has been seen as an exemplar of and inspiration for postmodern architecture (Venturi *et al.* 1977).

Cinema

Postmodern theory clearly holds what it considers important arguments about visual phenomena, and the most obvious films in which to look for signs of postmodernism are those which emphasise style, spectacle, special effects and images, at the expense of content, character, substance, narrative and social comment. Examples include films such as *Dick Tracey* (1990) or *9½ Weeks* (1986). But to look only at films which deliberately avoid realism and sell themselves on their surface qualities can obscure some of the other things which are going on in contemporary cinema.[10] The films directed and produced by Steven Spielberg and his associates, such as the *Indiana Jones* (1981, 1984 and 1989) and *Back to the Future* series (1985, 1989 and 1990), equally display elements of postmodernism. This is not only because of their style but because their major points of reference, and the sources they most frequently invoke, are earlier forms of popular culture such as cartoons, 'B' feature science-fiction films, and the Saturday morning, movie-house, adventure series people of Spielberg's generation would have viewed in their youth. It is likewise argued that these films appear to stress spectacle and action through their use of sophisticated techniques and relentless pursuit sequences, rather than the complexities and nuances of clever plotting and character development. Sometimes it is suggested that the narrative demands of classical realism are being increasingly ignored by postmodern cinema. Moreover, the *Back to the Future* series and other films such as *Brazil* (1985) and *Blue Velvet* (1986) are said to be postmodern because of the way they are based on confusions over time and space. Others, such as *Who Framed Roger Rabbit?* (1988), can be seen to be postmodern because of their deliberate use of distinct (cultural and technical) genres: the cartoon strip and the detective story. Yet others, such as *Body Heat* (1981), can be claimed to be postmodern because they are parasitic on the cinema's past, recycling – in this example – the crime thriller of the 1940s. They thus engage in a kind of 'retro-nostalgia'. Related to this are films which recycle themselves in a number of sequels once the magic box office formula has been discovered, such as the *Rocky* (1976, 1979, 1982, 1985 and 1990) or *Rambo* (1982, 1985 and 1988) films and the many other repeats which could be mentioned. This tendency is argued to be postmodern partly because it ignores the demands of artistic originality and novelty associated with modernism. But mainly, it is argued to be postmodern because it goes no further than recycling the recent past, making films which are merely imitations of other films rather than reflections of social reality.

A frequently cited example of the postmodern film is *Blade Runner* (1982) (Harvey 1989: chapter 18; Instrell 1992). Among the more noticeable characteristics of this film (which is about Los Angeles in the early part of the twenty-first century), we can note how its architectural look, or production design, clearly mixes styles from different periods. The buildings which house the major corporation have lighting characteristic of contemporary skyscrapers but the overall look of ancient temples, while the 'street talk' consists of words and phrases taken from a whole range of distinct languages. These architectural and linguistic confusions can be said to contribute to an elusive sense of time since we appear to be in the past, the present and the future at the same time. It is a science fiction film which is not obviously futuristic in its design. This effect is accentuated in two ways. First, the 'non-human humans' in the film are not mechanical robots but 'replicants', almost perfect simulations of human beings. Second, the genre of the film is not clear.[11] It has been defined as a science fiction film, but it is also a detective film. Its story unfolds as a detective story, the hero has many of the character traits we associate with the 'tough-guy' policeman or private investigator, and his voice-over, which relates the investigation, draws upon the idioms and tone of film noir.

Television

One way of considering television as an example of postmodernism is to see it as a postmodern medium in its own right. Television's regular daily and night-time flows of images and information bring together bits and pieces from elsewhere, and create its sequences of programmes on the basis of compilations and surface simulations. Equally, there are a number of instructive examples of television programmes which can be used to assess the emergence of postmodernism. One useful example is the police and crime series *Miami Vice* (1985–1990), although its distinguishing features may be found elsewhere.[12] There are many other examples of television programmes which could be used to assess the claims of postmodernist theory, such as the surreal cult series *Twin Peaks* (1990–1991) and *Wild Palms* (1993).

One of the most important claims made about *Miami Vice* is that it was heavily reliant upon style and surface. Commentators have noted its visual 'sense' and striking imagery, pointing to the overall look and ambience which the series managed to achieve. For example, its executive producer, Michael Mann – who subsequently went on to produce the even more 'hyper-real' *Crime Story* (1989) – when asked once about the main rule he worked to when making the programme, is reputed to have replied, 'no earth tones'.[13] The series was carefully projected by its colour, locations and camera work. When it first came on in America, one critical response was to suggest it didn't conform to normal television. This refers to the way it seemed more in keeping with the grander stylistic and adventurous conventions of cinema rather than the cosy, intimate and more 'realistic' routines of television. It was noticeably different from more seemingly realistic police series such as *Hill Street Blues* (1981–1989). It has also been compared with film noir. This visual appeal was crucial to the series and was added to by the designer clothes worn by its detective heroes, and the imaginative day and night-time images of Miami. The visual pleasures derived from style and 'look' – locations, settings, people, clothes, interiors, the city – were a crucial motivation in the making and appreciation of the series. The use of an obtrusive pop and rock music sound track added to these pleasures, representing something of a departure for the police and crime series. More than this, it did not so much reject narrative as such, but rather parodied and stylised the established conventions of the genre, while abounding with self-conscious references to popular culture. For example, the conventions of the gangster film were often parodied, while one episode was a more or less straightforward remake of the western *High Noon* (1952).

Advertising

This example is drawn from television advertising, and can be used as another way to try to exemplify the emergence of postmodernism in contemporary popular culture. The argument here is that advertisements used to tell us how valuable and useful a product was. However, they now say less about the product directly, and are more concerned with sending up or parodying advertising itself by citing other adverts, by using references drawn from popular culture and by self-consciously making clear their status as advertisements. This argument recognises that advertising is always involved in selling things to people, but suggests that these features distinguish those elements of postmodernism which can be found in contemporary television advertising.

Advertising has, of course, always been seen as a superficial exercise, more involved with surface and style than anything else. But the point at issue is the changing content and tone of advertising, the move away from the simple and direct selling of a product on the basis of its value to the consumer, whatever the visual style and trick effects used. Although the intention is still to sell, it is contended that nowadays the postmodern effect is achieved by seemingly overt efforts within advertising to undermine this purpose. Once Guinness was supposed to be good for us and the advert told us so. Now this is much less clear and the adverts are more obscure and less obviously relevant to the product in question. Postmodern adverts are more concerned with the cultural representations of the advert than any qualities the product advertised may have in the outside world, a trend in keeping with the supposed collapse of 'reality' into popular media culture. The stylish look of advertisements, their clever quotations from popular culture and art, their mini sagas, their concern with the surfaces of things, their jokey quips at the expense of advertising itself, their self-conscious revelation of the nature of advertisements as media constructions, and their blatant recycling of the past, are all said to be indicative of the emergence of postmodernism in television advertising.

Pop music

From the point of view of postmodern theory, the recent history of popular music can be seen to be marked by a trend towards the open and extensive mixing of styles and genres of music in very direct and self-conscious ways.[14] This has ranged from the straightforward remixing of already recorded songs from the same or different eras on the same record, to the quoting and 'tasting' of distinct musics, sounds and instruments in order to create new sub- and pan-cultural identities. Good examples include eclectic successions of pop and rock-'n'-roll records, mixing, collage constructions, reggae sound systems, rap, house, hip hop and techno. It is also necessary to include in this category the so-called 'art rock' musical innovations and mixing of styles associated with groups and performers such as Talking Heads, Laurie Anderson and the Pet Shop Boys.

Whatever the respective merits of these new departures, these examples can be argued to be postmodern. They are concerned with collage, pastiche and quotation, with the mixing of styles which remain musically and historically distinct, with the random and selective pasting together of different musics and styles, with the rejection of divisions between serious and fun or pop music, and with the attack on the idea of rock as a serious artistic music which merits the high cultural accolade of the respectful concert (an attack closely associated with punk). By contrast, 'modernist' popular music can be understood as an attempt to fashion new and distinct forms out of previous styles. So what was distinctive about rock-'n'-roll, for example, was not the fact that it, too, borrowed from and based itself upon already existing musical styles, but that it used these styles to construct something new. Rock-'n'-roll, it is commonly suggested, arose out of the cross-cutting influences exerted by country and western, on the one hand, and urban rhythm and blues, on the other. The result was not, it is argued, a postmodern amalgam in which country and rhythm and blues stayed recognisably the same, but a novel and original fusion called rock-'n'-roll. Similarly with soul music. This is said to have arisen out of the coming together of gospel and blues within black American culture. Yet again the consequence was said to be something strikingly new and different, not a sound which maintained the relatively separate identities of gospel and blues. Put very simply and crudely, the argument about the transition between modernism and postmodernism in pop music can be seen as a movement from rock-'n'-roll in the late 1950s, and the Beatles, Tamla Motown, Bob Dylan and folk rock in the 1960s, to music mixing, house, hip hop, 'art rock' and 'straight' pop in the 1980s.

The emergence of postmodernism

So far, the meaning of the term postmodernism and indications of its presence in some leading examples of popular media culture have been outlined. Just how extensive and general these indications are, however, is something which is questioned below. Before that we need to look at another aspect of postmodern theory. This is its understanding of the social and historical conditions under which postmodernism is supposed to have emerged.[15]

Consumerism and media-saturation

Postmodernism has links with some long-standing arguments about how the scale and effects of consumerism and media-saturation have been vital aspects of the modern development of industrial, capitalist societies. One illustration of this is the attempt to account for the emergence of postmodernism by the claim that during the twentieth century, the economic needs of capitalism have shifted from production to consumption. This suggests that the major need of capitalist societies was to establish their conditions of production. The machines and factories for the manufacturing of goods had to be built and continually updated; heavy industries concerned with basic materials, such as iron and steel, and energy, had to be fostered; the infrastructure of a capitalist economy – roads, rail, communications, education, a welfare state, etc. – had to be laid down; and the workforce had to be taught the 'work ethic', the discipline required by industrial labour. All this meant that consumption had to be sacrificed to the needs of production.

Once a fully functioning system of capitalist production has been established, however, the need for consumption begins to grow, and people need to acquire a leisure or consumer ethic in addition to a work ethic. It would be simple minded to suggest that consumption is only a fairly recent development in the history of capitalism or that the problems of capitalist production have necessarily been resolved. But the point being made is that in an advanced capitalist society such as Britain, the need for people to consume has become as important, if not strategically more important, than the need for people to produce. Increased affluence and leisure time, and the ability of major sections of the working class to engage in certain types of conspicuous consumption, have in their turn served to accentuate this process. Hence, the growth of consumer credit, the expansion of agencies such as advertising, marketing, design and public relations, encouraging people to consume, and the emergence of a postmodern popular culture which celebrates consumerism, hedonism and style.

In this process, the media obviously become more important. The rise of modern mass communications, and the associated proliferation of popular media culture, therefore become central to the explanatory framework of postmodern theory. What is inferred from this is that the mass media have become so significant for communication and information flows within and between modern societies (and consequently the popular culture they broadcast and promote increasingly defines and channels everyday life in these societies) that they, along with consumerism, have given rise to the characteristic features of postmodernism described above. The world, it is argued, will consist more and more of media screens and popular cultural images – TVs, VDUs, videos, computers, computer games, personal stereos, adverts, theme parks, shopping malls, 'fictitious capital' or credit – which are part and parcel of the trends towards postmodern popular culture.

New middle-class occupations

Consumerism and media-saturation have been conceived of as over-abstract processes, but they can be given some social grounding if changes in the class and occupational structures are taken into consideration.[16] From this point of view, the increasing importance of consumption and the media in modern societies has given rise to new occupations (or changed the role and character of older ones) involved with the need to encourage people to consume, more frequently, a greater number and variety of commodities. The idea here is that some groups have to be held responsible for producing postmodernism, however unaware they may be about what they are doing. Hence it can be suggested that certain 'postmodern' occupations have emerged which function to develop and promote postmodern popular culture. These occupations involve the construction of postmodernism. They are claimed to be both creating and manipulating or playing with cultural symbols and media images so as to encourage and extend consumerism. This argument tries to account for the growing importance of occupations such as advertising, marketing, design, architecture, journalism and television production, others such as accountancy and finance associated with increased consumer credit, and those such as social work, therapists of one kind or another, teachers, lecturers and so on, associated with the definition and selling of notions of psychological and personal fulfilment and growth. All these occupations are said to be among the most important in determining the taste patterns for the rest of the society. They exert an important influence over other people's life-styles and values or ideologies (while expressing their own as well).

These new middle-class occupations, which cater for the variety of consumer markets already existing or in the process of being formed, are crucial to the development of a postmodern popular culture. They entail being conversant with the media and popular culture, both of which have to be used and manipulated in order for their appropriate occupational work to be carried out. This is further linked to the proposition that the cultural ideologies and identities of these occupational groups are becoming increasingly postmodern. At least, certain significant sections within these groups can be described in this way. The nature of the work they carry out and the need to distinguish themselves as a status group from others in the hierarchy of taste both help their elaboration of a postmodern ideology and life-style. Their quest for cultural power leads them towards postmodernism and away from the cultures of other classes, such as the high culture of the traditional middle-class intelligentsia.[17]

The erosion of identity

The interpretation of identity has become a key issue in the debates raised by postmodern theory.[18] The specific claims that have been made about identity in these debates furnish us with another set of reasons for the emergence of postmodernism. The overall case that can be examined here does not claim that a simple process of decline has occurred but that a limited and dependable set of coherent identities have begun to fragment into a diverse and unstable series of competing identities. The erosion of once secure collective identities has led to the increasing fragmentation of personal identities. It is argued that we have witnessed the gradual disappearance of traditional and highly valued frames of reference in terms of which people could define themselves and their place in society, and so feel relatively secure in their personal and collective identities. These traditional sources of identity – social class, the extended and nuclear family, local communities, the 'neighbourhood', religion, trade unions, the nation state – are said to be in decline as a result of tendencies in modern capitalism such as increasingly rapid and wide-scale rates of social change. Economic globalisation, for example, the tendency for investment, production, marketing and distribution to take place on an international basis above and beyond the nation state or the local community, is seen as an important reason for the gradual erosion of these traditional sources of identity. Transnational economic processes erode the significance of local and national industries and, thereby, the occupational, communal and familial identities they could once sustain.

This argument then goes on to suggest that these problems are exacerbated because no equivalent and workable forms emerge which can take the place of traditional sources of identity. No new institutions or beliefs arise to give people a secure and coherent sense of themselves, the times in which they live and their place in society. Those features of contemporary societies which are novel or which represent the prominence of previously secondary trends, such as the demands of consumerism or watching television, are not thought to offer satisfactory and worthwhile alternatives. In fact, they encourage the features associated with postmodernism. Consumerism by its very nature is seen to foster a self-centred individualism which disrupts the possibilities for solid and stable identities. Television has similar effects because it is both individualistic and universal. People relate to television purely as individual viewers cut off from wider and more genuine social ties, while television relates back to people as individual and anonymous members of an abstract and universal audience. In both cases, the wider collectivities to which people might belong, and the legitimate ideas in which they might believe, tend to be ignored, eroded or fragmented. Neither consumerism nor television form genuine sources of identity and belief, but since there are no dependable alternatives, popular culture and the mass media come to serve as the only frames of reference available for the construction of collective and personal identities.

The limits of postmodernism

This survey of the emergence of postmodernism within contemporary popular culture is not extensive, but it is clearly possible to find examples which clarify the claims of postmodernist theory. We can now question these claims. There are at least two ways to do this: one will be to take a critical look at some of the central arguments of postmodern theory; the other will be to examine critically the claims it makes about a particular area of popular culture.

First of all, the idea that the mass media take over 'reality' clearly exaggerates their importance. The mass media are important, but not that important. This idea that the media are all important sometimes seems to be merely an ideology which expresses the interests of media professionals. It has less to commend it as a serious analysis because it fails to identify the precise character of this importance, and does not provide empirical evidence for the claims it makes. It also ignores the point that other factors, such as work and the family, contribute to the construction of 'reality'. The related idea that popular media culture regulates consumption rests upon unsubstantiated assumptions about people's behaviour as consumers. Equally, it fails to recognise how useful the commodities which people buy are for them, and neglects the fact that the ability to consume is restricted by economic and cultural inequalities. Moreover, the notion that 'reality' has imploded inside the media such that it can only be defined by the media is equally questionable. Most people would still be able to distinguish between the 'reality' created by the media, and that which exists elsewhere. Of course, if reality has really 'imploded' into the media, how would we know it has happened? We could only rely on the media to tell us that it had, but why should we trust them?

Those theorists who think postmodernism is emerging seem to be echoing many of the anxieties and fears expressed much earlier by mass culture and Frankfurt School critics.[19] This is evident in a number of the arguments put forward by postmodern theory. For example, the ideas that collective and personal identities are being eroded, that modern popular culture is a trash culture, that art is under threat and that the enlarged role of the mass media allows them to exercise a powerful ideological influence over their audiences, all provide clear evidence for this point. Neither are cultural pessimism, and concern over working-class consumption, new issues; nor is the implied distinction between a modernist past when the world was a better place to live in, and the postmodern present and future when things can only go on getting worse and worse. Not only is too much significance given to consumerism and the power of media such as television, but the claims that are made are rarely substantiated by any evidence. In addition, little attention is given to such things as the nature of people's daily lives, popular attitudes towards consumption, the continuity of identities and the possibility of alternative identities emerging in the course of time.

Another major difficulty with postmodernism lies in its assumption that metanarratives are in decline. In the first place, what is postmodernism, after all, if it is not another metanarrative? It presents a definite view of knowledge and its acquisition, together with a general account of the significant changes it sees occurring in modern societies. It presumes to tell us something true about the world, and knows why it is able to do this. It is therefore difficult to see why postmodernism should not be thought of as a metanarrative. If it is indeed another metanarrative, how can metanarratives be in decline? It could be suggested that postmodernism is the last of the metanarratives. But would it be possible to argue this except on the basis of another metanarrative, since it involves making a claim to know something? It would seem that, far from metanarratives being in decline, they are something we cannot do without. And if, despite its protestations, postmodernism is a metanarrative, there is no reason why we should discard other metanarratives such as Marxism and modernism.

It is apparent that developments in technology and communications have had significant effects on the speed with which information, images and people can be transported around the world. They are therefore in line with postmodernist claims about space and time. As a result, the sense that people now have of time and space must have changed when compared with previous generations. But again the opportunities to experience these changes may be unequally distributed. They may be more available to some classes and occupational groups than to others. Moreover, why should these changes be qualitatively distinct from those associated with the invention of the aeroplane and the cinema? We need to know about the history within which these changes can be understood, and not succumb to a surprisingly positivistic faith in technology. If we are going to talk about changes, then we must presumably engage in some kind of historical evaluation. Another reason to be sceptical of the claims of postmodern theory is that the effects of these dramatic changes in time and space upon people's lives remain relatively unexamined, the changes in people's consciousness seemingly being assumed to follow automatically from technological changes.

Postmodernist claims about the breakdown of the distinction between art and popular culture have a degree of plausibility, particularly since they seem to relate to the practices and ideologies of certain occupational groups. However, the claims appear to be largely confined to these groups. There are, in fact, a number of difficulties with the idea that such a breakdown is occurring. First, if art and popular culture can still be distinguished from each other, then how far can the breakdown be said to have gone? Second, postmodern culture has been distinguished from other types of culture such as pre-modern and modern. Therefore the possibility of using criteria to distinguish between cultural products does not disappear with postmodernism. If we take the postmodern argument at face value, the potential for cultural discrimination must remain under postmodernism. Otherwise, how can postmodernism be distinguished from other types of culture? Third, the postmodern popular culture produced by certain occupational groups within the cultural industries is clearly not just concerned with a celebratory populism or a know-nothing relativism. The quotes and references that are part of this process are meant to appeal to those 'clever' enough to spot the source of the quote or reference. Rather than dismantling the hierarchy of aesthetic and cultural taste, postmodernism erects a new one, placing itself at the top. Last, it can be argued that most people do discriminate in their cultural consumption and appreciation, even if they do not do so in order to conform with the demands of the hierarchy of art and mass culture, or of postmodernism.

If we look at the examples of popular culture discussed above, there appear to be changes in the direction of postmodernism, most notably in the areas of architecture and advertising. However, this conclusion is not true of most areas of popular culture. In particular, its relevance to an account of changes in the cinema is limited, as we can show by looking briefly at this example. No doubt there are aspects of contemporary cinema which can be called postmodern, but a number of significant problems emerge if the history of cinema is taken into consideration.[20] The changes which are called postmodern are either not as novel as is claimed or are simply misunderstood.

Popular cinema has always been concerned with presenting spectacle to a large audience. From the start, cinema appealed to audiences on the basis of the spectacular events it brought to the screen. To say that postmodernism is concerned with spectacle is to forget this history and to misunderstand the nature of cinema. Obviously, the spectacles screened today are different from those at the turn of the century in their technical achievements. None the less, despite these different technical and cultural contexts, there is no reason to suppose that one era has been more concerned with spectacle than another. Furthermore, stories remain an important aspect of the appeal of contemporary cinema. The *Back to the Future* films may exemplify postmodern claims about confusions over time and space but they are equally held together by effective and complex narratives. Likewise, a spectacular film such as *Blade Runner* has a story about the misguided attempts by science to replicate human life, and the tragic fates its 'replicants' suffer, a theme which goes back to Mary Shelley's *Frankenstein* novel.

From the postmodern point of view, contemporary cinema indulges in nostalgia, living off its past, ransacking it for ideas, recycling its images and plots and cleverly alluding to it in self-conscious postmodern parodies. This view also means that postmodern popular culture is identifiable by its self-conscious awareness of its status as a cultural product. Yet again, this exaggerates the novelty of these developments and misinterprets their character and their history. The repeat and the sequel have been part of the way cinema has worked from its earliest stages. Initially it made use of other types of popular culture such as the stage, the newspaper and the novel, and very soon these media fed off each other for ideas and stories. As it grew, cinema remade films that had been made before. For example, that model of narrative realism *The Maltese Falcon* (1941) was in fact the third film to be made from Hammett's original novel, while between 1908 and 1920 six film versions of Robert Louis Stevenson's *Dr Jekyll and Mr Hyde* were released (Maltin 1991; Wood 1988). Similarly, the history of cinema throws up numerous examples of the film sequel, including those which involved a whole series of repeats. The *Sherlock Holmes* (1922–1985), *Tarzan* (1918–1989) and *Thin Man* (1934–1947) series are obvious examples, but even a cursory survey will reveal a number of other cases (Maltin 1991). Similarly, *King Kong* (1933) spawned *Son of Kong* (1933) and *Mighty Joe Young* (1949). It is also an example of a film which reflects self-consciously upon its status as a cultural product because it deals directly with film-making and spectacle (Kawin 1986).

Insofar as it is possible to generalise, film genres can be said to depend upon a delicate blend of repetition and surprise. As Neale has argued, the historically variable character of genres, the mixing together of genres, the difficulty of allocating particular films to specific genres, together with the confused or hybrid nature of film genres as a whole, are all features to be found throughout the history of cinema rather than being unique to recent films (Neale 1990). Similarly, the parody of genres has a much longer history than is allowed for by postmodern theory, as does the period film which tries to reconstruct an earlier period of history in a highly stylised manner. Westerns and gangster films readily come to mind as relevant examples in this context. Neither is what postmodern theory has to say about nostalgia films, those films said to be parasitic on the past history of cinema, that convincing.[21] There are clearly films which can be called nostalgia films. But many films which are evaluated in this way seem to be more importantly concerned with reinventing and reviving genres, and establishing their contemporary relevance, than with repeating what has gone before. For example, *Body Heat* (1981) is sometimes seen as a nostalgia film but, far from merely recycling the past, it is a film which tries to update cinematic images and themes about sex, desire and fate.

This discussion has tried to indicate some of the difficulties confronted by postmodernism and its interpretation of modern cinema. The signs of postmodernism in certain areas of contemporary popular culture may well be quite partial and specific. It is reasonable to suppose that an examination of other areas will reveal problems similar to those arising from this brief survey of cinema. While it cannot be dismissed completely, postmodernism seems subject to severe theoretical and empirical limitations. It is certainly inadequate as a basis for developing a sociology of popular culture.

Some recent theoretical developments

This concluding section of the chapter deals with some of the fall-out from postmodernism. Along with, and following on from postmodern theory, there have been a number of recent attempts to analyse popular culture, and we can now look at one or two examples.

Discourse and popular culture

So far, post-structuralism has only been mentioned in passing, mainly because it has not been that directly involved in the analysis of popular culture. However, there are one or two signs that theorists and researchers working in this area are turning to some of its ideas for new ways of interpreting popular culture. In particular, the work of Michel Foucault (1926–1984), the French post-structuralist philosopher and historian of ideas, whose ideas are central to the critique of structuralism and Marxism, has been used for this purpose, and we can consider briefly one study to assess critically the arguments involved in this perspective.[22]

Foucault's ideas have become increasingly prominent in the social sciences, but their impact is much less evident in the sociology of popular culture and the mass media. However, one study which indicates what the application of post-structuralism to this area involves is Ang's attempt to use Foucault's notion of discourse to analyse the audience.[23] For Foucault, discourses are particular ways of organising knowledge in the context of serving specific types of power relationships.

Ang's analysis looks at institutional discourses about television audiences. These audiences do not exist naturally, nor can they be taken for granted. Rather they are constructed by particular discourses which seek to know them in order to exert power over them. For example, advertisers define audiences as consumers, and gather knowledge about their purchasing habits, because they want to sell commodities to them. However, because audiences are constructed in this manner by the combination of knowledge and power within these discourses, it does not mean that real audiences will behave in the way such discourses think they will. Audiences can also be understood by the way they resist the discursive powers which try to construct them in ways these powers want.

Basing her critique upon Foucault's ideas, Ang writes:

> in Foucault's work . . . we find a . . . detailed emphasis upon the way in which power and knowledge are intertwined through concrete discursive practices – that is, situated practices of functional language use and meaning production. In these discursive practices, elusive fields of reality are transformed into discrete objects to be known and controlled at the same time. But this can only happen in specific, power-laden institutional contexts, that delimit the boundaries of

> what can actually be said. More concretely, it is only in and through the discourses that express the institutional point of view that the dispersed realities of audiencehood come to be known through the single, unitary concept of 'television audience'. . . . But what should be stressed is that the move towards more scientific ways of knowing the audience within television institutions is not simply a sign of progress from ignorance to knowledge . . . Rather, what is at stake here is a politics of knowledge. In the way television institutions know the audience, epistemological issues are instrumental to political ones: empirical information about the audience such as delivered by audience measurement could become so important only because it produces a kind of truth that is more suitable to meet a basic need of the institutions: the need to control.
>
> (1991: 8 and 10)

Ang considers how the major television institutions involved in the organisation, production and communication of programmes operate to control their audiences by treating them as objects of discourses. They construct, produce and distribute knowledge about their audiences so as to control them in keeping with their institutional requirements. The ideas and habits of which television watching is composed are so complex and varied that they have to be defined by the discourses of television institutions if they are to be managed and controlled. According to Ang, the domination of these discourses has meant that the real or ordinary television audience has not figured as prominently as it should have in analyses and discussions of watching television. These discourses speak on behalf of, but not for, the television audience. By exposing the discourses of the audience developed by the powerful television institutions, discourses which have also influenced academic studies of the audience, she hopes to shift attention back to the ordinary television viewer. To achieve this, it is necessary for research to look at 'the social world of actual audiences', and 'to develop forms of knowledge about television audiencehood that move away from those informed by the institutional point of view' (ibid.: 12).

This understanding of how media organisations work contrasts with the way Marxism treats them as either channels for a dominant ideology or expressions of the demands of profitability. In Ang's analysis, they work according to a much more general drive to exercise power, although in practice there is no reason why it cannot incorporate the arguments of other approaches. Ang tries to substantiate her argument by examining commercial and public service television in America and Europe. However, her use of the concept of power remains vague, abstract and diffuse, general problems encountered by the Foucauldian concept. If television institutions seek to control audiences by discursive forms of knowledge, what are the particular reasons which make them do this? Is there a universal drive to exercise power which characterises all institutions? Or are there more specific social and historical reasons to explain why this should happen, such as the demands of profitability and the constraints of the commodity form? Although Ang does provide evidence of the latter, a theory of this process still needs to suggest the interests which motivate power. Similarly, why should the power of institutions be resisted? What are the interests which motivate resistance to discursive power?

What is more, there is a tendency for this approach to see everything as being discursively constructed, a problem made more acute by the notorious imprecision of the concept of discourse itself. Despite itself, this argument seems usually to end up with nothing but discourses. The realities of power are then dissolved into discourses. For example, Ang suggests that to confront the institutional construction of audiences it is necessary to consider 'the social world of actual audiences'. However, this is, in its turn, another discursive construction, although preferable to the former: 'we cannot presume to be speaking with the authentic voice of the "real audience", because there is no such thing' (ibid.: 165).

None of us may be able to speak for an authentic audience, but there must be audiences somewhere outside discourses. If the institutional discourses of television audiences are empirically inadequate, how can we know this except by claiming to know why they are inadequate? We don't have to refer to other discursive constructions but to the process of acquiring empirical knowledge. Ang accepts that institutional and academic knowledge about audiences is not completely useless (for example, ibid.: 11), but how can this claim be substantiated if all knowledge is discursively constructed and we can never produce knowledge about real audiences? In fact, the claim which is made can only be based upon some criterion which can distinguish between knowledge which is more useful and that which is less useful, and so between truth and falsehood. Also, is Ang presenting us with just another discourse which we can ignore; or knowledge which will enlighten us about audiences?

The 'dialogical' approach to popular culture

This approach is based upon the dialogue which arises between texts and audiences. Barker has alluded to the potential offered by Foucault's notion of discourse (as 'a specific expression of knowledge as power, as in the way children are "defined" by intelligence and aptitude tests' (1989: 220)) for media and cultural studies, and we can treat this approach as an extension of the previous one. He writes of Foucault: 'his way of thinking about power has great potential, and has opened the way to new kinds of research' (ibid.: 213). This potential lies in how Foucault's concept of power shows

> the way we can be turned into objects to be studied. Our talk becomes a symptom, our dreams, thoughts, and sensations become the property of 'experts'. That is power. It is not to deny that there are forms of direct physical control, punishment, armies, police forces. But the first and most common form of power lies in these linkings of power/knowledge.
>
> (ibid.)

However, Barker's mentors are also Volosinov and Propp as well as Foucault. He presents an extensive empirical and critical account of theories which have tried to analyse comics as a form of popular culture. As a result of the failings he notes in these other theories, he puts forward an approach to popular culture which owes much, as he acknowledges, to Volosinov's idea of dialogical analysis.[24]

The objective of Barker's book is to develop a theory of ideology which does not contain the deficiencies of previous theories, and which can provide an adequate basis for the analysis of comics. To this end, he combines Volosinov's dialogical approach and Propp's emphasis on the importance of narrative forms into a conceptual framework which also owes a small debt to Foucault (ibid.: chapter 12).[25] His argument has much in common with that put forward by Frazer (1987), although, rather than turning to discourse analysis, he prefers to retain the concept of ideology. Accordingly, he suggests we can understand comics in terms of a 'contract' between the reader and the text, which is based on a dialogue between them. The meaning of the text arises from this social relationship. A good impression of Barker's argument can be gained from the following:

> A 'contract' involves an agreement that a text will talk to us in ways we recognise. It will enter into a dialogue with us. And that dialogue, with its dependable elements and form, will relate to some aspect of our lives in our society. . . . I have been illustrating the way specific comics offer a contract to some aspect of the social lives of their readers. . . . It is from this that I want to formulate the central hypotheses of the book: (1) that the media are only capable of exerting power over audiences to the extent that there is a 'contract' between texts and audiences, which relates to some specifiable aspect(s) of the audience's social lives; and (2) the breadth and direction of the influence is a function of those socially constituted features of the audience's lives, and comes out of the fulfilment of the contract; (3) the power of 'ideology' therefore is not of some single kind, but varies entirely – from rational to emotional, from private to public, from 'harmless' to 'harmful' – according to the nature of the 'contract'. . . . if all comics, all media, involve a dialogue between text and reader, then to study one side without implicitly assuming the other, would be like listening

> to one end of a telephone conversation without thinking about the other person's part . . . we need to understand ideology as dialogical.
>
> (ibid.: 261)

Barker thus bases his analysis of popular culture on the use of the concept of 'dialogue', formulated initially by Volosinov to develop a theory of language and ideology, in order to study the relationship between texts and readers. He tries to overcome the difficulties confronted by previous theories of ideology, and encourage empirical research.

However, if we refer back to our discussions of Foucault, Ang and Frazer, a number of questions can be raised about this approach. First of all, we might ask what part power has to play in the forming of contracts between texts and audiences since power is supposedly so important for discourse analysis? Can this relationship be regarded as a reasonably equal one? Or if not, what are the bases of the inequalities within which it is shaped? No doubt Barker's notion of the contract is one way of understanding the relationship between audiences and popular culture. It does not dismiss them as 'cultural dopes', nor does it lapse into a celebration of their freedom to choose whatever culture they want. But it does need to say more about how the contract is formed and transformed by wider power relations. Related to this is a problem regarding the role of production. Texts are not usually produced by readers, but are the result of industrial and cultural production. What, then, do these processes contribute to the dialogue between text and audience? Barker stresses the importance of studying the production histories of cultural forms which 'summarise the interactions of producers (their purposes, institutional structures, external constraints, relations with creators, writers, artists, etc.), their audiences (traditions of reading, definitions of the medium, etc.) through which the form is produced and reproduced' (ibid.: 275). And his book contains accounts of the production histories of a number of comics. But the roles they play in the dialogues and contracts with which he wishes to analyse popular culture are not fully or consistently discussed. His stress upon the significance of production histories, the structures and transformations of cultural forms, 'the social characteristics of the audience' (ibid.), and the concept of the contract between text and readers, make his argument more substantial and wide-ranging than those offered by either Foucauldian or dialogical theories. But it implies that there may be as many production histories as there are types of popular culture and so gives up on generalising theoretically about production and consumption; and it is still a long way from considering how the relationships he discusses are influenced by the way popular culture becomes a commodity.

Cultural populism

This is defined by McGuigan as follows: 'cultural populism is the intellectual assumption, made by some students of popular culture, that the symbolic experiences and practices of ordinary people are more important analytically and politically than Culture with a capital C' (1992: 4). In fact, McGuigan's book is part of a recent critical backlash against the emergence of a populist approach to the analysis of popular culture. He complains about

> a discernable narrowing of vision in cultural studies, exemplified by the drift into an uncritical populist mode of interpretation. I support the wish to understand and value everyday meanings, but, alone, such a wish produces inadequate explanations of the material life situations and power relations that shape the mediated experiences of ordinary people.
>
> (ibid.: 244)

For McGuigan, populism understands popular cultural forms as an expression of the interests, experiences and values of ordinary people, and this is precisely what is wrong with it. It becomes an uncritical endorsement rather than a critical dissection of popular culture.

Populism argues that popular culture cannot be understood as a culture which is imposed upon the thoughts and actions of people. Whether this imposition is said to result from the demands of capitalist production and consumption for profits and markets, from the needs of capitalism or patriarchy for ideological control, from the interests of a bourgeois class, from the playing out of the class struggle or from the dictates of an universal mental structure, it is none the less inadequate as a way of understanding popular culture. According to populism, popular culture cannot be understood unless it is viewed, not as an imposition, but as a more or less genuine expression of the voice of the people. The critical response to the mass culture critics' condemnation of the Americanisation of British culture can be cited as an example of populism. From this point of view, the attempt to wrest something positive from American popular culture is not to be dismissed as a slavish and misguided imitation of American life, but welcomed as the assertion of pleasure and creativity in a culture which allows popular participation and celebration for ordinary people. That American popular culture is popular with the British working class is no reason to disregard it, or to write it off as the imposition of economic and ideological power. For populists, this dismissive attack can be safely left in the hands of middle-class intellectuals. In their eyes, these intellectuals don't realise that not only do they have an inadequate explanation, since it does not take into consideration the wishes and desires of the people, but the very fact that it is associated with intellectuals is reason enough to be suspicious about its status as an argument.

One of the problems with cultural populism, for McGuigan, is that it has become increasingly influential in the study of popular culture. He sees it exemplified by some of the work of the Centre for Contemporary Cultural Studies at Birmingham University on youth subcultures and popular television, as well as by the ideas of Fiske,[26] whose views are often taken as perfect illustrations of the claims and limitations of populism (ibid.: 70–75 and chapters 3 and 4). The target of McGuigan's critique is:

> an uncritical populist drift in contemporary cultural studies . . . [in which] ordinary people use the symbolic resources available to them under present conditions for meaningful activity . . . thus, emancipatory projects to liberate people

> from their alleged entrapment, whether they know they are entrapped or not, are called into question. . . . Economic exploitation, racism, gender and sexual oppression, to name but a few, exist, but the exploited, estranged and oppressed cope . . . very well . . . making valid sense of the world and obtaining grateful pleasure from what they receive.
>
> (ibid.: 171)

While he makes a number of criticisms of this perspective, McGuigan's main complaints concern its neglect of the 'macro-processes of political economy', its failure to 'account for both ordinary people's everyday culture and its material construction by powerful forces beyond the immediate comprehension and control of ordinary people', and its complicity with 'economic liberalism's concept of "consumer sovereignty"' (ibid.: 172, 175 and 176; for a similar critique, see Golding and Murdock 1991: 28; cf. Strinati 2000).

Interestingly enough, the theories discussed in this book do not take a populist position on the role of the audience in their explanations of popular culture. Whether it is defined as a political strategy or an analysis of culture, populism has a long history, as the critique of mass culture theory's attack on Americanisation showed. Yet it is difficult to find in the major theories of popular culture an explicit statement of the populist approach. Even semiology, which is argued to have played a part in the development of the Birmingham Centre's cultural populism, says the audience takes for granted the cultural signs which surround it and fails to perceive the ideological work they are doing.[27] Populism has clearly figured in the ideologies of the producers of popular culture as a way of justifying what they produce – 'giving people what they want' – and it can equally be an ideology of audiences (Ang 1989). This perhaps suggests that populism is more important as an ideology than it is as a theory. But in view of the generally dismissive attitude taken by a number of theories towards the popular audience, it is perhaps not that surprising if some writers have been prompted to turn to populism as a response to the elitism to be found generally in theories of popular culture.

Ironically enough, populism represents a mirror image of elitism and this shows up its critical failings, for it is basically an overreaction to elitism. Whereas theories have often seen audiences as full of passive unthinking dupes, open to manipulation and ideological control by the mass media and the culture they spread, populism has turned this around, seeing audiences as self-conscious, active subversives, exploiting media culture for their own ends, and resisting and reinterpreting messages circulated by cultural producers. Whereas elitism has patronised the audience by calling it stupid, populism has patronised the audience by calling it subversive. Populism has still presumed to speak on behalf of, not to, audiences. If the elitist conception of the audience is wrong, then so is the populist one, and for similar reasons. They both operate in terms of unfounded caricatures, and without an adequate empirical and historical appreciation of the social and cultural nature of audiences (cf. Barker 1989).[28] Indeed, it is possible to think of the popularity of popular culture as a real sociological problem, without thereby becoming a populist.

Another aspect of this problem is the way populism has prevented a more adequate account of consumption from being included in theorising about popular culture. The critique of populism has equated it with consumption. This has meant that any attempt to understand the role of consumption in determining forms of popular culture has been regarded as another example of populism, and therefore dismissed. This is a feature of the political economy perspective, and is clearly justified by some of the more extreme statements of the populist position. But by concentrating upon those writers who see consumption as a type of populist subversion, exponents of this critique neglect authors such as Bourdieu (1984) and Miller (1987) (cf. Campbell (1987), Moorhouse (1991) and Stacey (1994)), whose discussion of consumption is not at all populist. As Miller notes, for example, remarking upon the critique of consumption to be found in modern social theories such as postmodernism:

> these global approaches almost always move from an attack on contemporary material culture as trivial or inauthentic to an implied (though rarely explicit) denigration of the mass

> of the population whose culture this is. By contrast, the analysis of particular domains of consumption . . . allows for a more sensitive discrimination between those elements of consumption which appear to generate close social relations and social groupings (such as those among children and neighbourhoods) and those which, by analogy with the critique of ideology, appear to act to prevent sections of the population from representing their interests, and to suppress any expression of those perspectives which might help to develop such interests.
>
> (1987: 16; cf. 10)

It would also be interesting to see how consumption would fit into the political economy approach.[29] And while the social sciences have shown relatively little interest in the process of cultural and material consumption (ibid.: 7), Bourdieu's work (1984) might be useful in this context as it tries to connect cultural consumption with cultural production.[30]

The argument that the major determinant of popular culture is the need for the cultural industries to make a profit is not just an argument about production, or about how and why cultural goods are produced. It is also an argument about consumption, or about how and why the goods produced make a profit by finding large enough markets. The analysis of popular culture requires an emphasis on both, particularly since it is doubtful whether power and control over production by themselves are sufficient to determine patterns of cultural consumption. Apart from anything else, the latter are also an important influence on what gets produced. And it is the combination of production and consumption within the structure of the commodity, rather than an abstract will to power, which may well explain why, for example, television institutions (Ang 1991) produce discourses about their audiences.

Further reading

Boyne, R. and Rattansi, A. (eds) (1990) *Postmodernism and Society*, Basingstoke, Macmillan.

Collins, J. (1992) 'Postmodernism and television', in R. Allen (ed.), *Channels of Discourse, Reassembled*, London, Routledge (second edition).

Connor, S. (1989) *Postmodernist Culture*, Oxford, Basil Blackwell.

Featherstone, M. (1991) *Consumer Culture and Postmodernism*, London, Sage.

Fiske, J. (1991) 'Postmodernism and television', in J. Curran and M. Gurevitch (eds), *Mass Media and Society*, London, Edward Arnold.

Gitlin, T. (1989) 'Postmodernism: roots and politics', in I. Angus and S. Jhally (eds), *Cultural Politics in Contemporary America*, New York and London, Routledge.

Harvey, D. (1989) *The Condition of Postmodernity*, Oxford, Basil Blackwell.

Hebdige, D. (1988) *Hiding in the Light: On Images and Things*, London, Routledge (part 4).

Jameson, F. (1991) *Postmodernism*, London and New York, Verso.

Lash, S. (1990) *The Sociology of Postmodernism*, London and New York, Routledge.

—— and Urry, J. (1987) *The End of Organized Capitalism*, Cambridge, Polity Press.

Strinati, D. (1993) 'The big nothing?: contemporary culture and the emergence of postmodernism', *Innovation* vol. 6, no. 3.

Conclusion

THE FIRST EDITION OF this book did not contain a conclusion which brought the various arguments together in a fitting climax. It merely went over in passing some recent developments in theories of popular culture in order to outline the directions some work in this area was taking. Since the book is now going into a second edition, it seems appropriate to include a proper conclusion, one which conveys the author's position on the usefulness of the theories discussed, and gives some indication of the path future work might thus take. This conclusion highlights both the value of certain theoretical contributions and the shortcomings of a good deal of popular cultural theory. The first edition presented critiques of all the theories because the book provided an introductory outline, and a critical assessment of all the theories covered inevitably followed. However, in most instances the criticisms were somewhat negative. Therefore, this conclusion suggests that, from the point of view of sociology at least, a number of the theories assessed either have little to contribute, as is the case with mass culture theory, semiology, the Marxist theory of ideology, and postmodernism, or still need to develop a more specific framework for analysing popular culture, as is the case with feminism. Other theories, such as those presented by the Frankfurt School and political economy, do provide important insights with, for example, their particular stress on the commodity form and social class, but these are probably best developed by a theoretical approach which tries to go beyond them. This conclusion cannot claim to have such an approach, nor is it yet possible to envisage one. However, some suggestions can be made.

It is possible to read and use this book without worrying about this conclusion. But if the reader's interest is in what the author thinks about the question of where do we go from here, then what follows might be helpful. This objective will not be approached by criticising the particular theories again, but by briefly making some general points about a theory of popular culture. Another way of understanding the aim of this conclusion is through my response to a student who complained about my teaching of the course on which this book is based, and who rebuked me for not saying that some theories were better than others. In effect, I was accused of being a postmodernist and a relativist because it appeared I thought all the theories were as good or as bad as each other, and that there was little to choose between them. My response was that I thought I had been adopting the proper liberal approach in suggesting that all theories might have something to contribute to the study of popular culture, even if some, in the end, might – just might – be more important than others. But the accusation that I was a postmodernist and a relativist was too much, and made me reconsider my position. If this is what happens when you try to be liberal, I thought I might as well argue my own case, while treating all the theories as fairly as I could. Hence, the short argument – if indeed it can be called an argument – developed in this conclusion.

This argument proposes that one of the best ways of explaining the causes, structure and direction of popular culture is by an approach and theory which is sociological. This means a number of things: that such a theory presents a relatively logical and coherent explanation of popular culture by referring to particular sets of social relationships; and that such an explanation is open to, or can be sustained or undermined by, social and empirical proof. It also means that non-sociological arguments are, in principle, open to sociological critiques, and the reverse also applies; also, as will have been noted, the valuable contribution made by some disciplines, such as history, is acknowledged, and is not, and need not, be questioned, while the potential contribution of other disciplines, such as biology, genetics and psychology, is beyond the competence of the author to discuss at all. So it is non-sociological contributions other than these which are at issue. (In the first instance, this argument has little to do with evaluating popular culture, that is, objectively deciding what is good or bad culture, a question which is almost impossible to answer anyway.)

As we have seen, many of the theories and propositions covered in this book fail to meet one or more of these criteria, being either illogical, contradictory, empirically implausible, or oblivious of the need for empirical proof. They are also often open to a sociological critique. In some instances, such as mass culture theory, the exposition has presented a more coherent account than that found in the relevant literature, but this has not afforded it a great deal of theoretical rigour. And the contradictory or illogical character of key arguments can also be found in postmodernism. With other examples, such as the Frankfurt School and the Marxist theory of ideology, scant regard is paid to historical or empirical information. Something similar happens with semiology, though here it seems to be the case that empirical corroboration is often a function of the method used rather than empirical reality; while it is equally open to a sociological critique. This does not mean that certain theories, such as that of the Frankfurt School, should be rejected completely; for example, its stress on the significance of the commodity is clearly important. But it does mean that theories like this need none the less to be re-examined if their insights are to be useful. Feminism is less open to many of the problems so far identified, though, as we have seen, an appropriately feminist theory of popular culture has yet to be developed. The theory which offers the best way forward, or, more accurately, the one which, after critical assessment, is prone to fewer problems, is that of political economy.

Apart from anything else, it is the most empirically and historically minded of all the theories we have considered; and the relation of its concepts to empirical reality, and its openness to evidence and argument, are key tests of any theory.

It is possible to read the book in the light of these claims. However, the potential contribution of political economy still needs to be criticised further if it is to provide the basis for an alternative theory of popular culture. We have already noted some of the problems encountered by this approach in Chapter 4 above. There are one or two other criticisms that can be made in this context. One concerns what is actually meant by the idea of political economy. Certainly, in conversation with other academics interested in this area, the phrase 'political economy' seems to be shorthand for either sociology or an approach which is not textually based. Also, in some accounts, the economy is evident but not the politics; still further, for some, political economy is a synonym (or euphemism) for Marxism. Whatever the precise outcome – and this is not a question which can be resolved here (nor is it one which seems worth bothering with) – the confusion about what is being claimed on behalf of 'political economy' suggests a lack of clarity in its focus which brings me to the next critical point. Although political economy claims to focus upon the political economy as the main way of explaining the mass media and popular culture, its main explanatory variable seems to be ownership and control, a somewhat restricted focus for such an approach. Admittedly, the market and profitability feature as explanatory variables, but they are not consistently related to ownership and control. Also, the significance of the way popular culture has come to be dominated by its status as a commodity, as something which has to be bought and sold, and which has to be produced to be consumed, is not given enough emphasis.

This may be related to another problem, which concerns why the ownership and control of the mass media is considered so important. It is something which is obviously important; but for political economy it is important because it shows that a ruling class is able to exercise power over the mass media and popular culture and thereby exercise power over the society as a whole.

Even if this control may not always be direct, it can ensure the relative absence of alternative ideas, images and values which are critical of the dominant ones. The conclusion which can be drawn from this is that the political economy approach is based upon another variant of the dominant ideology thesis whose Althusserian and Gramscian inspired versions we criticised in Chapter 4. This time, and despite the reservations made, the thesis is more clearly reliant upon the direct role played by a unified and highly powerful ruling class: how else, for example, are we to take the claim that evidence about ownership and control vindicates Marx's argument that 'the ruling ideas in society are the ideas of the ruling class'? Regardless of its stated intentions, political economy is dependent upon a dominant ideology theory and not a theory of political economy in order to explain the nature of popular culture and the mass media in capitalist societies. Whereas Althusser relies upon a conspiracy of the structure – the function of ideology in reproducing capitalism – and Gramsci relies upon a conspiracy of the struggle – the guaranteed outcome of the conflict over hegemony, political economy relies upon a conspiracy of the subject – the ruling class using its control of ideas to secure its power. This can also be seen as a major problem with the political economy approach, since it is difficult to fit this in with the stress it places upon some of the factors mentioned earlier, such as the influence of the commodity.

This argument is not saying that ideology is not important: what it is saying is that the dominant ideology thesis as such faces critical limitations as a theory of popular culture. Nor is it meant to imply that the economy is necessarily more important than ideology: what it is implying is that concern about the hierarchy of this relationship – the base–superstructure scheme – is only a problem for Marxism. If we are not committed to this theory (though it has obvious contributions to make), then there ceases to be a problem. And the view taken by this book is that we can take some crucial points from Marxism, such as ideas about production, consumption and the commodity, without getting entangled in the theoretical baggage of its theory of ideology and the base–superstructure dilemma.

To conclude this argument, some further general and critical points are worth considering. The main problem with a number of theories of popular culture is that they are textual and cultural, and not sociological or historical, even if they sometimes pretend otherwise. Indeed, most theories of popular culture do not avoid this problem, which can be argued to be a consequence of treating popular culture as something which can explain other things as opposed to something which needs to be explained. Of course, there is nothing wrong with textual analyses which are just that, and provide insights into the structure and meaning of texts, and have no pretensions to be anything else, for example, sociology. However, this is not always so, as the example of 'cultural studies' shows: this tries to be multi-disciplinary but ends up being undisciplined; it endeavours to give textual analysis a significance it cannot possess.

The problems associated with textual analysis of this kind have been discussed at length elsewhere, for example in the companion volume to this, *An Introduction to Studying Popular Culture* (Strinati 2000: 255–256), which provides an empirical and historical illustration of the specific theoretical stance being taken in this conclusion. It is also possible to find examples of such problems in the various critiques in this book. We can therefore confine ourselves to a few concluding comments.

The main problem this issue raises is that, without a sociology of popular culture, the relationship between popular culture and 'society' remains assumed and unexamined: it becomes a question of faith and assertion, not argument and empirical research. The fact that popular culture is produced by commercial industries for markets of consumers must be a major factor influencing this relationship; and if this is so, it must play a crucial part in shaping any meanings and ideas contained in the popular culture produced and consumed. This is not to say that this fact is the only influence, but since it is the one which most clearly motivates the relationship, it is one which it is necessary to understand. Also, reflection (and kindred ideas such as construction), may not be the most appropriate way to understand this relationship. Concepts such as ideology may also be as important, if not more important, in explaining this relationship, because the texts of popular culture may often be false, inaccurate, misleading, deceptive or illusory. In addition, the textual analysis of popular culture need not take account of how power influences the relationship between popular culture and society. To close this second edition, we can therefore conclude that the future development of theories of popular culture needs to be more adequately grounded in sociology, both in its theorising and in empirical research.

Notes

Introduction

1 Some idea of the scale of contemporary popular media culture is given by the fact that 98 per cent of homes in Britain now have a television set while almost two-thirds have a video recorder (the *Guardian*, 20 September 1991), and that, on average, every member of the population watched over 26 hours of television a week in 1992 (BFI 1993; 50).

2 For assessments of the nature of international media and cultural inequalities see Sreberny-Mohammadi (1991) and Drummond and Paterson (1986: part 1).

3 On audience research see, for example, Lewis (1990), Morley (1991 and 1992), Moores (1993), Stacey (1994) and Walkerdine (1986).

4 See also Storey (1993, 1997 and 2003).

5 For discussions of this idea see Abercrombie *et al*. (1980), Hill (1990) and Abercrombie (1990).

1 Mass culture and popular culture

1 The sources for these points are Burke (1978) and Williams (1976), which have already been referred to in the main text.

2 The sources for the mass culture debate are equally relevant to my discussion of mass society theory and the critiques of both mass society and mass culture theory. Among the most useful sources are the following: Bennett (1982), MacDonald (1957), Brookeman (1984), Frith (1983), Rosenberg and White (1957), Eliot (1979), Hoggart (1958), F.R. Leavis (1930), Q.D. Leavis (1932), Williams (1963), Johnson (1979), Ang (1989), Modleski (1986a) and Strinati (1992a).

3 This was particularly true for the Frankfurt School, which is discussed in the next chapter.

4 For one of the best accounts of Hollywood cinema see Bordwell *et al.* (1988).

5 For a comparison of liberal and totalitarian political regimes see Bendix (1969), Kornhauser (1960) and Bennett (1982). On the relation between intellectuals and mass culture see Ross (1989) and Turner (1992).

6 As Bennett (1982: 32) has commented:

> The range and diversity of the theorists who are normally regarded as having contributed to the development of mass society theory is forbidding. We have thus, to name but a few, cultural theorists such as Matthew Arnold, T.S. Eliot, Friedrich Nietzsche and Ortega y Gasset; political theorists such as John Stuart Mill and Alexis de Tocqueville; the students of crowd or mass psychology from Gustave le Bon to Wilheim Reich and Hannah Arendt; and, finally, such representatives of the Italian school of sociology as Vilfredo Pareto and Gaetano Mosca.

Together with the works cited in note 2 above, for other sources on mass society theory see Giner (1976), Kornhauser (1960), Swingewood (1977), Bell (1965) and Shils (1957 and 1962).

7 This quote is taken from MacDonald (1957), an article which is drawn upon extensively in this chapter in order to exemplify mass society and mass culture theory. It should, however, be noted, as Ross (1989: 52–53) points out, that MacDonald produced a number of versions of this essay as his views changed over time.

8 For the main sources on mass culture theory, and the subsequent critique, see notes 2 and 6 above.

9 For interesting accounts of the work of F.R. Leavis and Q.D. Leavis see Mulhern (1981) and Sansom (1992).

10 The main sources used for the discussion of Americanisation are: Strinati (1992a), Hebdige (1988), Webster (1988), Bigsby (1975), Morley and Robins (1989), and Hoggart (1958).

11 According to the English subtitles to Wenders' film *Kings of the Road* (1976), the actual phrase used is 'the yanks colonised our sub-conscious'.

12 The actor who played the gangster hero in *Scarface* was in fact Paul Muni.

13 Harry Palmer is the name given to the working-class spy hero in the films made from Deighton's novels, *The Ipcress File* (1965), *Funeral in Berlin* (1967) and *Billion Dollar Brain* (1967). (According to Michael Caine, who played the character in the films, he coined the name himself: the *Guardian*, 17 August 1994; the hero is not named in the novels.) Much of Hammett's detective fiction is also characterised by his trait of not giving a name to his detective hero.

14 The process of standardisation is discussed more fully in the next chapter on the Frankfurt School.

15 See A. Collins (1993), who has extended Ang's distinction to include an ideology of entertainment which is still populist but which sees no reason why it should be defensive about its cultural tastes and preferences.

16 Nor is this meant to imply that the tradition of ethnographic research on audiences can be ignored (see, for example, Moores (1993) and note 3 above). But it is to suggest that much theory has not incorporated this research into its arguments.

2 The Frankfurt School and the culture industry

1 See, for example, Caughie (1991), Gendron (1986), Modleski (1986b) and Murdock and Golding (1977: 18).

2 For example, Benjamin had fled to Paris in the 1930s, and was then forced to flee France by the advance of the German army in 1940. On the point of entering Spain on his way to America, but worried about the possibility of escape, he committed suicide in the same year.

3 An important source for my discussion of the Frankfurt School has been Adorno (1991; especially chapters 1 and 3). Other sources I have found useful are: Bennett (1982), Craib (1984: chapter 11), Gendron (1986), Jay (1973: chapter 6), Slater (1977: chapter 5), Bottomore (1989: chapter 2), Swingewood (1991: 283–290), Horkheimer and Adorno (1973; originally published in 1947), Abercrombie *et al.* (1980), Held (1980: chapter 3), Larrain (1979: 200–210), Eagleton (1991: 125–136), Thompson (1990: 97–109), Brookeman (1984: chapter 8), Dant (1991: 87–98) and Marcuse (1972).

4 For discussions of Marx's theory of commodity fetishism in addition to those to be found in the texts cited in the previous note (in particular, Eagleton, Held and Larrain) see Elster (1985: 95–99) and Mepham (1979).

5 Of all of his work it is Marcuse (1972) which is by far the most relevant for the concerns of this chapter.

6 For a short historical account of doo-wop see Hansen (1981).

7 The critique advanced in the main text draws upon the sources cited in note 3 above.

8 For relevant accounts of genre see Neale (1980 and 1990), Cook (1985), Berger (1992), Palmer (1991: chapter 7) and Krutnik (1991: chapter 1).

9 On this view of the audience see Chapter 5 below and note 3 to the Introduction.

10 For examples of this argument see Palmer (1988) and Messenger Davies (1989).

11 For a perceptive discussion of the 'debate' between Adorno and Benjamin see Wolin (1994: chapter 6).

12 The limitations of Benjamin's case concern the problems raised by Adorno in his debate with Benjamin. See Wolin (ibid.).

3 Structuralism, semiology and popular culture

1 A very useful source on Saussure is Culler (1976). See also Saussure (1974). I am well aware of other developments in semiology (Hawkes: 1977), as well as other comparable thinkers like Durkheim (1858–1917) and Freud (1856–1939), but Saussure's work forms a particularly illustrative case to discuss in the context of this chapter.

2 Some of these problems are assessed by Culler. See Culler (1976: 79–89 and chapter 4).

3 For this discussion, apart from the works of Lévi-Strauss cited in the main text, I have relied on the following: Leach (1970), Hawkes (1977), Sperber (1979), Badcock (1975), Craib (1984: chapter 7), Swingewood (1991: chapter 11), Barker (1989: 147–159), Wright (1975) and Woollacott (1982).

4 One famous sociological study which uses the distinction between the sacred and the profane to define religion and to analyse totemism was carried out by Durkheim (1915).

5 For his popular novels see Eco (1983) and (1990a). It can be suggested that, compared with Eco, Bennett and Woollacott (1987) provide a more convincing and comprehensive analysis of James Bond.

6 However, see also Lévi-Strauss (1963: 282), where he stresses the need to take seriously a culture's 'home-made' models of itself.

7 Apart from the works by Barthes cited in the main text, I have relied upon: Culler (1983), Sturrock (1979), Barthes (1967, 1977 and 1983), Woollacott (1982), Hawkes (1977), Dyer (1982: chapter 6), Fiske and Hartley (1978), Craib (1984: chapter 7), Wright (1975), Barker (1989: 124–128), Rylance (1994) and Williamson (1978). See also Masterman (1984) for an indication of Barthes's influence.

8 In fact, Barthes here appears to clarify something which would have otherwise remained implicit. See Barthes (1968: section 4).

9 The sources for this critique are to be found in note 3 above. Leach (1970) is particularly useful in this context.

10 The sources for this critique are to be found in note 7 above. See also Moorhouse (1991: 7–9).

11 For his development of this idea of polysemy see Barthes (1977: 15–51); cf. Fiske (1989a).

12 For an example of a study which combines semiological and ideological forms of analysis see Hebdige (1979). Some writers like McGuigan (1992: 91, 96–97, and 100–107), and Moores (1993: 134–138) have tended to see this study as holding to a populist conception of the consumers of popular culture, in that – for Hebdige – subculture represents a subversive rearrangement by its adherents of codes and signs to be found elsewhere in popular culture, including the realm of dominant ideas and symbols. However, it seems to me that this is an inference drawn by the

analyst in terms of the dictates of semiological and ideological analysis, rather than an explanation which takes account of the actual interpretations and preferences of these consumers. It is worth quoting Cohen on this point:

> I sometimes have a sense of working-class kids suffering an awful triple fate. First, their actual career prospects are grim enough; then their predicament is used, shaped and turned to financial profit by the same interests which created it; and then – the final irony – they find themselves patronized in the latest vocabulary imported from the Left Bank. (1980: xxviii)

4 Marxism, political economy and ideology

1 Although it obviously counts as a school of Marxist theory, I have confined my discussion of the Frankfurt School to a separate chapter for a number of reasons. First, it represents an earlier attempt to develop a Marxist theory of culture and ideology than the variants of western Marxism considered in this chapter which have had a similar objective in view. Second, it employs a distinctive usage of Marx's theory of commodity fetishism. Third, it thus appears both to be more distinct from other Marxist approaches and to share a lot in common with mass culture theory. These reasons, however, should not allow us to exaggerate the extent of these differences.

2 The literature on this is massive. Apart from the work of Marx cited in the main text, some useful secondary sources are: McLellan (1986: chapter 2), Elster (1985) and (1986: chapter 9), Larrain (1979; chapter 2), Eagleton (1991: chapter 3), Dant (1991: chapter 4), Barrett (1991: part 1), Thompson (1990: 33–44), Swingewood (1991: 72–80) and Mepham (1979).

3 I am using this work as an example of a contemporary Marxist account which is explicitly based upon the explanatory priority Marxist theory accords to the economy. Other examples which could have been used include media imperialism. See, for example, Drummond and Paterson (1986: part 1), Mattelart *et al.* (1984) and Tomlinson (1991: chapter 2). For an interesting exchange on the political economy approach see Budd and Steineman (1989)

and Fiske (1989a). It is fair to point out that Murdock and Golding have altered their position since the mid-1970s. See Golding and Murdock (1991), which is discussed briefly in the main text. See also Murdock (1993), which sets out arguments I find it difficult to disagree with.

4 The difficulties in dealing with a phenomenon like language in terms of the base–superstructure model are instructive. Language covers the whole range of 'levels' from biology to pure, immaterial utterances. How is it possible to decide which is the most important?

5 Apart from the work of Althusser cited in the main text, the sources I have relied on are: Althusser (1969 and 1970), Anderson (1979), Craib (1984: chapters 8 and 9), McLellan (1986: chapter 3), Bennett (1982 and 1979: 112–123), Barrett (1991: chapter 5), Larrain (1979: 154–164), Eagleton (1991: 136–158), Swingewood (1991: 306–311), Dant (1991: 76–85), Cormack (1992: chapter 1) and Abercrombie *et al.* (1980).

6 For an example of this, see Centre for Contemporary Cultural Studies (1978). It is also worth consulting issues of *Screen* for the mid-1970s.

7 The sources used for this critique are cited in note 5 above.

8 Apart from Gramsci (1971), which is cited in the main text, particularly useful texts on Gramsci are Bennett (1986), and Simon (1982). Other useful sources are: Anderson (1979) and (1976–1977), Joll (1977: chapters 8 and 9), Ransome (1992), Williams (1977: 108–114), Swingewood (1991: 205–214), Eagleton (1991: 112–123), Barrett (1991: chapter 4), Cormack (1992: chapter 1), Buci-Glucksmann (1980) and Abercrombie *et al.* (1980).

9 For examples of this see Hall *et al.* (1978) and Hall and Jacques (1983).

10 For biographical information on Gramsci see Fiori (1973), Joll (1977), Buci-Glucksmann (1980), Simon (1982) and Ransome (1992).

11 For useful discussions of Gramsci's concept of hegemony, apart from his own writings, see the sources cited in note 8 above, in particular Anderson (1976–1977), Simon (1982), Buci-Glucksmann (1980) and Williams (1977).

12 For discussions of this topic see Clarke (1986 and 1992). For other examples of the application of Gramsci's concept of hegemony to popular television see Seiter (1986) and Gitlin (1994).

13 The sources for a critical assessment of Gramsci's writings are to be found in note 8 above, in particular Anderson (1976–1977) and Abercrombie *et al*. (1980), but it is noticeable that there is a relative lack of critical commentaries on his work in the secondary literature.

14 For an interesting account of fatalism and social theory, see Lockwood (1982).

15 For assessments of culturalism (along with structuralism) and its relation to the importance of Gramsci's work for the study of popular culture see Bennett (1986) and Hall (1981).

5 Feminism and popular culture

1 Examples of this literature include Greer (1971), de Beauvoir (1972), Mitchell (1975), Spender (1980) and Friedan (1963), the last being particularly important from the point of view of media and cultural studies.

2 For discussions of different types of feminism and feminist analysis see Van Zoonen (1991), McIntosh (1978) and Lengermann and Niebrugge-Brantley (1992).

3 For a full statement of what this approach entails see Tuchman (1981).

4 We have already seen this argument put forward by Barthes in the chapter on structuralism and semiology.

5 The source for this is the *Guardian*, 21 November 1990, p. 6.

6 Books written by women are 'readerly' because they do not demand any 'work' to be performed by their readers. They are therefore easy to 'consume', and therefore easy to 'write'. The stress placed upon the importance of production as opposed to consumption is a feature of other theories of popular culture like Marxism.

7 I have here relied upon Baehr (1981) and Gill (1988).

8 For some important discussions of patriarchy see Kuhn and Wolpe (1978), Hartman (1979), Walby (1990) and Barrett (1988).

9 For sources on the pornography debate see Dworkin (1980), Seaton (1986), Benn (1986) and Ross (1989: chapter 6).

10 For a discussion of the debate between Marxism and feminism see Sargent (1981).

11 The source for this is McRobbie's essay '*Jackie* magazine: romantic individualism and the teenage girl', in McRobbie (1991a; originally

published in 1978). However, McRobbie has since retracted much of the substance of this argument. See her later essay '*Jackie* and *Just Seventeen*: girls' comics and magazines in the 1980s', in ibid.

12 The concept of 'positioning' is very similar to Althusser's concept of 'interpellation'.

13 It could, of course, be claimed that, from a semiological point of view, codes like these could be invented ad nauseum, there being no rational, objective or empirical criteria to limit the choice apart from the limits of the text itself.

14 This method could presumably be used to generate 'hidden' meanings ad infinitum, the only stopping point being the preferred ideological reading of the analyst.

15 On the basis of his own study of the magazine and its stories, Barker also questions the empirical validity of McRobbie's conclusions, in particular her claim that *Jackie* discourages female friendships in favour of boyfriends and marriage. Barker (1989: 157, 179–181 and 247–249).

16 See note 12 to Chapter 3, above.

17 For a more extended discussion of the issues raised by Frazer's article see Stacey (1994).

18 On these developments and their implications see McRobbie (1991b) and (1993).

19 The studies Stacey has in mind are: Winship (1981), Partington (1991) and Nava (1992). Stacey's own study (1994) is an equally important example of this approach, as is Winship (1992).

6 Postmodernism, contemporary popular culture and recent theoretical developments

1 A version of this discussion of postmodernism appeared in *Innovation* vol. 6, no. 3, 1993.

2 See *Screen* vol. 28, no. 2, 1987, and *Theory, Culture and Society* vol. 5, nos. 2–3, 1988.

3 See, for example, the *London Evening Standard Magazine*, September 1989.

4 Good examples of this are Denzin (1991) and Jameson (1991).

5 One convenient indication of this is the way in which the concept of 'postmodernism' in the title of Jameson's original article on this theme (1984) has attracted much more attention than the other equally problematic terms it contained, namely 'late' capitalism, and cultural 'logic'.

6 Featherstone (1988), for example, has related the discussion of postmodernism to the more general debate about the overall shape and direction of industrial, capitalist societies.

7 Among the sources used for this discussion, apart from those cited in notes 2 and 4 above, are: Harvey (1989: especially part 1), Gitlin (1989), Lash and Urry (1987: 285–300), Hebdige (1988: part 4), Boyne and Rattansi (1990), Lash (1990), Collins (1989), Connor (1989), Docherty (1993), Jencks (1986), Twitchell (1992), Pfeil (1985), Hutcheon (1989), Lyotard (1984) and Baudrillard (1988). On Baudrillard see Gane (1991a) and (1991b). I have found Gitlin, and Lash and Urry particularly helpful in providing an initial orientation and an organisational structure for my discussion of postmodernism, and Harvey and Connor very useful in filling in more of the substance and detail.

8 I do not have the space here to present an extensive account of modernism (see, however, the section on architecture below), although it is obviously relevant to any consideration of postmodernism. For assessments of modernism see the sources cited in note 7, particularly Harvey (1989), Lash and Urry (1987), Lash (1990) and Gitlin (1989). See also Murdock (1993).

9 For discussions of modernist and postmodernist architecture see, for example, Jencks (1984 and 1986), Portoghesi (1982 and 1983) and Venturi *et al*. (1977).

10 Among the sources consulted for this section see Lash and Urry (1987), Harvey (1989), Corrigan (1991), Baudrillard (1987), Denzin (1991) and Jameson (1991: chapter 9). For further details of the films discussed see the relevant issues of the *Monthly Film Bulletin* and *Sight and Sound*.

11 This refers to the original film which went on theatrical release, and not the so-called director's cut which came out in 1992.

12 For a general consideration of this area see Connor (1989: chapter 6), Collins (1992) and Fiske (1991). For assessments of *Miami Vice*, see Butler (1985) and Fiske (1987: 255–262).

13 There is no actual source for this quote other than my own memory, but a comparable quote can be found in Butler (1985: 133).

14 For discussions of postmodernism and popular music see Connor (1989: 185–190), Hebdige (1987 and 1988: part 4) and Stratton (1989); cf. Laing (1985: chapter 1).

15 In considering the reasons for the emergence of postmodernism I have used those sources cited in note 7 above. For some evidence on media-saturation see note 1 to the Introduction.

16 In the considerable literature on postmodernism this has received less than its fair share of attention. See, however, Gitlin (1989), Lash and Urry (1987), Harvey (1989: 348; cf. 290), Lash (1990) and Pfeil (1985). See also Bourdieu (1984) and Featherstone (1991: especially chapter 2); cf. Collins (1993) and Frith and Savage (1993).

17 It has to be said that, in the light of what we know at the moment, these claims remain highly speculative. But see Bourdieu (1984) and Miller (1987).

18 See, for example, Harvey (1989: 86–87), Lash and Urry (1987), and Gitlin (1989). For post-structuralist views on identity see Sarup (1988).

19 On mass culture theory and the Frankfurt School see the respective chapters in the main text.

20 I have relied upon a number of sources for this assessment. These include historical studies of Hollywood cinema like Kerr (1986), Bordwell *et al*. (1988), Balio (1985) and Neale (1985), as well as reference books and film guides, in particular Maltin (1991). It would be instructive if the claims of postmodernist theory could be subject to a similar kind of critical assessment in other areas of popular media culture.

21 This is particularly the case with Jameson's arguments. See Jameson (1991: chapter 9).

22 For discussions and assessments of Foucault's work see Foucault (1980), Barrett (1991: chapters 6 and 7), Rabinow (1984), Ritzer (1992: 507–515), Smart (1983 and 1988) and Dant (1991: 120–134). It should be noted that Foucault's ideas, as with post-structuralism more generally, have developed in critical opposition to structuralism and Marxism.

23 For other examples of discourse analysis which are derived from differing notions of discourse see Frazer (1987), Gill (1993) and Fairclough (1989).

24 Volosinov also appears to go by the name of Bakhtin, and there seems to be some confusion in the literature on this. For discussions of the work of Bakhtin (Volosinov) and its relevance for the study of culture see Stam (1988 and 1989), Morson (1986) and Morson and Emerson (1989).

25 Note that Barker sees a number of similarities between the ideas of Bakhtin (Volosinov) and Propp (1989: 274–275); cf. Wright (1975).

26 For a possible example of this see Fiske (1989b). However, Fiske (1989a and 1991) suggest that this may be an oversimplification of his views.

27 For example, there is Cohen's (1980) critique of Hebdige's (1979) semiologically inspired study of youth subcultures, which is referred to in note 12 to Chapter 3, above.

28 For another example of a more sophisticated empirical and historical approach to the study of audiences see Allen (1990).

29 Miller's arguments could be applied to a number of the theories discussed in this book.

30 For detailed and interesting discussions of Bourdieu's work see Robbins (1991), Jenkins (1992) and Garnham and Williams (1986).

Bibliography

Abercrombie, N. (1990) 'Popular culture and ideological effects', in N. Abercrombie, S. Hill and B.S. Turner (eds), *Dominant Ideologies*, London, Unwin Hyman.

—— Hill, S. and Turner, B.S. (1980) *The Dominant Ideology Thesis*, London, Allen and Unwin.

Adorno, T. (1991) *The Culture Industry*, London, Routledge.

Allen, R. (1990) 'From exhibition to reception: reflections on the audience in film history', *Screen* vol. 31, no. 4.

Althusser, L. (1969) *For Marx*, Harmondsworth, Penguin.

—— (1971) *Lenin and Philosophy and Other Essays*, London, New Left Books.

—— and Balibar, E. (1970) *Reading* Capital, London, New Left Books.

Anderson, P. (1976–1977) 'The antinomies of Antonio Gramsci', *New Left Review* no. 100.

—— (1979) *Considerations on Western Marxism*, London, Verso.

Ang, I. (1989) *Watching* Dallas, London, Routledge.

—— (1991) *Desperately Seeking the Audience*, London, Routledge.

Arnold, M. [1869] (1932) *Culture and Anarchy*, Cambridge, Cambridge University Press.

Badcock, C. (1975) *Lévi-Strauss: Structuralism and Sociological Theory*, London, Hutchinson.

Baehr, H. (1981) 'The impact of feminism on media studies – just another commercial break?', in D. Spender (ed.), *Men's Studies Modified*, Oxford, Pergamon Press.

Balio, T. (ed.) (1985) *The Hollywood Film Industry*, Madison, University of Wisconsin Press.

Barker, M. (1989) *Comics: Ideology, Power and the Critics*, Manchester, Manchester University Press.

Barrett, M. (1988) *Women's Oppression Today*, London, Verso.

—— (1991) *The Politics of Truth*, Cambridge, Polity Press.

Barthes, R. (1967) *Writing Degree Zero*, London, Cape (originally published in 1953).

—— (1968) *Elements of Semiology*, New York, Hill and Wang (originally published in 1964).

—— (1973) *Mythologies*, London, Paladin Books (originally published in 1957).

—— (1977) *Image–Music–Text*, London, Fontana.

—— (1983) *Barthes: Selected Writings*, ed. S. Sontag, London, Fontana.

—— (1988) *The Semiotic Challenge*, Oxford, Blackwell.

Baudrillard, J. (1987) *The Evil Demon of Images*, Sydney, Power Publications.

—— (1988) *Selected Writings*, ed. M. Poster, Cambridge, Polity Press.

Beauvoir, S. de (1972) *The Second Sex*, Harmondsworth, Penguin.

Bell, D. (1965) 'America as a mass society: a critique', in *The End of Ideology*, New York, Free Press (revised edition).

Bendix, R. (1969) *Nation Building and Citizenship*, New York, Anchor Books.

Benjamin, W. [1936] (1973) 'The work of art in the age of mechanical reproduction', in *Illuminations*, London, Fontana.

Benn, M. (1986) 'Campaigning against pornography', in J. Curran, J. Ecclestone, G. Oakley and A. Richardson (eds), *Bending Reality: The State of the Media*, London, Pluto Press.

Bennett, T. (1979) *Formalism and Marxism*, London and New York, Methuen.

—— (1982) 'Theories of the media, theories of society', in M. Gurevitch, T. Bennett, J. Curran and J. Woollacott (eds), *Culture, Society and the Media*, London, Methuen.

—— (1986) 'Introduction: "the turn to Gramsci"', in T. Bennett, C. Mercer and J. Woollacott (eds), *Popular Culture and Social Relations*, Milton Keynes, Open University Press.

—— and Woollacott, J. (1987) *Bond and Beyond: The Political Career of a Popular Hero*, Basingstoke, Macmillan.

Berger, A. (1992) *Popular Culture Genres: Theories and Texts*, London, Sage.

Bigsby, C. (ed.) (1975) *Superculture*, Bowling Green, Ohio, Bowling Green University Press.

Booker, C. (1969) *The Neophiliacs: A Study of the Revolution in English Life in the Fifties and Sixties*, London, Collins.

Bordwell, D., Staiger, J. and Thompson, K. (1988) *The Classical Hollywood Cinema*, London, Routledge.

Bottomore, T. (1989) *The Frankfurt School*, London, Routledge.

Bourdieu, P. (1984) *Distinction*, London, Routledge.

—— (1993) *The Field of Cultural Production*, Cambridge, Polity Press.

Boyne, R. and Rattansi, A. (eds) (1990) *Postmodernism and Society*, Basingstoke, Macmillan.

British Film Institute (BFI) (1993) *British Film Institute: Film and Television Handbook 1994*, London, British Film Institute.

Brookeman, C. (1984) *American Culture and Society since the 1930s*, London and Basingstoke, Macmillan.

Buci-Glucksmann, C. (1980) *Gramsci and the State*, London, Lawrence and Wishart.

Budd, M. and Steineman, C. (1989) 'Television, cultural studies and the "blind spot"', in G. Burns and R. Thompson (eds), *Television Studies: Textual Analysis*, New York, Praeger.

Bullock, A. and Stallybrass, O. (eds) (1977) *The Fontana Dictionary of Modern Thought*, London, Fontana.

Burke, P. (1978) *Popular Culture in Early Modern Europe*, London, Temple Smith.

Butler, J. (1985) 'Miami Vice: the legacy of film noir', *Journal of Popular Film and Television*, Fall issue.

Campbell, C. (1987) *The Romantic Ethic and the Spirit of Modern Consumerism*, Oxford, Basil Blackwell.

Caughie, J. (1991) 'Adorno's reproach: repetition, difference and television genre', *Screen* vol. 32, no. 2.

Centre for Contemporary Cultural Studies (1978) *On Ideology*, London, Hutchinson.

Chandler, R. (1980) *Pearls are a Nuisance*, London, Pan Books.

Clarke, A. (1986) 'This is not the boy scouts: television police series and definitions of law and order', in T. Bennett, C. Mercer and J. Woollacott (eds), *Popular Culture and Social Relations*, Milton Keynes, Open University Press.

—— (1992) '"You're nicked!": television police series and the fictional representation of law and order', in D. Strinati and S. Wagg (eds), *Come On Down?: Popular Media Culture in Post-war Britain*, London, Routledge.

Cohen, P. (1980) *Folk Devils and Moral Panics: The Creation of the Mods and Rockers*, Oxford, Martin Robertson (second edition).

Collins, A. (1993) 'Intellectuals, power and quality television', *Cultural Studies* vol. 7, no. 1.

Collins, J. (1989) *Uncommon Cultures: Popular Culture and Post-modernism*, New York and London, Routledge.

—— (1992) 'Postmodernism and television', in R. Allen (ed.), *Channels of Discourse, Reassembled*, London, Routledge (second edition).

Connor, S. (1989) *Postmodernist Culture*, Oxford, Basil Blackwell.

Cook, P. (ed.) (1985) *The Cinema Book*, London, British Film Institute.

Cormack, M. (1992) *Ideology*, London, Batsford.

Corrigan, T. (1991) *A Cinema Without Walls*, London, Routledge.

Craib, I. (1984) *Modern Social Theory*, London and New York, Harvester Wheatsheaf.

Culler, J. (1976) *Saussure*, London, Fontana.

—— (1983) *Barthes*, London, Fontana.

Curran, J., Gurevitch, M. and Woollacott, J. (1982) 'The study of the media: theoretical approaches', in M. Gurevitch *et al.* (eds), *Culture, Society and the Media*, London, Methuen.

Curran, J. and Gurevitch, M. (eds) (1991) *Mass Media and Society*, London, Edward Arnold.

Dant, T. (1991) *Knowledge, Ideology and Discourse*, London and New York, Routledge.

Deighton, L. (1978) *The Ipcress File*, London, Triad Granada (originally published in 1962).

Denning, M. (1987) *Cover Stories: Narrative and Ideology in the British Spy Thriller*, London and New York, Routledge and Kegan Paul.

Denzin, N. (1991) *Images of Postmodern Society: Social Theory and Contemporary Cinema*, London, Sage.

DiMaggio, P. (1986) 'Cultural entrepreneurship in nineteenth century Boston: the creation of an organizational base for high culture in America', in R. Collins, J. Curran, N. Garnham, P. Scannell, P. Schlesinger and C. Sparks (eds), *Media, Culture and Society: A Critical Reader*, London, Sage Publications.

Docherty, T. (1993) *Postmodernism: A Reader*, New York and London, Harvester Wheatsheaf.

Drummond, P. and Paterson, R. (eds) (1986) *Television in Transition*, London, British Film Institute.

Durkheim, E. (1915) *The Elementary Forms of the Religious Life*, London, George Allen and Unwin.

Dworkin, A. (1980) 'Pornography and grief', in L. Lederer (ed.), *Take Back The Night*, New York, William Morrow.

Dyer, G. (1982) *Advertising as Communication*, London and New York, Methuen.

Dyer, R. (1973) *Light Entertainment*, London, British Film Institute.

Eagleton, T. (1991) *Ideology: An Introduction*, London and New York, Verso.

Eco, U. (1979) 'The narrative structure in Fleming', in *The Role of the Reader*, Bloomington, Indiana, University of Indiana Press.

—— (1983) *The Name of the Rose*, London, Secker and Warburg.

—— (1990a) *Foucault's Pendulum*, London, Pan Books.

—— (1990b) *The Limits of Interpretation*, Bloomington, Indiana, University of Indiana Press.

Eliot, T. S. (1979) *Notes towards the Definition of Culture*, London, Faber and Faber.

Elster, J. (1985) *Making Sense of Marx*, Cambridge, Cambridge University Press.

—— (1986) *An Introduction to Karl Marx*, Cambridge, Cambridge University Press.

Fairclough, N. (1989) *Language and Power*, London and New York, Longman.

Featherstone, M. (1988) 'In pursuit of the postmodern', *Theory, Culture and Society* vol. 5, nos 2–3.

—— (1991) *Consumer Culture and Postmodernism*, London, Sage.

Fiori, G. (1973) *Antonio Gramsci: Life of a Revolutionary*, New York, Schocken Books.

Fiske, J. (1987) *Television Culture*, London and New York, Methuen.

—— (1989a) 'Popular television and commercial culture: beyond political economy', in G. Burns and R. Thompson (eds), *Television Studies: Textual Analysis*, New York, Praeger.

—— (1989b) *Understanding Popular Culture*, Boston and London, Unwin Hyman.

—— (1991) 'Postmodernism and television', in J. Curran and M. Gurevitch (eds), *Mass Media and Society*, London, Edward Arnold.

—— and Hartley, J. (1978) *Reading Television*, London and New York, Methuen.

Foucault, M. (1980) *Power/Knowledge: Selected Interviews and other Writings 1972–1977*, ed. C. Gordon, New York, Harvester Wheatsheaf.
Franklin, S., Lury, C. and Stacey, J. (eds) (1991) *Off-centre: Feminism and Cultural Studies*, London, HarperCollins.
Frazer, E. (1987) 'Teenage girls reading Jackie', *Media, Culture and Society* vol. 9.
Friedan, B. (1963) *The Feminine Mystique*, Harmondsworth, Penguin.
Frith, S. (1983) *Sound Effects: Youth, Leisure and the Politics of Rock*, London, Constable.
—— and Savage, J. (1993) 'Pearls and swine: the intellectuals and the mass media', *New Left Review* no. 198.
Gamman, L. and Marshment, M. (eds) (1988) *The Female Gaze: Women as Viewers of Popular Culture*, London, The Women's Press.
Gane, M. (1991a) *Baudrillard: Critical and Fatal Theory*, London, Routledge.
—— (1991b) *Baudrillard's Bestiary: Baudrillard and Culture*, London, Routledge.
Garnham, N. and Williams, R. (1986) 'Pierre Bourdieu and the sociology of culture; an introduction', in R. Collins, J. Curran, N. Garnham, P. Scannell, P. Schlesinger and C. Sparks (eds), *Media, Culture and Society: A Critical Reader*, London, Sage Publications.
Gendron, B. (1986) 'Theodor Adorno meets the Cadillacs', in T. Modleski (ed.), *Studies in Entertainment*, Bloomington, Indiana, Indiana University Press.
Gill, R. (1988) 'Altered images?: women in the media', *Social Studies Review* vol. 4, no. 1.
—— (1993) 'Ideology, gender and popular radio: a discourse analytic approach', *Innovation* vol. 6, no. 3.
Giner, S. (1976) *Mass Society*, London, Martin Robertson.
Gitlin, T. (1989) 'Postmodernism: roots and politics', in I. Angus and S. Jhally (eds), *Cultural Politics in Contemporary America*, New York and London, Routledge.
—— (1994) 'Prime time ideology; the hegemonic process in television entertainment', in H. Newcomb (ed.), *Television: The Critical View*, New York and Oxford, Oxford University Press (fifth edition).
Golding, P. and Murdock, G. (1991) 'Culture, communications and political economy', in J. Curran and M. Gurevitch (eds), *Mass Media and Society*, London, Edward Arnold.
Goldthorpe, J., Lockwood, D., Bechhofer, F. and Platt, J. (1969) *The Affluent Worker in the Class Structure*, Cambridge, Cambridge University Press.

Gramsci, A. (1971) *Selections From the Prison Notebooks*, London, Lawrence and Wishart.
Greer, G. (1971) *The Female Eunuch*, New York, McGraw-Hill.
Gurevitch, M., Bennett, T., Curran, J. and Woollacott, J. (eds) (1982) *Culture, Society and the Media*, London, Methuen.
Hall, S. (1980) 'Encoding/Decoding', in S. Hall, D. Hobson, A. Lowe and P. Willis (eds), *Culture, Media, Language*, London, Hutchinson.
—— (1981) 'Cultural studies: two paradigms', in T. Bennett *et al.* (eds), *Culture, Ideology and Social Process*, Milton Keynes, Open University Press.
—— Critcher, C., Jefferson, T., Clarke, J. and Roberts, B. (1978) *Policing the Crisis: Mugging, the State and Law and Order*, London, Macmillan.
—— and Jacques, M. (eds) (1983) *The Politics of Thatcherism*, London, Lawrence and Wishart.
—— and Jefferson, T. (1976) *Resistance through Rituals: Youth Sub-cultures in Post-war Britain*, London, Unwin Hyman.
Hansen, B. (1981) 'Doo-Wop', in J. Miller (ed.) (1981) *The Rolling Stone Illustrated History of Rock and Roll*, London, Pan Books.
Hartman, H. (1979) 'The unhappy marriage of Marxism and feminism', *Capital and Class* Summer issue; reprinted in L. Sargent (ed.), *Women and Revolution: A Discussion of the Unhappy Marriage of Marxism and Feminism*, London, Pluto Press, 1981.
Harvey, D. (1989) *The Condition of Postmodernity*, Oxford, Basil Blackwell.
Hawkes, T. (1977) *Structuralism and Semiotics*, London, Methuen.
Hebdige, D. (1979) *Sub-culture: The Meaning of Style*, London, Methuen.
—— (1987) *Cut 'n' Mix: Culture, Identity and Caribbean Music*, London, Routledge.
—— (1988) *Hiding in the Light: On Images and Things*, London, Routledge.
Held, D. (1980) *Introduction to Critical Theory*, London, Hutchinson.
Hill, S. (1990) 'Britain: the dominant ideology thesis after a decade', in N. Abercrombie, S. Hill and B.S. Turner (eds), *Dominant Ideologies*, London, Unwin Hyman.
Hoggart, R. (1958) *The Uses of Literacy*, Harmondsworth, Penguin.
Horkheimer, M. and Adorno, T. (1973) *Dialectic of Enlightenment*, London, Allen Lane (originally published in 1947).
Hutcheon, L. (1989) *The Politics of Postmodernism*, London, Routledge.
Instrell, R. (1992) 'Blade Runner: the economic shaping of a film', in J. Orr and C. Nicholson (eds), *Cinema and Fiction*, Edinburgh, Edinburgh University Press.

Jameson, F. (1984) 'Postmodernism, or the cultural logic of late capitalism', *New Left Review* no. 146.
—— (1991) *Postmodernism*, London and New York, Verso.
Jay, M. (1973) *The Dialectical Imagination*, London, Heinemann.
Jencks, C. (1984) *The Language of Post-modern Architecture*, London, Academy Editions.
—— (1986) *What is Post-modernism?*, London, Academy Editions.
Jenkins, R. (1992) *Pierre Bourdieu*, London and New York, Routledge.
Johnson, L. (1979) *The Cultural Critics*, London, Routledge and Kegan Paul.
Joll, J. (1977) *Gramsci*, London, Fontana.
Kawin, B. (1986) 'Children of the light', in B. Grant (ed.), *Film Genre Reader*, Austin, University of Texas Press.
Kerr, P. (ed.) (1986) *The Hollywood Film Industry*, London and New York, Routledge and Kegan Paul.
Kornhauser, W. (1960) *The Politics of Mass Society*, London, Routledge and Kegan Paul.
Krutnik, F. (1991) *In a Lonely Street: Film Noir, Genre, Masculinity*, London and New York, Routledge.
Kuhn, A. and Wolpe, A.M. (eds) (1978) *Feminism and Materialism*, London, Routledge and Kegan Paul.
Laing, D. (1985) *One Chord Wonders*, Milton Keynes, Open University Press.
Larrain, J. (1979) *The Concept of Ideology*, London, Hutchinson.
Lash, S. (1990) *The Sociology of Postmodernism*, London and New York, Routledge.
—— and Urry, J. (1987) *The End of Organized Capitalism*, Cambridge, Polity Press.
Leach, E. (1970) *Lévi-Strauss*, London, Fontana.
Leavis, F. R. (1933) *Mass Civilization and Minority Culture*, London, Minority Press.
Leavis, Q.D. (1932) *Fiction and the Reading Public*, London, Chatto and Windus.
Le Carré, J. (1975) *Tinker, Tailor, Soldier, Spy*, London and Sydney, Pan Books (originally published in 1974).
Lengermann, P. and Niebrugge-Brantley, J. (1992) 'Contemporary feminist theory', in G. Ritzer, *Sociological Theory*, New York, McGraw-Hill (third edition).
Levine, L. (1988) *High Brow/Low Brow: The Emergence of Cultural Hierarchy in America*, Cambridge, Mass., Harvard University Press.

Lévi-Strauss, C. (1963) *Structural Anthropology*, New York and London, Basic Books.
—— (1969) *Totemism*, Harmondsworth, Penguin.
—— (1970) *The Raw and the Cooked*, London, Cape.
—— (1977) *Structural Anthropology*, vol. 2, London, Allen Lane.
Lewis, J. (1990) 'Are you receiving me?', in A. Goodwin and G. Whannel (eds), *Understanding Television*, London and New York, Routledge.
Lockwood, D. (1982) 'Fatalism: Durkheim's hidden theory of order', in A. Giddens and G. Mackenzie (eds), *Social Class and the Division of Labour*, Cambridge, Cambridge University Press.
Lowenthal, L. (1957) 'Historical perspectives of popular culture', in B. Rosenberg and D. White (eds) *Mass Culture*, Glencoe, Ill., Free Press.
Lyotard, J.-F. (1984) *The Postmodern Condition*, Manchester, Manchester University Press.
MacDonald, D. (1957) 'A theory of mass culture', in B. Rosenberg and D. White (eds) *Mass Culture*, Glencoe, Ill., Free Press.
McGuigan, J. (1992) *Cultural Populism*, London, Routledge.
McIntosh, M. (1978) 'The state and the oppression of women', in A. Kuhn and A.M. Wolpe (eds) *Feminism and Materialism*, London, Routledge and Kegan Paul.
McLellan, D. (1986) *Ideology*, Milton Keynes, Open University Press.
McRobbie, A. (1991a) *Feminism and Youth Culture*, Basingstoke, Macmillan.
—— (1991b) 'New times in cultural studies', *New Formations* 13, Spring issue.
—— (1993) 'Cultural studies for the 1990s', *Innovation* vol. 6, no. 3.
McShine, K. (1989) *Andy Warhol: A Retrospective*, New York, Museum of Modern Art.
Maltin, L. (1991) *Movie and Video Guide 1992*, London, Penguin Books.
Marcuse, H. (1972) *One Dimensional Man*, London, Abacus.
Marx, K. (1963) *Selected Writings in Sociology and Social Philosophy*, ed. T. Bottomore and M. Rubel, Harmondsworth, Penguin.
Masterman, L. (ed.) (1984) *Television Mythologies: Stars, Shows and Signs*, London, Comedia.
Mattelart, A., Delacourt, X. and Mattelart, M. (1984) *International Image Markets*, London, Comedia.
Mepham, J. (1979) 'The theory of ideology in *Capital*', in J. Mepham and D. Ruben (eds), *Issues in Marxist Philosophy*, vol. 3, Brighton, Harvester Press.

Merquior, J. (1985) *Foucault*, London, Fontana.
Messenger Davies, M. (1989) *Television is Good for Your Kids*, London, Hilary Shipman.
Miller, D. (1987) *Material Culture and Mass Consumption*, Oxford, Basil Blackwell.
Mitchell, J. (1975) *Psychoanalysis and Feminism*, Harmondsworth, Penguin.
Modleski, T. (1986a) 'Femininity as mas(s)querade: a feminist approach to mass culture', in C. MacCabe (ed.), *High Theory/Low Culture*, Manchester, Manchester University Press.
—— (ed.) (1986b) *Studies in Entertainment*, Bloomington, Indiana, Indiana University Press.
Moores, S. (1993) *Interpreting Audiences*, London, Sage Publications.
Moorhouse, H. (1991) *Driving Ambitions: An Analysis of the American Hot Rod Enthusiasm*, Manchester, Manchester University Press.
Morley, D. (1980) *The Nationwide Audience*, London, British Film Institute.
—— (1991) 'Where the global meets the local: notes from the sitting room', *Screen* vol. 32, no. 1.
—— (1992) *Television, Audiences and Cultural Studies*, London and New York, Routledge.
—— and Robins, K. (1989) 'Spaces of identity: communications technologies and the reconfiguration of Europe', *Screen* vol. 30, no. 4.
Morson, G. (ed.) (1986) *Bakhtin: Essays and Dialogues on his Work*, Chicago, Chicago University Press.
—— and Emerson, C. (eds) (1989) *Rethinking Bakhtin: Extensions and Challenges*, Evanston, Ill., North Western University Press.
Mulhern, F. (1981) *The Moment of Scrutiny*, London, Verso.
Mulvey, L. (1975) 'Visual pleasure and narrative cinema', *Screen* vol. 16, no. 3.
—— (1981) 'Afterthoughts on "visual pleasure and narrative cinema" inspired by Duel in the Sun', *Framework* Summer issue; reprinted in L. Mulvey, *Visual and Other Pleasures*, Basingstoke, Macmillan.
Murdock, G. (1993) 'Communications and the constitution of modernity', *Media, Culture and Society*, vol. 15.
—— and Golding, P. (1977) 'Capitalism, communication and class relations', in J. Curran, M. Gurevitch and J. Woollacott (eds), *Mass Communication and Society*, London, Edward Arnold.
Nava, M. (1992) *Changing Cultures*, London, Sage.
Neale, S. (1980) *Genre*, London, British Film Institute.
—— (1985) *Cinema and Technology*, London, Macmillan.

—— (1990) 'A question of genre', *Screen* vol. 31, no. 1.
Orwell, G. (1957) *Inside the Whale and Other Essays*, Harmondsworth, Penguin.
—— [1946] (1965) *The Decline of the English Murder and Other Essays*, Harmondsworth, Penguin.
Palmer, P. (1988) 'The social nature of children's television viewing', in P. Drummond and R. Paterson (eds), *Television and Its Audience*, London, British Film Institute.
—— (1991) *Potboilers: Methods, Concepts and Case Studies in Popular Fiction*, London and New York, Routledge.
Partington, A. (1991) 'Melodrama's gendered audience', in S. Franklin, C. Lury and J. Stacey (eds), *Off-centre: Feminism and Cultural Studies*, London, HarperCollins.
Penley, C. (1988) 'Introduction. The lady doesn't vanish: Feminism and film theory', in *Feminism and Film Theory*, New York and London, Routledge and the British Film Institute.
Pfeil, F. (1985) 'Makin' flippy-floppy: postmodernism and the baby-boom PMC', in M. Davis (ed.), *The Year Left: An American Socialist Yearbook 1985*, London, Verso.
Portoghesi, P. (1982) *After Modern Architecture*, New York, Rizzoli.
—— (1983) *Postmodern Architecture*, New York, Rizzoli.
Rabinow, P. (ed.) (1984) *The Foucault Reader*, London, Penguin.
Radway, J. (1987) *Reading the Romance: Women, Patriarchy and Popular Literature*, London, Verso.
Ransome, P. (1992) *Antonio Gramsci: A New Introduction*, New York and London, Harvester Wheatsheaf.
Reisman, D., Glazer, N. and Dewney, R. (1961) *The Lonely Crowd: A Study of the Changing American Character*, New Haven, Conn., Yale University Press (abridged edition).
Ritzer, G. (1992) *Sociological Theory*, New York, McGraw-Hill (third edition).
Robbins, D. (1991) *The Work of Pierre Bourdieu*, Milton Keynes, Open University Press.
Rosenberg, B. and White, D. (eds) (1957) *Mass Culture*, Glencoe, Ill., Free Press.
Ross, A. (1989) *No Respect: Intellectuals and Popular Culture*, New York and London, Routledge.
Ross Muir, A. (1988) 'The status of women working in film and television', in L. Gamman and M. Marshment (eds), *The Female Gaze: Women as Viewers of Popular Culture*, London, The Women's Press.

Rylance, R. (1994) *Roland Barthes*, New York and London, Harvester Wheatsheaf.

Sansom, A. (1992) *F.R. Leavis*, New York and London, Harvester Wheatsheaf.

Sargent, L. (ed.) (1981) *Women and Revolution: A Discussion of the Unhappy Marriage of Marxism and Feminism*, London, Pluto Press.

Sarup, M. (1988) *An Introductory Guide to Post-structuralism and Postmodernism*, New York and London, Harvester Wheatsheaf.

Saussure, F. de (1974) *Course in General Linguistics*, London, Fontana (originally published in English in 1959).

Seaton, J. (1986) 'Pornography annoys', in J. Curran, J. Ecclestone, G. Oakley and A. Richardson (eds), *Bending Reality: The State of the Media*, London, Pluto Press.

Seiter, E. (1986) 'The hegemony of leisure: Aaron Spelling presents Hotel', in P. Drummond and R. Paterson (eds), *Television in Transition*, London, British Film Institute.

Shils, E. (1957) 'Daydreams and nightmares: reflections on the criticism of mass culture', *The Sewanee Review* vol. 65, no. 4.

—— (1962) 'The theory of mass society', *Diogenes* 39.

Simon, R. (1982) *Gramsci's Political Thought: An Introduction*, London, Lawrence and Wishart.

Skeggs, B. (1993) 'Two minute brother: contestation through gender, "race" and sexuality', *Innovation* vol. 6, no. 3.

—— (1997) *Formations of Class and Gender*, London, Sage.

Slater, P. (1977) *Origin and Significance of the Frankfurt School*, London, Routledge and Kegan Paul.

Smart, B. (1983) *Foucault, Marxism and Critique*, London, Routledge and Kegan Paul.

—— (1988) *Michel Foucault*, London, Routledge.

Spender, D. (1980) *Man Made Language*, London, Routledge and Kegan Paul.

—— (ed.) (1983) *Feminist Theorists: Three Centuries of Key Women Thinkers*, New York, Random House.

Sperber, D. (1979) 'Claude Lévi-Strauss', in J. Sturrock (ed.), *Structuralism and Since*, Oxford, Oxford University Press.

Sreberny-Mohammadi, A. (1991) 'The global and the local in international communications', in J. Curran and M. Gurevitch (eds), *Mass Media and Society*, London, Edward Arnold.

Stacey, J. (1994) *Star Gazing: Hollywood Cinema and Female Spectatorship*, London, Routledge.

Stam, R. (1988) 'Mikhail Bakhtin and left cultural critique', in E. Ann Kaplan (ed.), *Postmodernism and Its Discontents*, London and New York, Verso.

—— (1989) *Subversive Pleasures: Bakhtin, Cultural Criticism and Film*, Baltimore, Maryland, Johns Hopkins University Press.

Storey, J. (1993) *An Introductory Guide to Cultural Theory and Popular Culture*, Athens, Georgia, University of Georgia Press.

—— (2003) *Inventing Popular Culture*, Oxford, Blackwell.

—— (1997) *An Introductory Guide to Cultural Theory and Popular Culture*, London, Prentice Hall, Harvester Wheatsheaf (second edition).

Stratton, J. (1989) 'Beyond art: postmodernism and the case of popular music', *Theory, Culture and Society* vol. 6.

Strinati, D. (1992a) 'The taste of America: Americanization and popular culture in Britain', in D. Strinati and S. Wagg (eds), *Come on Down? Popular Media Culture in Post-war Britain*, London, Routledge.

—— (1992b) 'Postmodernism and popular culture', *Sociology Review* vol. 1, no. 4.

—— (1993) 'The big nothing?: contemporary culture and the emergence of postmodernism', *Innovation* vol. 6, no. 3.

—— and Wagg, S. (eds) (1992) *Come On Down?: Popular Media Culture in Post-war Britain*, London, Routledge.

—— (2000) *An Introduction to Studying Popular Culture*, London, Routledge.

Sturrock, J. (ed.) (1979) *Structuralism and Since*, Oxford, Oxford University Press.

Swingewood, A. (1977) *The Myth of Mass Culture*, London, Macmillan.

—— (1991) *A Short History of Sociological Thought*, Basingstoke, Macmillan (second edition).

Thompson, J.B. (1990) *Ideology and Modern Culture*, Cambridge, Polity Press.

Tomlinson, J. (1991) *Cultural Imperialism*, London, Pinter Publishers.

Tuchman, G. (1981) 'The symbolic annihilation of women by the mass media', in S. Cohen and J. Young (eds), *The Manufacture of News,* London, Constable (revised edition).

—— Daniels, A. Kaplan and Benet, J. (eds) (1978) *Hearth And Home: Images of Women in the Mass Media*, New York, Oxford University Press.

Turner, B. (1992) 'Ideology and utopia in the formation of an intelligentsia: reflections on the English cultural conduit', *Theory, Culture and Society* vol. 9.

Turner, G. (1990) *British Cultural Studies: An Introduction*, Boston, Mass., Unwin Hyman.

Twitchell, J. (1992) *Carnival Culture: The Trashing of Taste in America*, New York, Columbia University Press.

Van Zoonen, L. (1991) 'Feminist perspectives on the media', in J. Curran and M. Gurevitch (eds), *Mass Media and Society*, London, Edward Arnold.

Venturi, R., Scott-Brown, D. and Izenhour, S. (1977) *Learning from Las Vegas*, Cambridge, Massachusetts Institute of Technology Press.

Walby, S. (1990) *Theorizing Patriarchy*, Oxford, Basil Blackwell.

Walkerdine, V. (1986) 'Video replay: families, films and fantasy', in V. Burgin, J. Donald and C. Kaplan (eds), *Formations of Fantasy*, London and New York, Methuen.

Webster, D. (1988) *Looka Yonder: The Imaginary America of Populist Culture*, London, Routledge.

White, J. (1986) *The Worst Street in North London*, London, Routledge and Kegan Paul.

Williams, R. (1963) *Culture and Society 1780–1950*, Harmondsworth, Penguin.

—— (1976) *Keywords: A Vocabulary of Culture and Society*, London, Fontana.

—— (1977) *Marxism and Literature*, Oxford and New York, Oxford University Press.

Williamson, J. (1978) *Decoding Advertisements: Ideology and Meaning in Advertising*, London and Boston, Marion Boyars.

Winship, J. (1981) 'Woman becomes an "individual" – femininity and consumption in women's magazines 1954–1969', stencilled paper no. 65, Centre for Contemporary Cultural Studies, University of Birmingham, 1981.

—— (1992) 'The impossibility of Best: enterprise meets domesticity in the practical women's magazines of the 1980s', in D. Strinati and S. Wagg (eds), *Come On Down?: Popular Media Culture in Post-war Britain*, London, Routledge.

Wolin, R. (1994) *Walter Benjamin: An Aesthetic of Redemption*, Berkeley and Los Angeles, University of California Press (second edition).

Wood, G. (1988) 'Horror film', in W. Gehring (ed.), *Handbook of American Film Genres*, New York, Greenwood Press.

Woollacott, J. (1982) 'Messages and meanings', in M. Gurevitch, T. Bennett, J. Curran and J. Woollacott (eds), *Culture, Society and the Media*, London, Methuen.

Worpole, K. (1983) *Dockers and Detectives: Popular Reading, Popular Writing*, London, Verso.

Wren-Lewis, J. (1983) 'The encoding/decoding model: criticisms and redevelopments for research on decoding', *Media, Culture and Society* vol. 5.

Wright, W. (1975) *Six-guns and Society: A Structural Study of the Western*, Berkeley, University of California Press.

Index